Your All-in-One Resource

On the CD that accompanies this book, you'll find additional resources to extend your learning.

The reference library includes the following fully searchable titles:

- *Microsoft Computer Dictionary*, 5th ed.
- *First Look 2007 Microsoft Office System* by Katherine Murray
- Windows Vista Product Guide

Also provided are a sample chapter and poster from *Look Both Ways: Help Protect Your Family on the Internet* by Linda Criddle.

The CD interface has a new look. You can use the tabs for an assortment of tasks:

- Check for book updates (if you have Internet access)
- Install the book's practice file
- Go online for product support or CD support
- Send us feedback

The following screen shot gives you a glimpse of the new interface.

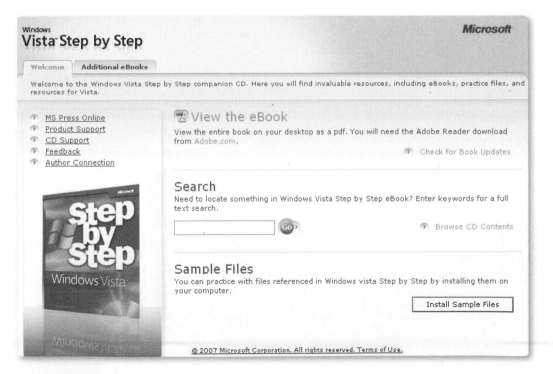

Microsoft®

Microsoft® Office Excel® 2007 Visual Basic® for Applications Step by Step

Reed Jacobson

PUBLISHED BY
Microsoft Press
A Division of Microsoft Corporation
One Microsoft Way
Redmond, Washington 98052-6399

Library of Congress Control Number: 2007924651

Printed and bound in the United States of America.

5 6 7 8 9 10 11 12 13 14 QGT 5 4 3 2 1 0

Distributed in Canada by H.B. Fenn and Company Ltd.

A CIP catalogue record for this book is available from the British Library.

Microsoft Press books are available through booksellers and distributors worldwide. For further information about international editions, contact your local Microsoft Corporation office or contact Microsoft Press International directly at fax (425) 936-7329. Visit our Web site at www.microsoft.com/mspress. Send comments to mspinput@microsoft.com.

Microsoft, Microsoft Press, ActiveX, Calibri, Excel, Groove, InfoPath, Internet Explorer, MS-DOS, OneNote, Outlook, PivotTable, PowerPoint, SharePoint, SQL Server, Visio, Visual Basic, Visual Studio, Win32, Windows, Windows Server, and Windows Vista are either registered trademarks or trademarks of Microsoft Corporation in the United States and/or other countries. Other product and company names mentioned herein may be the trademarks of their respective owners.

The example companies, organizations, products, domain names, e-mail addresses, logos, people, places, and events depicted herein are fictitious. No association with any real company, organization, product, domain name, e-mail address, logo, person, place, or event is intended or should be inferred.

The book expresses the author's views and opinions. The information contained in this book is provided without any express, statutory, or implied warranties. Neither the authors, Microsoft Corporation, nor its resellers, or distributors will be held liable for any damages caused or alleged to be caused either directly or indirectly by this book.

Acquisitions Editor: Juliana Aldous Atkinson
Developmental Editor: Sandra Haynes
Project Editor: Rosemary Caperton
Editorial and Production Services: Online Training Solutions, Inc.
Technical Reviewer: Jason Lee; Technical Review services provided by Content Master, a member of CM Group, Ltd

Body Part No. X13-68402

Contents

What do you think of this book? We want to hear from you!

Microsoft is interested in hearing your feedback so we can continually improve our books and learning resources for you. To participate in a brief online survey, please visit:

www.microsoft.com/learning/booksurvey/

2   Make a Macro Do Complex Tasks   37

3   Explore Workbooks and Worksheets   67

What do you think of this book? We want to hear from you!

Microsoft is interested in hearing your feedback so we can continually improve our books and learning resources for you. To participate in a brief online survey, please visit:

www.microsoft.com/learning/booksurvey/

About the Author

Reed Jacobson is a Senior Architect with Hitachi Consulting, an international management and technology consulting firm. He worked as a Software Application Specialist for Hewlett-Packard for 10 years and ran his own consulting firm for 5 years.

Reed received a BA degree in Japanese and Linguistics. He also received an MBA degree from Brigham Young University and a graduate fellowship to study Linguistics at Cornell University.

In addition to authoring this book, Reed is the author of *Excel Trade Secrets for Windows*, *Microsoft Excel Advanced Topics Step by Step*, *Microsoft Office 2000 Expert Companion*, and *Microsoft SQL Server Analysis Services Step by Step*. He has given presentations at Microsoft and other conferences, and has taught courses around the world.

Features and Conventions of This Book

This book has been designed to lead you step by step through all the tasks you are most likely to want to perform when creating macros in Microsoft Office Excel 2007. If you start at the beginning and work your way through all the exercises, you will gain enough proficiency to be able to perform many types of tasks by using macros. Each topic is self contained, but later chapters do assume that you know the information presented in earlier chapters. If you have worked with a previous version of Excel, or if you completed all the exercises and later need help remembering how to perform a procedure, the following features of this book will help you look up specific tasks related to Excel 2007 macros:

- **Detailed table of contents.** Look up the topic you want in the list of the topics and sidebars within each chapter.

- **Chapter thumb tabs.** Easily locate the beginning of the chapter you want.

- **Topic-specific running heads.** Within a chapter, quickly locate the topic you want by looking at the running head of odd-numbered pages.

- **Detailed index.** Look up specific tasks and features and general concepts in the index, which has been carefully crafted with the reader in mind.

- **Companion CD.** Find the practice files needed for the step-by-step exercises, as well as a fully searchable electronic version of this book and other useful resources.

If you are new to Excel 2007, you might not have had much time to explore the Microsoft Office Fluent user interface, which was introduced with the 2007 Microsoft Office system. The step-by-step instructions in this book often tell you to click buttons on the Office Fluent Ribbon, identifying the tab to click and the group in which the button is located. You should have no difficulty following these instructions.

You can save time when you use this book by understanding how the *Step by Step* series shows special instructions, keys to press, buttons to click, and so on. The table on the next page tells you what you need to know.

Convention	Meaning
	This icon indicates a reference to the book's companion CD.
USE	This paragraph before the first exercise in a chapter indicates the practice files that you will use when working through the exercises.
BE SURE TO	This paragraph before the first exercise in a chapter indicates any prerequisite requirements that you should attend to before beginning the exercise, or actions you should take to restore your system after completing the exercise.
OPEN	This paragraph before the first exercise in a chapter indicates files that you should open before beginning the exercise.
CLOSE	This paragraph at the end of a chapter provides instructions for closing open files or programs before moving on to another topic.
1 **2**	Blue numbered steps guide you through step-by-step exercises.
1 2	Black numbered steps guide you through procedures in expository text.
→	An arrow indicates an exercise that has only one step.
See Also	These paragraphs direct you to more information about a given topic in this book or elsewhere.
Troubleshooting	These paragraphs provide a helpful hint or information about other available options.
Tip	These paragraphs provide a helpful hint or shortcut that makes working through a task easier, or information about other available options.
Important	These paragraphs point out information that you need to know to complete a procedure.
Ctrl+Home	A plus sign (+) between two key names means that you must hold down the first key while you press the second key. For example, "press Ctrl+Home" means "hold down the Ctrl key while you press the Home key."
Program interface elements	In steps, the names of program elements, such as buttons, commands, and dialog boxes, are shown in black bold characters.
User input	Anything you should type appears in blue bold characters.
Italic	Italic font is used for emphasis and to introduce new terms.

Using the Book's CD

The companion CD included with this book contains the practice files you'll use as you work through the book's exercises, as well as other electronic resources that will help you learn how to use VBA macros with Microsoft Office Excel 2007.

What's on the CD?

The following table lists the practice files supplied on the book's CD. Note that some practice files are used in more than one chapter.

> **Tip** The *ExcelVBA07SBS* folder contains a subfolder named *Finished*. This folder contains the finished version of each chapter's workbook. The *Finished* folder is never explicitly referred to in the text, but it is there for your reference. If you have trouble getting a macro to work properly, you can look at the macros in the *Finished* folder to help troubleshoot the problem.

Chapter	In the *ExcelVBA07SBS* folder	In the *Finished* folder
Chapter 1: Make a Macro Do Simple Tasks	*Budget.xlsx*	*Chapter01.xlsm*
Chapter 2: Make a Macro Do Complex Tasks	*Nov2007.txt* *Orders.xlsx*	*Chapter02.xlsm*
Chapter 3: Explore Workbooks and Worksheets	None	None
Chapter 4: Explore Range Objects	*Ranges.xlsx*	*Chapter04.xlsm*
Chapter 5: Explore Data Objects	*Orders.xlsx* *Orders.accdb*	*Chapter05.xlsm*
Chapter 6: Explore Graphical Objects	*Graphics.xlsx* *MakeLogo.txt* *MakeMap.txt*	*Chapter06.xlsm*
Chapter 7: Control Visual Basic	*Flow.xlsx* *Flow.txt*	*Chapter07.xlsm*

Chapter	In the *ExcelVBA07SBS* folder	In the *Finished* folder
Chapter 8: Extend Excel and Visual Basic	*Structure.txt*	*Chapter08.xlsm*
Chapter 9: Launch Macros with Events	*Events.txt*	*Chapter09.xlsm*
Chapter 10: Use Dialog Box Controls on a Worksheet	*Loan.xlsx*	*Chapter10.xlsm*
Chapter 11: Create a Custom Form	*Budget.xlsx*	*Chapter11.xlsm*
Appendix: A Complete Enterprise Information System	*EIS.xlsm* *Orders.accdb*	None

Important The companion CD for this book does not contain the Microsoft Office Excel 2007 software. You should purchase and install that program before using this book.

Minimum System Requirements

Step-by-Step Exercises

In addition to the hardware, software, and connections required to run the 2007 Microsoft Office system, you will need the following to successfully complete the exercises in this book:

- Excel 2007
- 10 MB of available hard disk space for the practice files

2007 Microsoft Office System

For this book, you will not need the complete 2007 Microsoft Office system. You will need only Excel. The following is a reference for your convenience.

> **Tip** If you are a Microsoft .NET Developer and want to build an application based on Excel, the contents of Chapters 3, 4, 5, and 6 will be particularly useful to help you understand the Excel object model. To use Microsoft .NET to develop applications for Excel, you will need Microsoft Visual Studio 2005 with a .NET language, as well as Microsoft Visual Studio 2005 Tools for the 2007 Microsoft Office System (VSTO 2005 SE), which is downloadable from the Microsoft.com Web site.

The 2007 Microsoft Office system includes the following programs:

- Microsoft Office Access 2007
- Microsoft Office Communicator 2007
- Microsoft Office Excel 2007
- Microsoft Office Groove 2007
- Microsoft Office InfoPath 2007
- Microsoft Office OneNote 2007
- Microsoft Office Outlook 2007
- Microsoft Office Outlook 2007 with Business Contact Manager
- Microsoft Office PowerPoint 2007
- Microsoft Office Publisher 2007
- Microsoft Office Word 2007

No single edition of the 2007 Microsoft Office system installs all of the above programs. Specialty programs available separately include Microsoft Office Project 2007, Microsoft Office SharePoint Designer 2007, and Microsoft Office Visio 2007.

To run these programs, your computer needs to meet the following minimum requirements:

- 500 megahertz (MHz) processor
- 256 megabytes (MB) RAM
- CD or DVD drive
- 2 gigabyte (GB) hard disk space for installation (a portion of this disk space will be freed if you select the option to delete the installation files)

> **Tip** Hard disk requirements will vary depending on configuration; custom installation choices may require more or less hard disk space.

- Monitor with minimum 1024 × 768 screen resolution
- Keyboard and mouse or compatible pointing device
- Internet connection, 128 kilobits per second (Kbps) or greater, for download and activation of products, accessing Microsoft Office Online and online Help topics, and any other Internet-dependent processes
- Windows Vista or later, Microsoft Windows XP with Service Pack 2 (SP2) or later, or Microsoft Windows Server 2003 or later
- Windows Internet Explorer 7 or Microsoft Internet Explorer 6 with service packs

The 2007 Microsoft Office suites, including Office Basic 2007, Office Home & Student 2007, Office Standard 2007, Office Small Business 2007, Office Professional 2007, Office Ultimate 2007, Office Professional Plus 2007, and Office Enterprise 2007, all have similar requirements.

Installing the Practice Files

You need to install the practice files to a suitable location on your hard disk before you can use them in the exercises. Follow these steps:

1. Remove the companion CD from the envelope at the back of the book, and insert it into the CD drive of your computer.

   The Step By Step Companion CD License Terms appear. Follow the on-screen directions. To use the practice files, you must accept the terms of the license agreement. After you accept the license agreement, a menu screen appears.

   > **Important** If the menu screen does not appear, click the Start button and then click Computer. Display the Folders list in the Navigation Pane, click the icon for your CD drive, and then in the right pane, double-click the StartCD executable file.

2. Click **Install Practice Files**.

   > **Important** On a computer running Windows Vista, the default installation location of the practice files is *Documents\MSP\ExcelVBA07SBS*. On a computer running Windows XP, the default installation location is *My Documents\MSP\ExcelVBA07SBS*. If your computer is running Windows XP, whenever an exercise tells you to navigate to your *Documents* folder, you should instead go to your *My Documents* folder.

3. Click **Next** on the first screen, and then click **Next** to accept the terms of the license agreement on the next screen.

4. If you want to install the practice files to a location other than the default folder (*Documents\MSP\ExcelVBA07SBS*), click the **Change** button, select the new drive and path, and then click **OK**.

> **Important** If you install the practice files to a location other than the default, you will need to substitute that path within the exercises.

5. Click **Next** on the **Choose Destination Location** screen, and then click **Install** on the **Ready to Install the Program** screen to install the selected practice files.

6. After the practice files have been installed, click **Finish**.

7. Close the **Step by Step Companion CD** window, remove the companion CD from the CD drive, and return it to the envelope at the back of the book.

Using the Practice Files

When you install the practice files from the companion CD that accompanies this book, the files are stored on your hard disk in *Documents\MSP\ExcelVBA07SBS*. Each exercise is preceded by a paragraph that lists the files needed for that exercise and explains any preparations needed before you start working through the exercise. Here are examples:

> **USE** the *Budget.xlsx* workbook and the *Nov2007.txt* text file. These practice files are located in the *Documents\MSP\ExcelVBA07SBS* folder.
>
> **BE SURE TO** save *Budget.xlsx* as a macro-enabled workbook called *Chapter04* in the trusted folder that you created in Chapter 1.
>
> **OPEN** the *Chapter04.xlsm* workbook.

You can browse to the practice files in Windows Explorer by following these steps:

Start

1. On the Windows taskbar, click the **Start** button, and then click **Documents**.

2. In your **Documents** folder, double-click **MSP**, and then double-click **ExcelVBA07SBS**.

You can browse to the practice files from an Excel 2007 dialog box by following these steps:

1. In the **Favorite Links** pane in the dialog box, click **Documents**.

2. In your **Documents** folder, double-click **MSP**, and then double-click **ExcelVBA07SBS**.

Removing and Uninstalling the Practice Files

You can free up hard disk space by uninstalling the practice files that were installed from the companion CD. The uninstall process deletes any files that you created in the *Documents\MSP\ExcelVBA07SBS* folder while working through the exercises. Follow these steps:

Start

1. On the Windows taskbar, click the **Start** button, and then click **Control Panel**.

2. In **Control Panel**, under **Programs**, click the **Uninstall a program** task.

3. In the **Programs and Features** window, click **Microsoft Office Excel VBA 2007 Step by Step**, and then on the toolbar at the top of the window, click the **Uninstall** button.

4. If the **Programs and Features** message box asking you to confirm the deletion appears, click **Yes**.

> **Important** Microsoft Product Support Services does not provide support for this book or its companion CD.

Getting Help

Every effort has been made to ensure the accuracy of this book and the contents of its companion CD. If you do run into problems, please contact the sources listed below for assistance.

Getting Help with This Book and Its Companion CD

If your question or issue concerns the content of this book or its companion CD, please first search the online Microsoft Press Knowledge Base, which provides support information for known errors in or corrections to this book, at the following Web site:

www.microsoft.com/mspress/support/search.asp

If you do not find your answer there, send your comments or questions to Microsoft Press Technical Support at:

mspinput@microsoft.com

More Information

If your question is about Microsoft Office Excel 2007 or another Microsoft software product, and you cannot find the answer in the product's Help, please search the appropriate product solution center or the Microsoft Knowledge Base at:

support.microsoft.com

In the United States, Microsoft software product support issues not covered by the Microsoft Knowledge Base are addressed by Microsoft Product Support Services. Location-specific software support options are available from:

support.microsoft.com/gp/selfoverview/

Chapter at a Glance

Record a macro, **page 6**

Add a macro to the Quick Access Toolbar, **page 22**

Assign a shortcut key to a macro, **page 8**

Use a macro to convert formulas to values, **page 24**

Read a recorded macro, **page 9**

Use a macro to apply enhanced formatting to cells, **page 5**

Make changes to a recorded macro, **page 18**

Create your own Digital ID to sign a macro, **page 30**

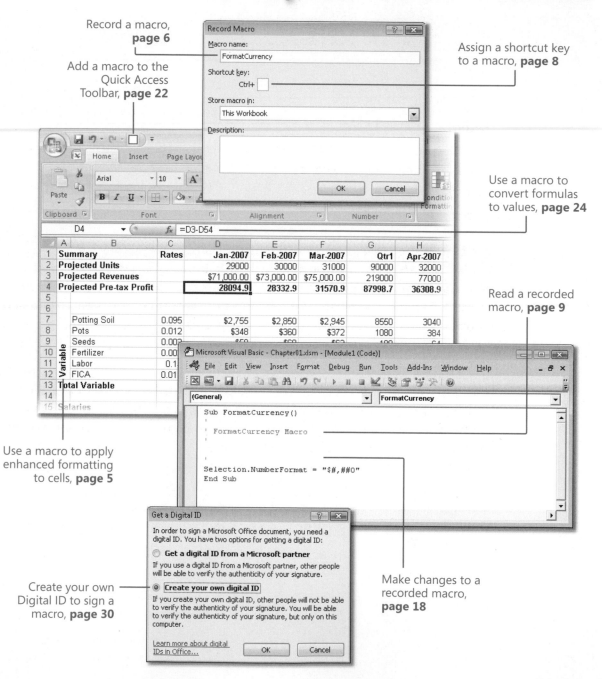

1 Make a Macro Do Simple Tasks

In this chapter, you will learn to:

✔ Record and run a macro.

✔ Understand and edit simple recorded macros.

✔ Run a macro by using a shortcut key.

✔ Manage macro security.

A couple of weeks ago, I misplaced the remote control to my digital video recorder. It was awful. I was trying to watch a perfectly legal, fair-use, time-shifted episode of *Desperate Housewives*, but I couldn't because the navigation controls are built into the remote control. Fortunately, when I was getting a fresh bag of popcorn from a cupboard in the kitchen a few days later, I discovered where I had set the remote. I'm so happy that I can again watch pre-recorded television. Not to mention changing the channel without having to stand up.

Microsoft Visual Basic for Applications (VBA) is the remote control for Microsoft Office Excel 2007. Sure, you can use Excel without ever using VBA, but the VBA remote control makes Excel more convenient to use. It also allows you to take advantage of features that can't be accessed through the standard user interface. Once you become acquainted with VBA, you'll wonder how you ever got along without it.

Important Before you complete this chapter, you need to install the practice files from the book's companion CD to their default locations. See "Using the Book's CD" on page xv for more information.

USE the *Budget.xlsx* workbook. This practice file is located in the *Documents\MSP\ ExcelVBA07SBS* folder. The workbook contains a single worksheet, named *Budget*. This worksheet includes a projected month-to-month budget for the year 2007.

BE SURE TO save the *Budget.xlsx* workbook with the name *Chapter01* in a new folder called *Work*. You put the workbook in a new folder so that you can be absolutely certain that nothing is in the folder except files that you put there. Later, this will allow you to trust any macro workbooks in that folder.

OPEN the *Chapter01.xlsx* workbook.

What's the Difference Between VBA and a Macro?

If VBA is the remote control for Excel, then what is a *macro*? And what is the difference between VBA and a macro? It's all very confusing. In essence, a macro is a computer program that gives automated instructions to the computer. The original macros were a way to use a few characters to represent a lot of instructions. They were called *macros* because the output was much bigger than the input.

In fact, the first spreadsheet macro programs really did just expand a short string of characters into a long set of actions. They were just shortcuts for the user interface commands. For example, if in the user interface you typed *R* (for "Range"), *N* (for "Name"), and *C* (for "Create"), you would enter *RNC* into the macro to automate the process. This approach was intuitive, but it also had inherent weaknesses. Not only were keystroke macros difficult to read, but they also didn't adapt well to a graphical user interface. What keystrokes would you use to represent dragging a rectangle with the mouse? They also made it difficult to enhance the user interface, because any changes to the menu structure would cause any previously created macros to fail.

To solve these problems, the early versions of Excel contained a new type of programming language—one that was independent of the user interface command names. For example, in Microsoft Excel version 4 (Excel 2007 is version 12), you could copy a range in at least three different ways: press Ctrl+C, click the Copy button on the Standard toolbar, or click Copy on the Edit menu. All of these methods were represented by the same instruction =COPY(). This new programming language was not technically a macro language in the old sense of expanding a few characters into a sequence of instructions. It was technically a set of functions, much like the functions used to perform tasks in spreadsheet cells. But saying "You can now automate simple tasks by writing custom programs based on special-ized spreadsheet functions" sounded scary, so the Excel team continued to refer to the custom programs as macros. The word *macro* came to mean *a program that users can write by themselves.*

Excel's early function-based macros were a major improvement over keystroke macros, but they still had two big drawbacks. First, Excel macros were very specific to Excel—the functions looked too much like spreadsheet formulas to be able to adapt to other applications, such as Microsoft Office Word. Second, the number of functions increased with each new version of Microsoft Office, and there was no good way to organize or group the thousands of possibilities.

To solve the first limitation—that function-based macros are specific to Excel—Microsoft introduced Visual Basic for Applications, or VBA, starting with Microsoft Excel version 5. VBA acts as a general-purpose language that is independent of the application. Suddenly, anyone who knows how to work with any version of Microsoft Visual Basic has a big head start in automating Excel, and anyone who learns how to write Excel macros in VBA can transfer that knowledge to other types of Visual Basic programming. In addition, although Excel was the first major application to use VBA, VBA is not tied directly to Excel; it works just as well with other VBA-enabled applications, such as Word and Microsoft Office PowerPoint.

To solve the second limitation of function-based macros—that there are too many commands to manage effectively—VBA works with an *object model*. The term *object model* sounds pretty scary, but it's really just a logical way to organize all the commands you can carry out in an application. In an object model, each different part of the application—for example, a workbook, a range, or a point on a chart—becomes an *object*, and each object has its own list of functions. You'll learn more later about what an object is and how objects relate to functions, but the point is that the object model organizes all the millions of possible commands around how each command is used—for example, you copy and paste a range of cells, but you don't copy and paste points on a chart.

Because of the object model, VBA doesn't need any special access to the internals of Excel. Rather, Excel exposes its capabilities to the outside world by means of the object model, and VBA talks to the object model.

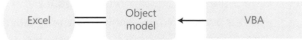

This means that an Excel VBA macro can control not only Excel, but also any application that provides an object model. All Microsoft Office applications, and several other Microsoft and non-Microsoft applications, provide appropriate object models.

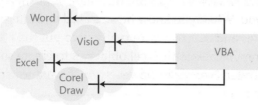

The VBA that comes with Excel isn't the only language that can communicate with the object model. Any language that supports Automation can control Excel. You can control Excel not only with the VBA hosted by Excel, but also with the VBA hosted by Word, with Microsoft Visual Basic version 6, or even with a language such as C++. With a simple translation layer, you can also talk to the Excel object model from Microsoft .NET applications written in C# or Microsoft Visual Basic .NET.

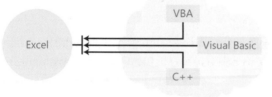

VBA and the .NET Framework

If .NET doesn't mean anything to you, skip this explanation and don't worry about it. If you are familiar with .NET, you may wonder how VBA macros relate to .NET programs. In Excel 2007, VBA is native code, and the object model is a Component Object Model (COM) interface. I don't know future plans for the product, but it is possible that a future version of Excel could use managed code such as C# or Visual Basic .NET as the embedded macro language. If that happens, most of what you learn for this version will still be valid, because the fundamentals of the object model will change only to the degree that the features in Excel change.

In this book, you will learn how to create VBA macros for your own use and to share with others in your workgroup. For most business users, writing macros in VBA is sufficient. If, however, you want to create a more sophisticated add-in, or if you want to create a stand-alone application that uses Excel in the background, you can create a .NET application in Microsoft Visual Studio. Microsoft Visual Studio 2005 includes a downloadable component called Visual Studio Tools for Office (VSTO), which includes the necessary Primary Interop Assembly (PIA) to communicate with the Excel object model. Microsoft Visual Studio 2005 Tools for the 2007 Microsoft Office System (VSTO 2005 SE) also includes tools that you can use to create custom task panes.

The object model exposes Excel's capabilities to VBA, but more importantly, it also exposes Excel's capabilities to you. When you know how to read and interpret an object model, you discover new features and quickly figure out how to put them to work. The best way to learn how VBA communicates with Excel objects is to create some simple macros by using the macro recorder. Eventually, however, you'll want to move beyond the limitations of the macro recorder.

Creating a Simple Macro

Excel has a large collection of tools conveniently available on the Ribbon or on short-cut menus. Sometimes, however, a built-in tool doesn't work quite the way you want. Creating a macro to enhance a built-in tool is a good way to get started with writing macros.

Format Currency by Using a Built-In Tool

On the Home tab of the Ribbon is a Number Format list from which you can choose any of several built-in formats. You can use the list to apply a Currency format to the selected cells.

1. In the *Chapter01* workbook, select cells **D3:F4** on the Budget worksheet.

2. On the **Home** tab of the Ribbon, click the **Number Format** arrow, and click **Currency**.

   Excel reformats the selected cells as Currency with two decimal places.

	A	B	C	D	E	F
1	Summary		Rates	Jan-2007	Feb-2007	Mar-2007
2	Projected Units			29000	30000	31000
3	Projected Revenues			$71,000.00	$73,000.00	$75,000.00
4	Projected Pre-tax Profit			$28,094.90	$28,332.90	$31,570.90
5						

Tip In addition to selecting Currency from the list, you can get the same result by clicking the Accounting Number Format button. The distinction between the Currency and Accounting formats can be confusing, especially because the Excel user interface (UI) is inconsistent. Here's how it works: Excel has two different types of formats that look like currency. One is called *Currency* and the other is called *Accounting*. The Currency format puts the currency symbol immediately in front of the number. The Accounting format puts the currency symbol to the far left of the cell. In Excel 2007, even though the name on the Ribbon button is *Accounting Number Format*, the default format it applies is Currency. To use the Accounting Number Format button to apply an Accounting format, click the arrow and choose one of the specific currency types—for example, $ English (U.S.). Unless you are doing specific accounting applications, the Currency format is usually easier to read.

Record a Macro to Format Currency

The standard Currency format has two decimal places. Two decimal places may be appropriate in something like a checkbook, where you know the exact amount you spent. But a budget worksheet contains estimates, and displaying estimated values to the penny seems silly. You can create a macro that formats the currently selected cells as Currency, but with no decimal places.

On the status bar, immediately to the right of the cell mode (Ready) indicator, in the bottom-left corner of the Excel window, is a button that will start the macro recorder. When no macro is currently recording, you can think of this as a Record Macro button. If the Record Macro button is not visible in the status bar, right-click the status bar, select the check box for Macro Recording, and click OK.

> **Troubleshooting** The Record Macro button is very close, both in appearance and in location, to the Insert Worksheet button, so be careful to click the right one.

1. On the Budget worksheet, select cells **D7:F8**.

Record Macro

2. On the status bar, click the **Record Macro** button.

3. Replace the default macro name with FormatCurrency, and then click **OK**.

A macro name must begin with a letter, and it can contain uppercase and lower-case letters, numbers, and underscores, but no spaces or other special characters.

The only apparent change is that the icon on the Record Macro button changes to a square, so you can now think of it as a Stop Recording button, which happens to be what the tool tip says it is. The Stop Recording button is like an "On the Air" button at a TV studio: You're recording.

4. Right-click in the selected range, and click **Format Cells**. If necessary, click the **Number** tab in the **Format Cells** dialog box.

5. Select **Currency** from the **Category** list.

6. Replace the value in the **Decimal Places** box with 0.

7. Select **Custom** from the **Category** list, and look in the **Type** box.

The characters $#,##0 represent a currency format with no decimal places. This is the format that gets applied to the selected cells.

See Also To learn more about format strings, click the Office Excel Help Button and type "number format codes" in the search box.

8. Click **OK** to format the selected cells as currency without decimal places.

9. On the status bar, click the **Stop Recording** button.

That's it. You have recorded a macro to format a selection with the currency format you want.

Run the Macro

Now you probably want to try the macro to see how it works.

Macros

1. On the Budget worksheet, select cells **D9:F10**.

2. On the **View** tab of the Ribbon, click the **Macros** button at the right end of the tab.

3. Select the **FormatCurrency** macro in the list, and click **Run**.

It worked! You ran your first macro, and the macro applied your customized currency format to the selected cells.

> **Tip** In the Excel Options dialog box, on the Popular page, is a check box labeled Show Developer Tab In The Ribbon. You can enable the Developer tab if you want, but it doesn't really make it any easier to write macros. The Developer tab contains three sections: The Code section includes buttons that are already easily available—either as the Record Macro button on the status bar or as the Macros button on the View tab of the Ribbon. The Controls section contains items that are very useful when adding controls to a worksheet. The XML section has nothing to do with creating macros.

Assign a Shortcut Key to the Macro

Running a macro from the Macro dialog box isn't much easier than directly assigning the number format. To make the macro easy to run, you can use a shortcut key.

1. On the **View** tab of the Ribbon, click the **Macros** arrow, and click **View Macros**.

2. Select the **FormatCurrency** macro in the list, and then click the **Options** button.

   The Macro Options dialog box allows you to change the macro's shortcut key assignment and its description. Other than the fact that you can't change the name, this dialog box looks very similar to the Record Macro dialog box, and in fact you can also assign a shortcut key at the time you first record a macro.

3. With the box below **Shortcut Key** selected, press Shift+C.

   As you can see by the label next to the box, this assigns Ctrl+Shift+C as the shortcut key.

Macro Options

Macro name:
  FormatCurrency

Shortcut key:
  Ctrl+Shift+ C|

Description:

OK   Cancel

> **Important** Excel uses many Ctrl key combinations as built-in shortcuts. For example, Ctrl+C is Copy and Ctrl+Z is Undo. If you assign one of these shortcuts to your macro, pressing the shortcut key combination runs your macro rather than the built-in command. If you always use Ctrl+Shift key combinations when you assign shortcut keys to your macros, you'll be less likely to override a built-in shortcut.

4. Click **OK** to return to the **Macro** dialog box, and then click **Cancel** to return to the worksheet.

5. Select cells **D11:F12**, and press Ctrl+Shift+C to run the macro.

Now you've successfully recorded, run, and enhanced a macro—all without seeing the macro itself. Maybe you'd like to actually see what you created.

Look at the Macro

The macro is hidden away in the workbook, and you need to open the Visual Basic editor to see it.

1. On the **View** tab of the Ribbon, click the **Macros** arrow, and click **View Macros**.

2. Click **FormatCurrency**, and then click **Edit**.

   The Visual Basic editor window opens. The Visual Basic editor appears to be a separate program, but it is "owned" by Excel—that is, if you quit Excel, the editor automatically shuts down. Inside the Visual Basic editor, a window captioned Module1 appears as well.

3. Maximize the Module1 window so that it fills the editor, and then resize the editor window so that you can see the Excel workbook in the background.

4. If any other windows are visible in the Visual Basic editor, close them now.

The window has the caption Module1. A *module* is the place where the recorder stores macros. Your macro is in the Module1 module. The macro looks like this:

```
Sub FormatCurrency()
'
' FormatCurrency Macro
'


'
    Selection.NumberFormat = "$#,##0"
End Sub
```

The four lines that start with apostrophes are *comments*. An apostrophe tells Visual Basic to ignore all subsequent text on the line. (The blank line among the comments, without even an apostrophe, is where the recorder would have put the shortcut key combination if you had assigned it when you recorded the macro.) The recorder inserts the comments to remind you to add comments as you write a macro. You can add to them, change them, or delete them as you want without changing how the macro runs. Comments appear in green to help you distinguish them from statements. Everything in Visual Basic that is not a comment is a *statement*. A statement tells Visual Basic what to do.

The first statement in the macro begins with *Sub*, followed by the name of the macro. This statement tells Visual Basic to begin a new macro. Perhaps the word *Sub* is used because a macro is typically hidden, or out of sight, like a *sub*marine. Or perhaps it is because macro-writers are sort of like hackers, and they are known to be *sub*versive. Or maybe *Sub* is just used for boring historical reasons. The final statement of the macro is *End Sub*. This statement tells Visual Basic to come back to the surface.

All the statements between Sub and End Sub form the *body* of the macro. These are the statements that do the real work. The first (and only) statement in the body of the FormatCurrency macro begins with Selection.NumberFormat.

The word *Selection* refers to some *thing* in Excel—in this case, the currently selected range of cells. The *thing* is called an *object*. Remember that objects are basically just a way of logically organizing the million of commands that are possible in Excel. Specifying Selection as the object says that the following instruction is going to have to do with a range of cells.

The word *NumberFormat* refers to an attribute—or *property*—of the range of cells. One way that Excel carries out an action is by assigning a new value to a property. In this case, it assigns the new format string to the NumberFormat property. In essence, the statement says, "Hey Excel, I've got a range here. Change the number format to look like this custom currency format, OK?"

This macro assumes that the current selection is a range of cells. If you happen to select a graphical shape and then run the macro, it fails. That's because when the macro says, "Hey Excel, I've got a rectangle here. Change the number format, OK?" Excel says, "No way! It doesn't make sense to change the number format of a rectangle, stupid!" Of course, it doesn't use those words. It says "Object doesn't support this property or method," but the meaning is about the same. Later, in Chapter 8, "Extend Excel and Visual Basic," you'll learn how to fix a macro so that you can give it to friends without the risk of having Excel tell them that they're stupid.

Save the Macro Workbook

If you've been following the instructions very carefully, you have not yet saved your workbook. If you have tried to save your workbook, you've received an ominous message about how a Visual Basic project cannot be saved in a macro-free workbook. This is a little bit annoying, but it is a nice new feature of the 2007 Microsoft Office release. As I'm sure you know, evil people have figured out that they can use Excel workbooks and Word documents to spread viruses and other infestations. I distinctly remember the time when I spread a virus all over my company because I got a workbook from a "trusted" colleague and so I told Excel it was OK to enable the macro. The problem was not that my colleague was untrustworthy; it was that he didn't even know that the workbook he sent me had a virus macro in it.

So now, in the 2007 Office release, a standard workbook is macro-free: it is guaranteed not to have any macros in it. There's no way it can spread a virus. If you do put a macro into a workbook, you must save it as a *macro-enabled* workbook.

> **Important** Macro-free workbooks happen to have the extension *.xlsx*, and macro-enabled workbooks have the extension *.xlsm*, but the file extension is not what matters. Macros are stored in a special section inside the workbook. Excel can easily tell whether the workbook contains a macro by looking at the content list of the workbook file; it doesn't even have to open the part of the workbook that contains the macro and could therefore be potentially dangerous. If you change the extension of a macro-enabled workbook to *.xlsx*, you just get an error when you try to open the workbook.

1. Click the **Microsoft Office Button**, point to the **Save As** arrow, click **Excel Macro-Enabled Workbook**, and click **Save**.

   This saves the workbook as *Chapter01.xlsm*.

2. Close the workbook, and use the **Recent Files** list on the **Office** menu to open it again.

   The file opens, but there's an alert message under the Ribbon that warns you that the macros are disabled for your safety.

3. On the security bar, click the **Options** button.

4. In the **Microsoft Office Security Options** dialog box, select **Enable This Content**.

5. Click **OK** to enable the macros and make the security bar disappear.

6. Select cells **D13:F13** and press Ctrl+Shift+C to format them as customize currency to make sure that the macro you created does work.

For your protection, Excel requires you to enable the macros each time you open the workbook. Even if you don't enable the macros, but then re-save the workbook, the macros don't go away. The next time you open the workbook you will still get the option to enable the macros. At the end of this chapter, you'll learn how to *trust* specific macro-enabled workbooks so that you don't have to enable the macros each time.

Changing Multiple Properties at Once

Now that you know how to save your work properly, let's get back to creating macros. The FormatCurrency macro you created earlier contains a statement that changes a single property (the number format) of a single object (the currently selected range of cells). Assigning a value to the property changes the object. Assigning a value to a property is a common way to carry out an action in VBA, and the recorder will often create a similar-looking statement when you record an action. But sometimes when you record a single action, the recorder assigns values to multiple properties all at once.

Create Sidebar Headings with a Command

A sidebar heading is a heading that is on the side of a group of rows, rather than at the top of a group of columns. Most of the time, headings are at the top, and therefore Excel has a Ribbon button that can merge and center several cells in a horizontal row. It's called the *Merge And Center button* and is in the Alignment group of the Home tab. But there is not a single button for creating sidebar headings. The Merge Cells option on the Merge And Center button list does allow you to merge vertically, and the Rotate Text Up option on the Orientation list allows you to rotate the text up, but there is not a command anywhere on the Ribbon that lets you create a sidebar heading in a single step. You can create a one-step sidebar heading action by recording a macro.

To better understand what's required, first walk through the steps to create the target format. Using the Alignment dialog box allows you to set both the text rotation and the cell merge at the same time.

1. Activate the Budget window.

2. Select the range **A6:A12**.

   The label *Variable* is at the top of the selected range.

	A	B	C	D
	A6		f_x	Variable
1	Summary		Rates	Jan-2007
2	Projected Units			29000
3	Projected Revenues			$71,000.00
4	Projected Pre-tax Profit			$28,094.90
5				
6	Variable			
7		Potting Soil	0.095	$2,755
8		Pots	0.012	$348
9		Seeds	0.002	$58
10		Fertilizer	0.002	$58
11		Labor	0.14	$4,060
12		FICA	0.011	$319
13	Total Variable			$7,598
14				

3. Right-click in the selection, and click **Format Cells**.

4. In the **Format Cells** dialog box, click the **Alignment** tab.

   The Alignment tab has several controls that control alignment, wrapping, orientation angle, text direction, shrinking, and merging.

5. Click the **Merge Cells** check box, and drag the red diamond in the orientation control to the top of the arc to set the orientation to 90 degrees.

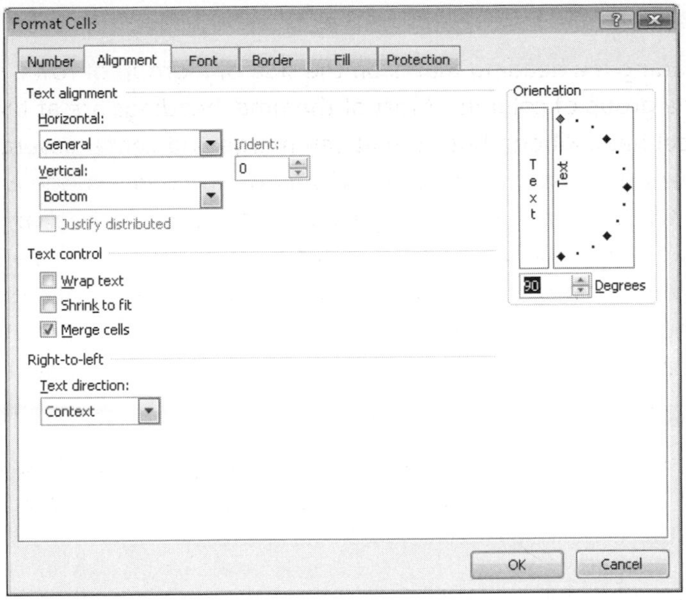
Format Cells
Number
Alignment
Font
Border
Fill
Protection
Text alignment
Horizontal:
General
Indent:
0
Vertical:
Bottom
Justify distributed
Text control
Wrap text
Shrink to fit
Merge cells
Right-to-left
Text direction:
Context
Orientation
Text
Text
90
Degrees
OK
Cancel

6. Click **OK** to merge and tilt the label.

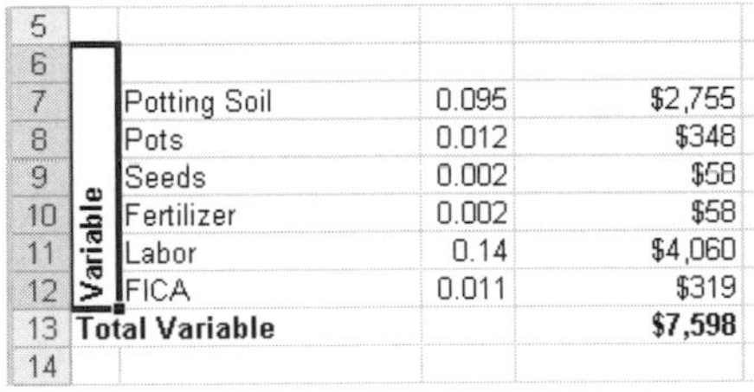

5				
6	Variable			
7		Potting Soil	0.095	$2,755
8		Pots	0.012	$348
9		Seeds	0.002	$58
10		Fertilizer	0.002	$58
11		Labor	0.14	$4,060
12		FICA	0.011	$319
13	**Total Variable**			**$7,598**
14				

A sidebar heading gives you some interesting layout opportunities. You can now record a macro to make it easy to create one whenever you like.

Record a Macro to Merge Cells Vertically

Rearrange your windows as necessary so that you can see both the Module1 window and the Excel window.

> **Tip** To rearrange the windows, minimize all the applications you have open except Excel and the Visual Basic editor, and activate Excel. Right-click the taskbar, and on the shortcut menu, click Show Windows Side By Side. (In Microsoft Windows XP, the command is Tile Windows Horizontally).

1. Select the range **A15:A20**, and then click the **Record Macro** button.

2. In the **Record Macro** dialog box, replace the default macro name with
SideBarHeading, replace the default description with Merge and Rotate cells
Vertically, and press Shift+S to set Ctrl+Shift+S as the shortcut key.

> **Important** If you assign the same shortcut key to two macros, the one that appears
> first in the Run Macro list is the one that runs. Also, a shortcut key is valid only while
> the workbook containing the macro is open.

3. Click **OK**.

In the module window, you can see that the recorder immediately
inserts the comment lines, the keyboard shortcut, and the Sub and End Sub
lines into the macro.

> **Tip** The first time you record a macro, Excel creates a new module. Each time
> you record an additional macro, Excel adds the new macro to the end of the same
> module. When you close and reopen the workbook, the macro recorder starts put-
> ting macros in a new module. There is no way for you to control where the record-
> er puts a new macro. Having macros in multiple modules shouldn't be a problem.
> When you use the Macro dialog box to select and edit a macro, it automatically
> takes you to the appropriate module.

4. Right–click the selection, and then click **Format Cells**.

5. In the **Format Cells** dialog box on the **Alignment** tab, select the **Merge Cells** check
box, set the orientation to 90 degrees, and click **OK**.

The recorder inserts several lines into the macro all at once.

6. Click the **Stop Recording** button, and save the *Chapter01* workbook.

The new macro in the Module1 window looks like this:

```
Sub SideBarHeading()
'
' SideBarHeading Macro
' Merge and Rotate cells Vertically
'
' Keyboard Shortcut: Ctrl+Shift+S
'
    With Selection
        .HorizontalAlignment = xlGeneral
        .VerticalAlignment = xlBottom
        .WrapText = False
        .Orientation = 90
        .AddIndent = False
        .IndentLevel = 0
```

```
        .ShrinkToFit = False
        .ReadingOrder = xlContext
        .MergeCells = True
End With
End Sub
```

The macro shows nine different properties that relate to cell alignment. Each property name is followed by an equal sign. These properties correspond to the controls you saw on the Alignment tab of the Format Cells dialog box.

All these properties pertain to the same object—the currently selected range of cells. This is the same object that the FormatCurrency macro uses, but in that macro, the property name comes right after the object, separated only by a period. This SideBarHeading macro is different because each property name just hangs there, preceded only by a dangling period.

The object for all these properties appears in a statement that begins with the word *With*. The group of statements from With to End With is called a *With structure*. Inside a With structure, you can put a dangling period in front of a property, and VBA just pretends that the object from the With statement is there. The macro recorder does that all the time, especially when you use a dialog box that has a lot of controls in it. A With structure makes the code easier to read because you can tell instantly that all the properties relate to the same object—in this case, the object is the currently selected range.

Eliminate Unnecessary Lines from the Macro

When you record a macro and make a change in a dialog box with a lot of controls, the recorder usually puts all the possible properties into the macro, even if you changed the values of only one or two of them. You can make your macro easier to understand if you eliminate unnecessary property assignments.

In the SideBarHeading macro, the only properties you need to change are Orientation and MergeCells, so you can delete all the other statements from the With structure.

1. Activate the Visual Basic editor window, and click as far to the left of the HorizontalAlignment statement as you can within the editor window. (Your mouse pointer should turn into a white arrow pointing northeast before you click.)

   This action selects the entire line, including the indent that precedes the text.

> **Troubleshooting** If you see a red circle in the margin after you click, you clicked too far into the gray area (and you need to learn the difference between North-East and North-West). Click in the red circle to remove it, and try again.

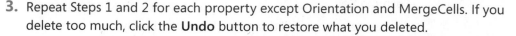

Macro Undo

2. Press the Delete key.

3. Repeat Steps 1 and 2 for each property except Orientation and MergeCells. If you delete too much, click the **Undo** button to restore what you deleted.

   The simplified macro (ignoring the comment lines, which you can delete if you want) should look like this:

```
Sub SideBarHeading()
    With Selection
        .Orientation = 90
        .MergeCells = True
    End With
End Sub
```

4. Activate the Excel window, and select cells **A25:A30**.

5. Press Ctrl+Shift+M.

   The macro adjusts the label. You can now create side-bar headings whenever you like (as long as this workbook is open).

6. Save the *Chapter01* workbook.

Now you've not only recorded a macro, but you've also deleted parts of it—and it still works. Next you'll record a macro and make *additions* to it.

Manipulating Recorded Properties

In a recorded macro, you can recognize a statement that assigns a value to a property because it always has an equal sign in the middle. Once you recognize a property in a recorded macro, you can easily change the way the macro works.

Record a Macro to Remove Window Elements

A typical Excel worksheet has several features that help you use the spreadsheet—the light gray gridlines that mark the boundaries of the cells, the row and column headings, and the formula bar. Most of the time, these are extremely helpful, but sometimes, you might want to remove them so that you can have a "clean" display. The Ribbon in Excel 2007 makes it very easy to turn each of these elements on or off, but you can create a macro that changes all three elements at the same time.

Arrange the workbook and macro windows so that you can see them both.

1. Click the **Record Macro** button.

2. Replace the default macro name with CleanDisplay, and click **OK**.

3. On the **View** tab of the Ribbon, clear the check boxes for **Gridlines**, **Headings**. and **Formula Bar.**

   All three elements will disappear from the display.

4. Click the **Stop Recording** button, and then save the *Chapter01* workbook.

5. Click the **Macros** button, select **CleanDisplay**, and then click **Edit** to look at the resulting code.

   Ignoring the comment lines, here's what it looks like:

```
Sub CleanDisplay()
    ActiveWindow.DisplayGridlines = False
    ActiveWindow.DisplayHeadings = False
    Application.DisplayFormulaBar = False
End Sub
```

The statements in this macro have a similar look to the one in the FormatCurrency macro. You can read the first one as "Let 'False' be the Display Gridlines state of the active window." This time you're not changing the selected cells but rather the active window. The second statement also changes something about the active window, but the third one changes something called the *Application*. In each case, you're changing the *property* of an *object*. A workbook window has different properties than a range of cells, and they have different properties than the application. The object is really just a way to group the properties. There's no such thing as a formula bar for a range of cells, and a single worksheet can have multiple windows, each with its own gridline and heading settings.

Run the Macro from the Visual Basic Editor

By looking at the macro, you can probably guess what you have to do to make it turn *on* these display features.

1. Replace each of the three occurrences of the word *False* with the word True.

   You can't use a shortcut key while you're in the Visual Basic editor, but the editor has its own shortcut for running whatever macro you're currently editing.

2. Press F5 to run the macro.

   The gridlines reappear in the current Excel worksheet. Pressing F5 from the Visual Basic editor is a fast way to run a macro while you're testing it.

> **Tip** In addition to using F5 to run the current macro in the Visual Basic editor, you can click the Run Sub/UserForm button in the toolbar. Also, if you want to be able to use the Macro dialog box to select a macro to run, click outside any macro before you press F5.

3. Press Ctrl+Z three times to change all the True values back to False.

4. Press F8 to run the macro.

The Sub statement turns yellow, but that's all. F8 *steps* through the macro, running one statement at a time. This lets you watch what the macro is doing.

5. Press F8 again to highlight the first statement in the body of the macro, but then put the mouse pointer over the word *DisplayGridlines* in the yellow statement.

You should see that the current state of the property is True.

6. Press F8 again to execute the statement (and highlight the next one). Again put the mouse pointer over the word *DisplayGridlines* in the statement that just executed.

You should see that the current state of the property is now False, because the macro just changed it.

7. Press F5 to run the rest of the macro.

One of the really cool things about a property is that you can use the exact same words to find out the current value of the property. This allows you to change your macro into one that *toggles* the value of the properties.

Use a Macro to Toggle the Value of a Property

If a property uses True and False as its values, you can toggle the value by using the VBA keyword *Not*. It's sort of like sarcastically saying, "That was a really funny joke—not!" You first ask Excel for the current value, and then you swap the value as you assign the value back to the property. Here's how:

1. Select **ActiveWindow.DisplayGridlines**, and copy it.

2. Select the word after the equal sign—it's probably the word *False*. Replace that word with **Not**, type a space, and then paste in the words you copied.

The resulting statement is

ActiveWindow.DisplayGridlines = Not ActiveWindow.DisplayGridlines

The Visual Basic keyword *Not* turns the value True into False and False into True.

3. Repeat the process for the other two statements: copy everything to the left of the equal sign, and paste it after the equal sign, replacing the current constant and inserting the word *Not*.

4. Change the name of the macro from *CleanDisplay* to ToggleCleanDisplay to better reflect the macro's new capabilities.

This is what the macro should look like now:

```
Sub ToggleCleanDisplay()
    ActiveWindow.DisplayGridlines = Not ActiveWindow.DisplayGridlines
    ActiveWindow.DisplayHeadings = Not ActiveWindow.DisplayHeadings
    Application.DisplayFormulaBar = Not Application.DisplayFormulaBar
End Sub
```

Macro Save

5. Click the **Save** button in the Visual Basic editor.

   This saves the workbook that contains the macros.

6. Click within the ToggleGrid macro, and then press F5 several times to test the macro.

The macro reads the old value of the property, changes it to the opposite with the keyword *Not*, and assigns the newly inverted value back to the property. By now, you should see a pattern to creating a simple convenience macro: First try out an action interactively. Once you know how to do the task, start the recorder. Do the task with the recorder on, and then stop the recorder and edit the recorded macro if necessary.

Eliminate Repeated Objects in a Recorded Macro

You may notice that your macro now contains the word *ActiveWindow* four different times. In each case, it is an object followed by a property. Based on what you've seen the macro recorder do, can you think of a way to only have to say *ActiveWindow* once? You move the object into a With structure, then let each property that needs the object begin with a dangling period, and then end the structure when you're finished. Here are the steps:

1. Put the insertion point just before the first occurrence of the word *ActiveWindow*, and type With, followed by a space.

2. Put the insertion point just before the first period and press Enter, creating a new line.

3. Delete all three remaining occurrences of the word *ActiveWindow*, but always leave the dangling period.

4. Just before the word *Application*, insert a new line, and type End With.

5. Press Tab to increase indentation, and Backspace to decrease indentation so that it is clear which statements are part of the structure. The finished structure should look like this:

```
With ActiveWindow
    .DisplayGridlines = Not .DisplayGridlines
    .DisplayHeadings = Not .DisplayHeadings
End With
```

6. Press F5 to test your changes.

It should toggle the same as before.

7. Create a With structure for the Application object, even though it occurs only twice—and both are in the same statement.

The finished structure should look like this:

```
With Application
    .DisplayFormulaBar = Not.DisplayFormulaBar
End With
```

8. Press F5 to test your changes, and save the *Chapter01* workbook.

Properties are a very powerful tool. When you detect a property assignment statement in a recorded macro, you can probably identify great opportunities for enhancing the macro.

Run a Macro from the Quick Access Toolbar

Keyboard shortcuts are convenient, but they are hard to remember. If you have a macro that you want to be able to run easily without having to remember a keyboard shortcut, you can add a custom button to Excel's Quick Access Toolbar. A particularly nice feature of the Quick Access Toolbar is that you can add a button that appears only when the workbook containing the macro is active. This helps you avoid cluttering up the Quick Access Toolbar with unusable buttons.

1. In the main Excel window, right-click anywhere in the **Quick Access Toolbar** (the row of buttons next to the Microsoft Office Button), and then click **Customize Quick Access Toolbar**.

This displays the Customize tab of the Excel Options dialog box.

2. In the **Customize Quick Access Toolbar** list, select **For Chapter01.xlsm**.

This will make the button visible only when the *Chapter01* workbook is active.

3. In the **Choose Commands From** list, select **Macros**, select **ToggleCleanDisplay**, and then click **Add**.

The macro name moves to the list on the right, but it shows a generic icon that may not help you remember what the macro does.

4. Select the **ToggleCleanDisplay** macro in the list on the right, and then click **Modify**.

5. In the **Modify** Button dialog box, select the white box icon (to symbolize a clean display), and then change the **Display Name** to Toggle Clean Display (which makes the tool tip easier to read without affecting the actual macro name).

6. Click **OK** twice to close both dialog boxes and return to Excel, which now has a new Toggle Clean Macro button in the Quick Access Toolbar.

Toggle Clean
Display

7. To try out the new **Toggle Clean Display** button, add a new workbook (which will make the button disappear), and then close it (which will make the button reappear).

Recording Methods in a Macro

So far, in all the macros you've created, the macro recorder has used property assignments to carry out actions. Sometimes assigning a value to a property is not the best way to carry out an action. For example, sometimes it is critical to make multiple changes simultaneously, and assigning properties is not the best way to keep everything synchronized. The ToggleCleanDisplay macro is a good example of that: because each property is independent of the others, it's very easy to get the toggle state inconsistent. Consequently, the Excel object model allows for a different way to carry out an action. This second method is called a—*method*. You can watch a method at work by using the macro recorder.

Convert a Formula to a Value by Using Menu Commands

For example, suppose that you want to freeze the formulas of some cells in the Budget worksheet at their current values. First change the formulas to values using menu commands—watching carefully how Excel does or does not prompt for additional information—and then create a macro that can change formulas to values for any arbitrary selection.

1. Start by activating the **Budget** window, and then select cell **D4**.

	A	B	C	D	E
	D4			f_x =D3-D54	
1	Summary		Rates	Jan-2007	Feb-2007
2	Projected Units			29000	30000
3	Projected Revenues			$71,000.00	$73,000.00
4	Projected Pre-tax Profit			28094.9	28332.9
5					

Notice the formula in the formula bar: =D3-D54.

2. Right-click the cell, and click the **Copy** command.

3. Right-click the cell again, and click the **Paste Special** command.

The Paste Special dialog box appears. This dialog box has four independent parts: the Paste group, the Operation group, the Skip Blanks check box, and the Transpose check box. You can choose only one option within each part, so you have four distinct choices you can make within this dialog box.

4. Select the **Values** option from the **Paste** group, and click **OK**.

   Excel pastes the value from the cell over the top of the existing cell, eliminating the formula that was in it. The moving border is still visible around the cell, indicating that you could paste the value again somewhere else.

5. Press the Esc key to get out of copy mode and clear the moving border.

   In the formula bar, cell D4 now contains the value 28094.9.

Copying and pasting cell values are actions that don't lend themselves to simple property assignments. When you execute the Copy command, what property would that be? Notice also that when you copy, you don't see a dialog box. Excel simply puts a moving border around the cells; you don't tell Excel *how* to do the copying.

When you execute the Paste Special command, on the other hand, you do see a dialog box. Excel needs additional information about exactly how you want the paste to behave. Think back to the Alignment tab of the Cell Format dialog box. That dialog box had multiple options, but the ones in Paste Special are different, because they *interact* with each other—if you select the Values option and the Add option and the Skip Blanks option all at the same time, they combine together to affect the one action of pasting. Given the interactive nature of all the dialog box controls, how would you do all that with a simple property assignment? When you record the same process in a macro, you'll see how a method looks different from a property.

Convert a Formula to a Value by Using a Macro

You can learn about how a macro uses methods by recording a macro that converts formulas to values. As you look at the recorded macro, you can compare the statements for actions that display or don't display a dialog box.

1. On the Budget worksheet, select cell **E4**.

   Notice the formula in the formula bar: =E3-E54.

2. Click **Record Macro**, replace the default name with **ConvertToValues**, press Shift+V to set the shortcut key to Ctrl+Shift+V, and then click **OK**.

3. Right-click cell **E4**, and click **Copy**.

4. Right-click cell **E4** again, then click **Paste Special**, click the **Values** option, and then click **OK**.

5. Press the Esc key to remove the moving border.

6. Click the **Stop Recording** button, and save the *Chapter01* workbook.

   In the formula bar, cell E4 now contains the value 28332.9.

7. Switch to the Visual Basic editor to look at the recorded macro.

> **Troubleshooting** If you closed the editor, go to the View tab of the Ribbon, click Macros, select ConvertToValue, and then click Edit.

Ignoring comments, the macro looks like this:

```
Sub ConvertToValues()
    Selection.Copy
    Selection.PasteSpecial Paste:=xlPasteValues, Operation:=xlNone, _
        SkipBlanks:=False, Transpose:=False
    Application.CutCopyMode = False
End Sub
```

The basic structure of this macro is the same as that of the other macros you've seen in this chapter: It starts with a Sub and ends with an End Sub, and has a bunch of statements in the middle. Also, the final statement in the body of the macro uses a familiar property assignment to set the value of the CutCopyMode property. This is how Excel interprets pressing Esc to remove the moving border around the cells.

The two statements that begin with Selection, however, are something new. Neither has a simple equal sign in it.

The statement Selection.Copy has two words, separated by a period. A word followed by a period is probably an object, and that's exactly what this is: a range of cells object. The word *Copy*, however, isn't a property; it's a method. That's why it doesn't have an equal sign after it. You don't assign anything to Copy; you just do it. Remember that the object is really just a way of grouping available commands. You can copy a range of cells, but you can't copy, say, a workbook window, so there's no such thing as ActiveWindow.Copy.

When you execute the Copy command in Excel, you don't see a dialog box asking you for any extra information. In the same way, when you use the Copy method in a macro, you don't give any extra information to the method.

The next statement begins with Selection.PasteSpecial. Once again, the word followed by a period—*Selection*—refers to an object. Once again, the word that follows the period—*PasteSpecial*—does not have a simple equal sign after it, so it's not a property. It's another method.

When you execute the Paste Special command in Excel, you see a dialog box that lets you give extra information to the command. In the same way, when you use the PasteSpecial method in a macro, you give the same extra information to the method. The extra pieces of information you give to a method are called *arguments*.

Using a method is like giving instructions to your nine-year-old son. With some instructions—such as "Come eat"—you don't have to give any extra information. With other instructions—such as "Go to the store for me"—you do have give more instructions: what to buy (milk), how to get there (on your bike), and when to come home (immediately). Giving an extra piece of information to your son is like giving an extra piece of information to an Excel method. In both cases, you end up with an argument.

The four arguments you use with the PasteSpecial method correspond exactly to the four distinct parts of the Paste Special dialog box. Each argument even has a name that matches the caption in the dialog box: Paste, Operation, SkipBlanks, and Transpose. When you use an argument, you don't actually have to include the argument name. This statement would function the same as

Selection.PasteSpecial xlPasteValues, xlNone, False, False

The names just make it easier to read, so the macro recorder includes them. If you do use a name for an argument, you put a colon-equal sign (:=) between the argument name and its value. The colon-equal sign may include an equal sign, but it's easy to tell them apart because the equal sign (used in a property assignment) always has a space on both sides.

Make a Long Statement More Readable

When a statement in a macro gets to be longer than about 70 characters, the macro recorder inserts a space and an underscore (_) after a convenient word and continues the statement on the next line. The underscore tells the macro that it should treat the second line as part of the same statement. You can manually break long statements into several lines, as long as you break the line after a space. You can also indent related lines with tabs to make the macro easier to read.

1. In the ConvertToValues macro, put each argument of the PasteSpecial statement on a separate line, using a space and an underscore character at the end of each line except the last.

```
Sub ConvertToValues()
    Selection.Copy
    Selection.PasteSpecial _
        Paste:=xlValues, _
        Operation:=xlNone, _
        SkipBlanks:=False, _
        Transpose:=False
    Application.CutCopyMode = False
End Sub
```

Splitting a statement into several lines doesn't change the way the macro runs; it just makes it easier to read.

2. In Excel, select cell **F4** and press Ctrl+Shift+V to run the macro. Look at the formula bar to make sure the formula changed to a value.

3. Save the *Chapter01* workbook.

Most of the macros in this chapter change the *property* of an object, but this macro executes the *method* of an object. Both properties and methods are separated from objects by periods, and both allow you to carry out actions. However, you assign a value to a property to carry out the action, whereas you simply execute a method, sometimes giving it arguments along the way.

Trusting Macro-Enabled Workbooks

If you frequently use workbooks that contain macros, having to enable the macros each time you open a workbook can be annoying—so annoying, in fact, that you might be tempted to disable the warning. Please don't do that. Eliminating the warning dramatically increases your computer's vulnerability to macro viruses. Excel 2007 provides two simple alternatives that allow you to safely eliminate the warning for workbooks that you trust. One alternative involves trusting the *location* of the macro workbooks. The other alternative involves trusting the *creator* (or publisher) of the workbook.

Designate a Trusted Location for Macros

The concept of a *trusted location* is that you designate a folder as a trusted, and then don't put macro-enabled workbooks into that folder if there is any chance that the workbook might be unsafe. Excel will then open any macro-enabled workbooks stored in that folder without a warning. Setting up the trusted location is a little bit complicated, but you only have to do it when you want to trust a new location.

1. Close the *Chapter01* workbook, and then re-open it.

2. In the warning bar, click the **Options** button, and then click the **Open the Trust Center** link at the bottom of the pop-up.

3. In the **Trust Center** dialog box, select the **Trusted Locations** group, and then click the **Add new location** button.

4. In the **Microsoft Office Trusted Location** dialog box, click the **Browse** button, navigate to the folder you created for the *Chapter01* macro-enabled workbook, and click **OK** to put the folder name into the **Path** box.

Microsoft Office Trusted Location

Warning: This location will be treated as a trusted source for opening files. If you change or add a location, make sure that the new location is secure.

Path:

C:\Users\Reed\Documents\MSP\ExcelVBA07SBS\Work

Browse...

☐ Subfolders of this location are also trusted

Description:

Date and Time Created: 13-Mar-07 17:59

OK   Cancel

5. Click the **OK** button three times to add the folder and close the dialog boxes.

The warning message should disappear.

6. Close the workbook, and then re-open it.

It should open without a warning.

7. Select cells **D16:F23** and press Ctrl+Shift+C to format the cells as customized currency.

This confirms that the macro still works.

If you put a workbook in a trusted location, you don't have to explicitly enable the macros. You have the responsibility to make sure that only trustworthy documents get into any of the trusted locations. Certain folders—such as the *Temporary Internet Files* folder—can never become trusted locations. You may want to look at the list folders Excel trusts by default and remove some of them as well, just to be safe.

Designate a Trusted Publisher for Macros

Specifying a trusted location is good for those situations where you can store all your macro-enabled workbooks in a very limited number of folders. It is also convenient when you receive macro-enabled workbooks from several different (trustworthy) colleagues. But if you create macro-enabled workbooks and need to store them in arbitrary locations, you can also designate yourself as a trusted publisher.

First, you need a macro-enable workbook that is not in a trusted location.

1. Click the **Microsoft Office Button**, point to **Save As**, and click **Macro-Enabled Workbook**.

2. Navigate to an un-trusted folder (such as the main folder that contains the practice files for this book), change the name of the workbook to Chapter01A.xlsm, and then click **Save**.

In order to trust yourself as a publisher, you must be able to prove who you are. To do that, you must first create a digital ID. The Microsoft Office Button contains a shortcut that allows you to create the digital ID you need.

1. In Excel, click the **Microsoft Office Button**, point to **Prepare**, and click **Add a Digital Signature**.

> **Troubleshooting** If you see a message that encourages you to go to the Microsoft Office Marketplace, click OK to go to the Get A Digital ID dialog box.

2. In the **Get a Digital ID** dialog box, select **Create your own digital ID**.

Creating your own digital ID is secure, but it is also valid only for you and on only the current computer. If a different user logs into your computer, the ID will not be valid for them. If you copy the workbook to a different computer, the ID will not be valid there. If you need a digital ID that can be used in multiple environments, you need to obtain one from a trusted source. You can either purchase a digital ID, or check with your company's Information Technology department to see if they can provide a digital ID for use within the company.

3. Click **OK** to display the **Create a Digital ID** dialog box, and enter your name, plus any additional information you choose.

4. Click **Create**, *and then stop.*

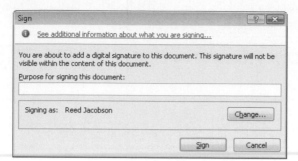

5. Do not click the Sign button. Do not pass Go. Do not collect $200. Click **Cancel**.

> **Important** Adding a digital signature to a workbook is different from adding one to the VBA project stored inside the workbook. The Prepare command on the Microsoft Office Button is a convenient way to create a new digital ID, but if you actually sign the document, you prevent any changes to the workbook cells. Conversely, when you add a signature to a VBA project, only the macros are signed and anyone can still make changes to the workbook. Make sure you go to the Visual Basic editor to add the actual signature.

6. Switch to the Visual Basic editor, click the **Tools** menu, and click **Digital Signature**.

The top portion of the Digital Signature dialog box shows whether the project is currently signed. The bottom portion shows digital signatures that are already trusted.

7. Click the **Choose** button, and then in the **Select Certificate** list, select the certificate you just created—it should have your name on it.

8. Click **OK**.

9. After confirming that the project is currently signed with your certificate, click **OK** again.

    You now have a digital ID, and you have used it to sign the project, but there is still one more step: You have not yet told Excel that you want to trust yourself as a publisher.

10. Switch back to Excel and close the *Chapter01A* workbook, saving the changes back to the untrusted location. (The change you made was to sign the VBA project.)

11. Re-open the workbook, and click **Options** on the **Security Warning** bar.

    An ominous-looking security alert appears, but all it really says is that "you have not yet chosen to trust" yourself.

12. Give it a lot of thought, but if you do decide to trust yourself to publish only macros that don't destroy your own computer, select **Trust All Documents From This Publisher**, and then click **OK**.

> **Troubleshooting** Depending on how you close and open the workbook, a different form of the security alert may appear immediately. Just click the Trust All From This Publisher button in the security alert and continue.

13. Close the workbook and open it again. No notice appears.

14. Select a suitable cell that contains a formula, and press Ctrl+Shift+V to make sure the macros work.

15. To confirm the Trusted Publishers list, click the **Microsoft Office Button**, and then click **Excel Options** at the bottom.

16. Select the **Trust Center** tab and click the **Trust Center Setting** button on the right.

17. Select the **Trusted Publishers** tab and see your certificate listed.

You can revoke the trust for a publisher at any time, just as you can revoke the trust for a location at any time.

18. Click **Cancel** twice to close the dialog boxes.

> **Important** You can use the Prepare command to create a digital ID, but you cannot use the same approach to delete a digital ID. To delete a digital ID from your computer, you must go to Internet Options in the Windows Control Panel. On the Content tab, click Certificates. The Certificates dialog box allows you to delete or import digital certificates from your computer, but it does not allow you to create a new personal digital ID. Creating a personal digital ID is part of the 2007 Microsoft Office system. If you remove a digital certificate from your computer, that does not remove it from the trusted publishers. You can still use the macro-enabled workbook, but making any subsequent changes to the macros destroys the signature on the project.

Security is important when you create any programs, including macros. Security is especially important when you share applications with others. If you are mostly creating macro-enabled workbooks for your own use, a personal digital ID is a simple, but flexible solution. If you are sharing macro-enabled workbooks with a small group of people, the trusted locations approach is probably a good solution. If you need to create macro-enabled documents for a wider audience, you'll probably want to obtain a properly authenticated digital signature to allow others to take advantage of your work.

> **CLOSE** the *Chapter01.xlsx* workbook.

Key Points

- The easiest way to start and stop recording macros is by using the small button in the status bar. To review or run macros, use the Macros button on the View tab.

- Dock, undock, hide and show windows freely in the Visual Basic editor. It's your working environment—make it work for you.

- When you have macros that relate to a single workbook, assign them to the Quick Access Toolbar for just that workbook. You might want to be more judicious about which macros you assign to the global Quick Access Toolbar.

- Don't be afraid to change what the macro recorder created—if you save a backup copy of the original, you can always restore it later. Delete unnecessary statement and property assignments. This will make your macro much easier to understand the next time you use it.

- Take advantage of the new security features to keep your computer—and your company's network—safe. Be very careful which folders and publishers you trust. If you receive a macro-enabled workbook from someone else—whether you trust them or not—open it with macros disabled and inspect the macros before you put the workbook into a trusted location.

Chapter at a Glance

Watch a macro run by stepping through it, **page 42**

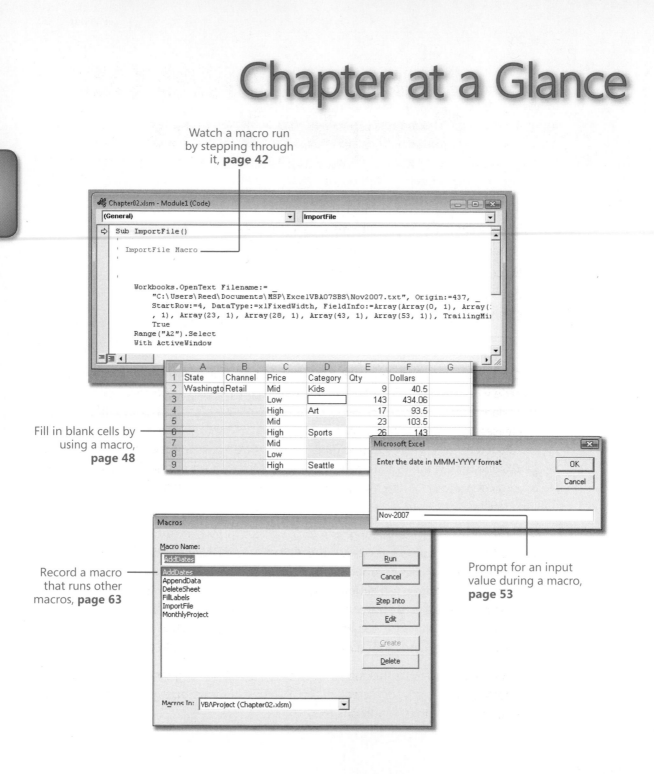

Fill in blank cells by using a macro, **page 48**

Prompt for an input value during a macro, **page 53**

Record a macro that runs other macros, **page 63**

2 Make a Macro Do Complex Tasks

In this chapter, you will learn to:

✔ Break a complex project into manageable pieces.

✔ Watch a macro run one statement at a time.

✔ Enter values into a macro while it's running.

✔ Record movements relative to the active cell.

✔ Create a macro that runs other macros.

Rube Goldberg was famous for inventing intricate contraptions with hundreds of parts that made what should have been a simple device appear wildly complex. For example, his cat "alarm clock" drops a ball into a bucket and the weight of the bucket lifts a lever that releases a spring that wakes up a cat. The Milton Bradley game company has had years of success with the Mousetrap game, which is based on a Rube Goldberg concept. Rube Goldberg contraptions are fun to look at. Two massive, perpetually working Rube Goldberg contraptions in the lobby of Boston's Logan International Airport have entertained travelers for hours.

Entertainment is one thing. Getting your job done is another. For example, the steps you might go through to get out a monthly report can be as complicated as a Rube Goldberg invention. First you import the monthly order file and add new columns to it. Then you sort it and print it and sort it a different way and print it again. Then you paste it at the end of the cumulative order-history file, and so forth. Each step has to be completed just right before the next one is started. Pretty soon, you start scheduling your vacations around the project because you don't want to train someone else to do it. Right?

One good use for macros is making cumbersome Rube Goldberg tasks simple. By putting the numerous steps involved in creating that Rube Goldberg monthly report in a macro, you can accomplish the task with one mouse click.

The secret to creating a macro capable of handling a long, intricate project is to break the project into small pieces, create a macro for each piece, and then glue the pieces together. If you just turn on the recorder, carry out 400 steps, and cross your fingers hoping for the best, you have about a 1-in-400 chance of having your macro work properly. Let's look at a hypothetical example.

As the bookkeeper at Lucerne Publishing, you have an elaborate month-end project that you'd like to automate so that you can delegate it to subordinates when you go on vacation. You get a monthly summary report of orders for the previous month from the order-processing system.

```
                    Company Confidential
                Order Summary for November 2007

State        Channel     Price  Category            Qty    Dollars
=========== =========== ====== ================ ======== =========
Washington   Retail      Mid    Kids                   9       40.5
                         Low                          143     434.06
                         High   Art                    17      93.5
                         Mid                           23     103.5
                         High   Sports                 26       143
                         Mid                            6        27
                         Low                            4        14
                         High   Seattle                13      71.5
                         Mid                            7      31.5
                         Low                           25      87.5
                         Mid    Dinosaurs              22        99
                         Low                           22        77
                         Mid    Humor                 143     554.32
                         Low                           13      45.5
                         Mid    Nature                 35     157.5
                         Low                           40       140
             Wholesale   Mid    Kids                   30      67.5
                         Low                           10      17.5
                         High   Art                   410   1,062.13
                         Mid                          900   1,848.48
                         High   Sports                 25     68.75
                         Mid                           30      67.5
                         Low                            5       8.75
```

The report shows sales information for each combination of state, channel, price range, and category. The order-processing system still exports the report as a text file. You prepare the file and add the new month's orders to a cumulative order-history database.

This chapter shows you how to record the separate tasks that make up this large, complex project as small, testable macros. Subsequently, you combine these small macros into one comprehensive macro. Along the way, you might learn some useful techniques for completing everyday tasks as well.

Important Before you complete this chapter, you need to install the practice files from the book's companion CD to their default locations. See "Using the Book's CD" on page xv for more information.

USE a new blank, macro-enabled workbook and the *Orders.xlsx* and *Nov2007.txt* files. These practice files are located in the *Documents\MSP\ExcelVBA07SBS* folder.

BE SURE TO save the new workbook as *Chapter02.xlsx* in the trusted *Work* folder that you created in Chapter 1. (If you didn't create a trusted folder, you will have to enable the macros each time you close and re-open the workbook. For details about macro-enabled workbooks and creating a trusted folder, see "Save the Macro Workbook" in Chapter 1, "Make a Macro Do Simple Tasks.")

OPEN the *Chapter02.xlsx* workbook.

Task One: Opening the Report File

The orders for the most recent month, November 2007, are in the *Nov2007* text file. The first task is to open the file, splitting it into columns as you do, and move the file into the workbook with the macro.

Open a Text File

Tip You might want to carry out Steps 3 through 6 as a dry run before recording the macro.

1. If the *Chapter02* workbook window is maximized, click the **Restore Window** button (for the workbook, not for the Excel application).

2. On the status bar, click the **Record Macro** button, type ImportFile as the macro name, and then click **OK**.

3. Click the **Microsoft Office Button**, and click **Open**.

4. Select **Nov2007.txt** in the list of files, and then click **Open**.

Step 1 of the Text Import Wizard appears. In Step 1, the first three rows of the file contain the report title and a blank line. You want to skip the first three rows.

5. Change the **Start import at row** value to 4.

6. Accept all the other default options, and click **Finish**.

The text file opens, with the columns split into Excel columns.

7. Drag up the bottom of the new window so that you can see the tabs at the bottom of the *Chapter02* workbook. Then drag the tab for the **Nov2007** worksheet on to the **Sheet1** tab of the *Chapter02* workbook.

	A	B	C	D	E	F	G	H
1	State	Channel	Price	Category	Qty	Dollars		
2	========	=======	=====	= ======	= =======	=========		
3	Washingto	Retail	Mid	Kids	9	40.5		
4			Low		143	434.06		
5			High	Art	17	93.5		
6			Mid		23	103.5		
7			High	Sports	26	143		
8			Mid		6	27		
9			Low		4	14		
10			High	Seattle	13	71.5		
11			Mid		7	31.5		
12			Low		25	87.5		

Nov2007.txt

Chapter02.xlsm

Nov2007

Sheet1   Sheet2   Sheet3

The Nov2007 worksheet moves to the *Chapter02* workbook, and the *Nov2007.txt* workbook disappears (because it lost its only worksheet, and a workbook can't exist without at least one sheet).

> **Tip** You'll have several copies of the Nov2007 worksheet after you test this macro several times. Multiple copies will be useful as you develop the macros for later project tasks. Once you have a worksheet named Nov2007 in the workbook, new copies are automatically named Nov2007 (2), Nov2007 (3), and so forth.

8. Row 2 contains equal signs that you don't need. Select cell **A2**. On the **Home** tab of the Ribbon, in the **Cells** group, click the **Delete** arrow, and then click **Delete Sheet Rows**.

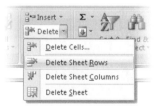

9. Select cell **A1**, and click the **Stop Recording** button to stop the recorder.

10. Save the *Chapter02* workbook.

You should now have the imported file split into columns and stripped of extraneous rows.

Watch a Macro Run by Stepping Through It

Rather than merely read a macro, you can step through it. This allows you to both read and test the macro as you watch it work. As you step through the macro, make notes of minor changes you might want to make to it.

When you step through a macro, the Visual Basic editor window appears over the top of the workbook. The Visual Basic editor window displays the selected macro and allows you to see which statement will execute next.

1. On the **View** tab of the Ribbon, click the **Macros** button, select **ImportFile** from the **Macro Name** list, and click **Step Into**.

The Visual Basic editor window appears on top of the workbook, with your recorded macro visible in the module. The statement that is ready to execute is highlighted in yellow, with a yellow arrow in the left margin.

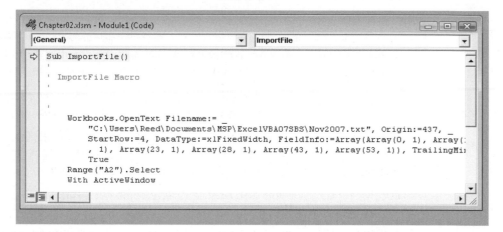

The highlighted statement, which is the first statement in the macro, contains the macro name.

```
Sub ImportFile()
```

2. Press F8 once or twice as needed to highlight the OpenText statement in the body of the macro.

In your recorded macro, specific details such as line divisions and locations of the file and windows will differ from those in this example.

```
ChDir "C:\MSP\ExcelVBA07SBS"
Workbooks.OpenText _
    Filename:="C:\MSP\ExcelVBA07SBS\Nov2007.txt", _
    Origin:=437, _
    StartRow:=4, _
    DataType:=xlFixedWidth, _
    FieldInfo:=Array(Array(0, 1), Array(11, 1), Array(23, 1), _
    Array(28, 1), Array(43, 1), Array(53, 1)), _
    TrailingMinusNumbers:=True
```

The ChDir statement is there because you changed to the folder containing the practice files. (ChDir stands for *Change Directory* because folders used to be called *directories*.) Since the OpenText statement contains the full path to the file, the ChDir statement is redundant, but it may come in handy later, so don't mark it for deletion.

The long OpenText statement opens the text file. You can probably identify the argument that specifies the file name. The Origin and DataType arguments were default values in the first step of the Text Import Wizard. The StartRow argument is where you specified the number of rows to skip. The FieldInfo argument specifies how to split the text file into columns. The TrailingMinusNumbers argument is irrelevant because there are no negative numbers in this file. Be grateful that the macro recorder can create this statement so that you don't have to!

The macro recorder divides this long statement into several lines by putting a space and an underscore at the end of each partial line. However, it doesn't divide the statement at the most logical places. When you edit the macro, you should redivide the statement into meaningful lines. You can use the way the statement is divided in the preceding OpenText statement as an example.

For this type of process, you open a different file each month. This month, you opened the *Nov2007* text file; next month, you'll open the *Dec2007* text file. Make a note to change the macro statement to let you select the specific file to open. You'll learn how to prompt for a file name in the next section.

3. Press F8 to open the file and highlight the next statement, which is the first line of this With structure:

```
With ActiveWindow
    .Width = 452.25
    .Height = 254.25
End With
```

These four statements were added when you moved the window out of the way. (Your Width and Height properties might have different values, and if you moved the window, there will be statements that change the Top and Left properties as well.) These are just accidental events that happen when you record a macro. It's a good idea to eliminate them from the finished macro.

4. Press F8 to step through any statements that move, resize, or activate windows. Make a note to delete all of them. This then highlights the next statement:

```
Sheets("Nov2007").Select
```

This statement makes the Nov2007 worksheet active, even though it was already the active sheet. (Macro recorders can't be too cautious.) You'll be able to delete this statement later also.

> **Tip** You can edit many statements while stepping through the macro. For example, you could delete the Select statement. Some changes, however, would force you to restart the macro. For example, you can't delete a With structure without restarting the macro (although you can delete individual statements inside a With structure). Visual Basic warns you if you try to make a change that would require you to restart the macro.

5. Press F8 to select the already-selected sheet, and make a note to delete the statement. This highlights the next statement:

```
Sheets("Nov2007").Move _
    Before:=Workbooks("Chapter02.xlsm").Sheets(1)
```

This statement moves the new sheet into the *Chapter02* workbook. But when you run this macro next month, the sheet won't be named Nov2007. It will be named Dec2007.

6. Press F8 to move the worksheet, and make a note to modify the macro so that it will work every month. This highlights the next statement:

```
Range("A2").Select
```

This statement selects cell A2 of the worksheet.

7. Press F8 to select cell **A2**. This highlights the next statement:

```
Selection.EntireRow.Delete
```

Because the selected range of cells consists of cell A2 and this statement deletes the entire row of the selected range of cells, this statement ultimately just deletes row 2.

8. Press F8 to delete the row. This highlights the final statement in the body of the macro:

```
Range("A1").Select
```

This statement selects cell A1. This is just a nice touch to leave the macro in the "default" location.

9. Press F5 to run the remainder of the macro.

In summary, here is your list of the changes you need to make to the recorded macro:

- Delete unnecessary statements.
- Allow the user to decide which file to open.
- Make the macro work with any month's file.

In the next section, you'll learn how to make these changes.

Select a File While Running a Macro

Excel provides a method that prompts the user to open a file, but Excel doesn't actually open the file. Instead it returns the name of the file, which you can turn over to the OpenText method.

1. Make the statement that begins with Workbooks.Open easier to read by dividing it into meaningful lines. Put a space and an underscore at the end of each partial line.

    Follow the ImportFile macro example in the section titled "Watch a Macro Run by Stepping Through It," earlier in this chapter.

2. Insert a new line immediately before the Workbooks.OpenText statement, and enter this statement:

    ```
    myFile = Application.GetOpenFilename("Text Files,*.txt")
    ```

    As soon as you type the period after Application, Visual Basic displays a list of all the methods and properties that can be used with an Application object. This feature is called *Auto List Members*. (The word *Members* refers to both methods and properties.) When you type the letter *G*, the list scrolls to show methods and properties that begin with that letter. At that point, you can press the Down Arrow key to select GetOpenFilename, and then press the Tab key to enter the method name into the macro.

    When you type the opening parenthesis, Visual Basic displays the possible arguments for the GetOpenFilename method. This feature is called *Auto Quick Info*. You can ignore it for now. Just type the words in parentheses as they appear at the beginning of this step.

    > **Tip** If you want to show all the files in the folder—not just the files with the *.txt* extension, just leave the parentheses after GetOpenFilename empty.

The Application.GetOpenFilename method displays the Open dialog box, just as if you had clicked the Open command on the Microsoft Office Button list The words in parentheses tell the method to display only text files—files ending with the *.txt* extension. (Be careful to type the quotation marks just as they appear at the beginning of this step.) The word *myFile* at the beginning of the statement is a variable, or placeholder, for storing the selected file name.

3. In the Workbooks.OpenText statement, select the entire file name, including the quotation marks, and delete it. In its place, type myFile.

The first part of the statement should look like this when you finish:

```
Workbooks.OpenText _
    Filename:=myFile, _
    Origin:=xlWindows, _
    StartRow:=4, _
```

By the time this statement executes, the variable *myFile* will contain the name of the file. Now that you have eliminated the full path from the OpenText method, the ChDir statement at the beginning becomes very handy—it automatically puts the GetOpenFilename function into the appropriate directory (assuming that the incoming text files always go to the same place).

4. Delete the statements that resize the window and the statement that selects the Nov2007 sheet.

5. Change the words *Sheets("Nov2007").Move* to ActiveSheet.Move.

ActiveSheet is a special word that refers to whatever sheet happens to be active. This allows your macro to work with a new sheet from any month.

When you're finished, the macro should look essentially like this:

```
Sub ImportFile()
    ChDir "C:\MSP\ExcelVBA07SBS"
    myFile = Application.GetOpenFilename("Text Files,*.txt")
    Workbooks.OpenText _
        Filename:=myFile, _
        Origin:=437, _
        StartRow:=4, _
        DataType:=xlFixedWidth, _
        FieldInfo:=Array(Array(0, 1), Array(11, 1), Array(23, 1), _
        Array(28, 1), Array(43, 1), Array(53, 1)), _
        TrailingMinusNumbers:=True
    ActiveSheet.Move Before:=Workbooks("Chapter02.xlsm").Sheets(1)
    Range("A2").Select
    Selection.EntireRow.Delete
    Range("A1").Select
End Sub
```

6. Save the *Chapter02* workbook.

> **Troubleshooting** If *Option Explicit* appears at the top of your module sheet, delete it before continuing.

7. Press F8 to step through the macro, and watch each statement work.

The macro should display the Open dialog box (displaying only text files), and then it should open the file that you select, delete the unwanted Row 2, and move the worksheet to the *Chapter02* workbook.

8. Press F5 to run through the macro in normal mode.

It should behave the same.

That concludes the macro for the first task of your month-end processing project. By now, you should have two or three copies of the Nov2007 worksheet in the *Chapter02* workbook. You're ready to move on to the next task.

Task Two: Filling In Missing Labels

When the order-processing system produces a summary report, it enters a label in a column only the first time that label appears. Leaving out duplicate labels is one way to make a report easier for a human being to read, but for the computer to sort and summarize the data properly, you need to fill in the missing labels.

	A	B	C	D	E	F	G
1	State	Channel	Price	Category	Qty	Dollars	
2	Washingto	Retail	Mid	Kids	9	40.5	
3			Low		143	434.06	
4			High	Art	17	93.5	
5			Mid		23	103.5	
6			High	Sports	26	143	
7			Mid		6	27	
8			Low		4	14	
9			High	Seattle	13	71.5	

You might assume that you need to write a complex macro to examine each cell and determine whether it's empty, and if so, what value it needs. In fact, you can use Excel's built-in capabilities to do most of the work for you. Because this part of the project introduces some powerful worksheet features, start by going through the steps before recording the macro.

Select Only the Blank Cells

Look at the places where you want to fill in missing labels. What value do you want in each empty cell? You want each empty cell to contain the value from the first nonempty cell above it. In fact, if you were to select each empty cell in turn and put into it a formula pointing at the cell immediately above it, you would have the result you want. The range of empty cells is an irregular shape, however, which makes the prospect of filling all the cells with a formula daunting. Fortunately, Excel has a built-in tool for selecting an irregular range of blank cells.

1. In a copy of the Nov2007 worksheet in the *Chapter02* workbook, select cell **A1**.

2. On the **Home** tab of the Ribbon, in the **Editing** group, click the **Find & Select** arrow, and then click **Go To Special**.

3. In the **Go To Special** dialog box, click **Current region**, and then click **OK**.

Excel selects the *current region*—the rectangle of cells including the active cell that is surrounded by blank cells or worksheet borders.

> **Tip** You also can press Ctrl+* to select the current region. Press and hold the Ctrl key while pressing either * on the numeric keypad or Shift+8 on the regular keyboard.

4. Once again, click the **Find & Select** arrow on the Ribbon, and then click **Go To Special**.

5. In the **Go To Special** dialog box, click the **Blanks** option, and then click **OK**.

   Excel subselects only the blank cells from the selection. These are the cells that need new values.

	A	B	C	D	E	F	G
1	State	Channel	Price	Category	Qty	Dollars	
2	Washingto	Retail	Mid	Kids	9	40.5	
3			Low		143	434.06	
4			High	Art	17	93.5	
5			Mid		23	103.5	
6			High	Sports	26	143	
7			Mid		6	27	
8			Low		4	14	
9			High	Seattle	13	71.5	

Excel's built-in Go To Special feature can save you—and your macro—a lot of work.

Fill the Selection with Values

You now want to fill each of the selected cells with a formula that points to the cell above. Normally when you enter a formula, Excel puts the formula into only the active cell. You can, however, if you ask politely, have Excel put a formula into all the selected cells at once.

1. With the blank cells selected and **D3** as the active cell, type an equal sign (=), and then press the Up Arrow key to point to cell **D2**.

The cell reference D2—when used in a formula in cell D3—actually means "one cell above me in the same column."

2. Press Ctrl+Enter to fill the formula into all the currently selected cells.

When more than one cell is selected, if you type a formula and press Ctrl+Enter, the formula is copied into all the cells of the selection. (If you press the Enter key without pressing and holding the Ctrl key, the formula goes into only the one active cell.) Each cell with the new formula points to the cell above it.

	A	B	C	D	E	F	G
1	State	Channel	Price	Category	Qty	Dollars	
2	Washington	Retail	Mid	Kids	9	40.5	
3	Washington	Retail	Low	Kids	143	434.06	
4	Washington	Retail	High	Art	17	93.5	
5	Washington	Retail	Mid	Art	23	103.5	
6	Washington	Retail	High	Sports	26	143	
7	Washington	Retail	Mid	Sports	6	27	
8	Washington	Retail	Low	Sports	4	14	
9	Washington	Retail	High	Seattle	13	71.5	

3. Press Ctrl+* to select the current region.

4. Right-click any selected cell, and click **Copy**. Right-click any selected cell, click **Paste Special**, click the **Values** option, and then click **OK**.

5. Press the Esc key to get out of copy mode, and then select cell **A1**.

Now the block of cells contains all the missing-label cells as values, so the contents won't change if you happen to re-sort the summary data.

Record Filling In the Missing Values

In this section, you'll select a different copy of the imported worksheet and follow the same steps, but with the macro recorder turned on.

1. Select a copy of the Nov2007 worksheet (one that doesn't have the labels filled in), or run the **ImportFile** macro again.

2. Click the **Record Macro** button, type FillLabels as the name of the macro, and then click **OK**.

3. Select cell **A1** (even if it's already selected), and press Ctrl+* to select the current region.

4. Click the **Find & Select** arrow on the Ribbon, click **Go To Special**, click the **Blanks** option, and then click **OK**.

5. Type an equal sign (=), press the Up Arrow key, and press Ctrl+Enter.

6. Press Ctrl+*, right-click, and click **Copy**. Then right-click, click **Paste Special**, click the **Values** option, and then click **OK**.

7. Press the Esc key to get out of copy mode, and then select cell **A1**.

8. Click the **Stop Recording** button, and then save the *Chapter02* workbook.

   You've finished creating the FillLabels macro.

Watch the FillLabels Macro Run

Now read the macro while you step through it.

1. Select (or create) another copy of the imported worksheet.

2. On the **View** tab of the Ribbon, click the **View Macros** button, select the **FillLabels** macro, and then click **Step Into**.

   The Visual Basic editor window appears, with the header statement of the macro highlighted.

3. Press F8 to move to the first statement in the body of the macro:

   ```
   Range("A1").Select
   ```

   This statement selects cell A1. It doesn't matter how you got to cell A1—whether you clicked the cell, pressed Ctrl+Home, or pressed various arrow keys—because the macro recorder always records just the result of the selection process.

4. Press F8 to select cell A1 and highlight the next statement:

   ```
   Selection.CurrentRegion.Select
   ```

This statement selects the current region of the original selection.

5. Press F8 to select the current region and move to the next statement:

```
Selection.SpecialCells(xlCellTypeBlanks).Select
```

This statement selects the blank special cells of the original selection. (The word *SpecialCells* is a method that handles many of the options in the Go To Special dialog box.)

6. Press F8 to select just the blank cells and move to the next statement:

```
Selection.FormulaR1C1 = "=R[-1]C"
```

This statement assigns =R[-1]C as the formula for the entire selection. When you entered the formula, the formula you saw was =C2, not =R[-1]C. The formula =C2 really means "get the value from the cell just above me," but only if the active cell happens to be cell C3. The formula =R[-1]C also means "get the value from the cell just above me," but without regard for which cell is active.

You could change this statement to Selection.Formula = "=C2" and the macro would work exactly the same—provided that the order file you use when you run the macro is identical to the order file you used when you recorded the macro and that the active cell happens to be cell C3 when the macro runs. However, if the command that selects blanks produces a different active cell, the revised macro will fail. The macro recorder uses R1C1 notation so that your macro will always work correctly.

See Also For more information about R1C1 notation, see the section titled "R1C1 Reference Style" in Chapter 4, "Explore Range Objects."

7. Press F5 to execute the remaining statements in the macro:

```
Selection.CurrentRegion.Select
Selection.Copy
Selection.PasteSpecial Paste:=xlPasteValues, _
    Operation:=xlNone, SkipBlanks:=False, Transpose:=False
Application.CutCopyMode = False
Range("A1").Select
```

These statements select the current region, convert the formulas to values, cancel copy mode, and select cell A1.

See Also The final statements in this macro are identical to the PasteSpecial macro from the section titled "Convert a Formula to a Value by Using a Macro" in Chapter 1, "Make a Macro Do Simple Tasks."

You've completed the macro for the second task of your month-end project. Now you can start a new macro to carry out the next task—adding dates.

Task Three: Adding a Column of Dates

The order summary report you import doesn't include the dates in each row because that would not be useful to people using the report. But you want to add the data to a master order history list, and the master list does include dates in each row because it contains data for multiple months.

Add a Constant Date

First you'll create a macro that fills the range with the date *Nov-2007* by inserting a new column A and putting the date into each row that contains data.

1. Select a worksheet that has the labels filled in, click the **Record Macro** button, type AddDates as the name of the macro, and then click **OK**.

2. Select cell **A1**. On the **Home** tab of the Ribbon, click the **Insert** arrow, and click **Insert Sheet Columns**.

    Excel inserts a new column A, shifting the other columns to the right.

3. Type Date in cell **A1**, and then press Enter.

4. Press Ctrl+* to select the current region.

5. On the **Home** tab of the Ribbon, click the **Find & Select** arrow, and click **Go To Special**. Click the **Blanks** option, and click **OK** to select only the blank cells.

    These are the cells that need date values.

6. Type Nov-2007, and press Ctrl+Enter.

    Excel fills the date into all the rows. (Excel displays the date as Nov-07, but it stores the full date, as you can verify by looking at the formula bar.)

7. Select cell **A1**, and then click the **Stop Recording** button to stop the recorder.

Step Through the Macro

To understand what the macro recorder created, look at the macro as you step through it.

1. With cell **A1** selected, on the **Home** tab of the Ribbon, click the **Delete** arrow, click **Delete Sheet Columns**, and then click **OK**.

2. On the **View** tab of the Ribbon, click the **View Macros** button, select the **AddDates** macro, and then click **Step Into**.

If you ignore the comments, this is what the macro should look like:

```
Sub AddDates()
    Range("A1").Select
    Selection.EntireColumn.Insert
    ActiveCell.FormulaR1C1 = "Date"
    Range("A2").Select
    Selection.CurrentRegion.Select
    Selection.SpecialCells(xlCellTypeBlanks).Select
    Selection.FormulaR1C1 = "Nov-2007"
    Range("A1").Select
End Sub
```

This macro is pretty straightforward. Notice that the statement that enters the word *Date* uses the word *ActiveCell* as the object, changing the "formula" of only the active cell, whereas the statement that enters the actual date uses the word *Selection* as the object, changing the "formula" of the entire range of selected cells. When you enter a formula using the Enter key alone, the macro uses the word *ActiveCell*. When you enter a formula using Ctrl+Enter, the macro uses the word *Selection*. (If the selection consists of only a single cell, *ActiveCell* and *Selection* are equivalent.)

In addition, using just the Enter key changes the selection to the next cell down. That's why the Range("A2").Select statement is in the macro. It doesn't hurt anything, but it is also unnecessary. Removing unnecessary statements from a recorded macro makes it easier to read, and easier to modify in the future if you ever need to.

3. Delete the **Range("A2").Select** statement from the macro.

4. Press F8 repeatedly to step through the macro.

The recorder always records the insertion of a value into a cell by using the FormulaR1C1 property—even if you enter a constant—just in case you might have entered a formula.

Prompt for the Date

Your recorded macro should work just fine—assuming that you always run it using the *Nov2007* text file. But the next time you actually use this macro, you'll be working with December orders, not November orders. You need to change the macro so that it puts in the correct date. One way to do that is to have the macro ask you for the date as it runs.

1. Insert a new line after the comments in the AddDates macro, and enter this new statement:

```
myDate = InputBox("Enter the date in MMM-YYYY format")
```

InputBox is a Visual Basic function that prompts for information while a macro runs. The words in parentheses are the message it displays. The variable myDate stores the date until the macro is ready to use it.

See Also For more information about the InputBox function—including how to make the macro work properly when you click Cancel, see the section titled "Ask Yourself a Question" in Chapter 7, "Control Visual Basic."

2. Select and delete the text **"Nov-2007"** in the macro. Be sure to delete the quotation marks.

3. Type *myDate* where the old date used to be.

   The revised statement should look like this:

   ```
   Selection.FormulaR1C1 = myDate
   ```

4. Activate a worksheet that needs to have the date column added. (Delete the old date column, or run the **FillLabels** macro, as needed.)

5. On the **View** tab of the Ribbon, click the **Macros** button, select the **AddDates** macro, and then click **Run**.

   The macro prompts for the date.

6. Type *Nov-2007*, and click **OK**.

Microsoft Excel	
Enter the date in MMM-YYYY format	OK
	Cancel
Nov-2007	

   The macro inserts the date into the appropriate cells in column A.

7. Save the *Chapter02* workbook.

> **Tip** In this example, the name of the imported file contains the name of the month. Consequently, it is possible to extract the name of the month from the worksheet name without prompting the user. To do that, change the statement that includes the InputBox function to this: myDate=Left(ActiveSheet.Name,7). Left is a VBA function that is essentially identical to the Excel function with the same name. In this case, it extracts the first seven letters from the worksheet's name, returning "Nov2007". Depending on the stetting in you have for Regional Options in Windows, Excel will interpret that string as a date. Prompting for the date avoids making assumptions about the file name or the type of string Excel can interpret as a date, but if you can make those assumptions, you can make the macro run with less interaction from you.

This completes your third task. Now you're ready to append the new data to the database.

Task Four: Appending to the Database

Now that you've added monthly dates to the imported Nov2007 worksheet, it has the same columns as the order-history master list, so you can just copy the worksheet and append it to the first blank row below the database. Of course, you don't want to include the column headings.

Append Data to a Master List

First you'll remove the headings and copy the remaining data from the Nov2007 worksheet. Then you'll open the master list workbook, select the first blank cell below the existing list, and close the database file.

1. Select one of the **Nov2007** worksheets that has the labels filled in and the dates added, click the **Record Macro** button, type AppendData as the macro name, and then click **OK**.

2. Select cell **A1**. Then on the **Home** tab of the Ribbon, click the **Delete** arrow, and click **Delete Sheet Rows**.

   This deletes the heading row so that you won't include it in the range you copy to the database.

3. Press Ctrl+* to select the current region, right-click a cell in the selected region, and click **Copy**.

4. Click the **Microsoft Office Button**, and click **Open**. If necessary, navigate to the *ExcelVBA07SBS* folder.

5. From the **Files Of Type** list, select **All Excel Files**, select **Orders.xlsx** from the list of files, and then click **Open**.

   The *Orders.xlsx* workbook opens with cell A1 selected.

6. Press Ctrl+Down Arrow to go to the last row of the database.

7. Press the Down Arrow key to select the first cell below the database. (It should be cell **A3267**.)

	A	B	C	D	E	F	G	H
3263	October-07	Washington	Retail	Mid	Dinosaurs	15	$67.50	
3264	October-07	Washington	Retail	Mid	Kids	13	$58.50	
3265	October-07	Washington	Retail	Mid	Seattle	6	$27.00	
3266	October-07	Washington	Retail	Mid	Sport	5	$22.50	
3267								

8. On the **Home** tab of the Ribbon, click **Paste** to append the rows you previously copied, and then press the Esc key to remove the copy message from the status bar.

	A	B	C	D	E	F	G	H
3263	October-07	Washington	Retail	Mid	Dinosaurs	15	$67.50	
3264	October-07	Washington	Retail	Mid	Kids	13	$58.50	
3265	October-07	Washington	Retail	Mid	Seattle	6	$27.00	
3266	October-07	Washington	Retail	Mid	Sport	5	$22.50	
3267	Nov-07	Washington	Retail	Mid	Kids	9	40.5	
3268	Nov-07	Washington	Retail	Low	Kids	143	434.06	
3269	Nov-07	Washington	Retail	High	Art	17	93.5	

9. Click the **Microsoft Office Button**, click **Close**, and then click **No** when asked whether you want to save changes.

   For now, you don't want to save the database with the new records to the *Orders* text file because you want to first test the macro.

10. Select cell **A1**, and then click the **Stop Recording** button to turn off the recorder.

Step Through the AppendData Macro

Step through the macro to see it work, and note any changes you should make.

1. Activate a worksheet with the labels filled in and the dates added. (Run the **ImportFile**, **FillLabels**, and **AddDates** macros as necessary.)

2. Click the **View Macros** button, select the **AppendData** macro, and click the **Step Into** button. Look at the first five lines of the macro:

```
Sub AppendData()
    Range("A1").Select
    Selection.EntireRow.Delete
    Selection.CurrentRegion.Select
    Selection.Copy
```

   These statements are similar to statements you've seen in earlier macros.

3. Press F8 five times to execute these first five simple statements in the macro.

   In the Visual Basic editor window, the statement that opens the master list should be highlighted:

```
Workbooks.Open Filename:="C:\MSP\ExcelVBA07SBS\Orders.xlsx"
```

   This statement opens the master list workbook.

> **Tip** If you remove the path from the file name, leaving only the actual file, the macro looks for the file in the current folder. That would be useful if you move the project to a new folder. However, if the master list is always in the same location, but the source file may be in different locations, it is better to leave the full path of the master file.

4. Press F8 to execute the statement containing the Open method and highlight the next statement:

```
Selection.End(xlDown).Select
```

This statement is equivalent to pressing Ctrl+Down Arrow. It starts with the active cell, searches down to the last nonblank cell, and selects that cell.

5. Press F8 to select the bottom cell in column **A** of the existing list and highlight the next statement:

```
Range("A3267").Select
```

This statement selects cell A3267. That is the first cell below the database this month, but next month it will be wrong. This is the statement the recorder created when you pressed the Down Arrow key. What you wanted was a statement that moves one cell down from the active cell. Make a note to fix this statement.

6. Press F8 to select cell **A3267** and highlight the next statement.

The next two statements work together:

```
ActiveSheet.Paste
Application.CutCopyMode = False
```

These statements paste the new rows into the database and remove the status bar message.

7. Press F8 twice to paste the data and highlight the next statement:

```
ActiveWorkbook.Close
```

This statement closes the active workbook. If you've made changes to the workbook, it also prompts you to save the changes. Make a note to add an argument that provides the answer automatically.

8. Press F8 to close the database workbook. Click **No** when asked whether you want to save changes. This highlights the next statement.

Only two statements remain in the macro:

```
    Range("A1").Select
End Sub
```

9. Press F5 to run the remainder of the macro.

The macro works now only because you're running it under circumstances identical to those when you recorded it, with the same current month file and the same database file. Here's a recap of the changes you'll need to make:

● Select the first row under the existing list, regardless of how many rows are in the list.

● Don't prompt when closing the database.

Record a Relative Movement

Take a closer look at the two statements in AppendData that find the first blank cell under the database. Imagine what will happen when you run this next month, when the master list will have 3444 rows. The statement

```
Selection.End(xlDown).Select
```

will select cell A3444, the appropriate bottom row, but then the statement

```
Range("A3267").Select
```

will select the absolute cell A3267 anyway.

When you select a cell, the macro recorder doesn't know whether you want the *absolute* cell you selected or a cell *relative* to where you started. For example, when you select a cell in row 1 to change the label of a column title, you always want the same absolute cell, without regard to where you started. But when you select the first blank cell at the bottom of a database, you want the macro to select a cell *relative* to where you started.

The macro recorder can't automatically know whether you want to record absolute cell addresses or relative movements, but you can tell the recorder which kind of selection you want. The strategy for fixing the macro is to use the recorder to create a new, temporary macro that contains a statement with the appropriate relative movement. You can use the new recorded statement to replace the offending statement in the current macro, and delete the temporary macro.

1. Click the **Record Macro** button, type TempMacro as the macro name, and then click **OK**.

2. On the **View** tab of the Ribbon, click the **Macros** arrow, and click **Use Relative References**.

When the Relative References option is activated, the recorder creates new cell selections that are relative to the starting selection. You want to record the action of moving down one cell. That's an action you can record from any cell, on any worksheet (except, of course, a cell in the bottommost row of the worksheet).

3. Press the Down Arrow key once. That's enough to record the relative movement you need.

4. Click the **Stop Recording** button. Then on the **View** tab of the Ribbon, click the **Macros** arrow, and click the **Use Relative References** button to deselect it.

> **Tip** The Use Relative References button has a slightly different colored background while it is active—that is, while relative references are being recorded. But you can't see the button while you're recording the macro. If you enable the Developer tab, as described in the section titled "Enable the Developer Tab in the Ribbon" in Chapter 9, "Launch Macros with Events," the Use Relative References button is directly visible on the Ribbon, but only while the Developer tab is active. To always be able to see at a glance whether Relative References are currently in effect or not—and to switch the state at will—add the Use Relative References command to the Quick Access Toolbar. To do that, simply right-click the Use Relative References command on the Macros list, and then click Add To Quick Access Toolbar.

5. Edit the **TempMacro** macro, and look at the change.

The new statement you recorded should look like this:

```
ActiveCell.Offset(1,0).Range("A1").Select
```

This statement means, "Select the cell below the active cell." It really does. At this point, you don't need to understand everything about how this statement works. Just trust the recorder.

See Also For more information about relative ranges see the section titled "Relative References" in Chapter 4, "Explore Range Objects."

6. Select the new statement, and copy it.

Sometimes when you record new temporary macros, it can be hard to find the original macro. The Visual Basic editor has a Procedure list that can help you find a macro by using the macro name.

7. Open the **Procedure** list (below the toolbars on the right side of the **Module** window), and select **AppendData**.

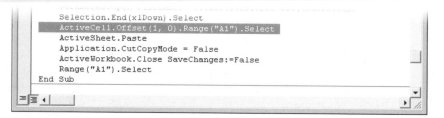

8. Select **Range("A3267").Select**, delete it, and paste the new statement in its place.

```
         Selection.End(xlDown).Select
         ActiveCell.Offset(1, 0).Range("A1").Select
         ActiveSheet.Paste
         Application.CutCopyMode = False
         ActiveWorkbook.Close SaveChanges:=False
         Range("A1").Select
    End Sub
```

9. Delete the entire **TempMacro** macro (using the **Procedure** list, if necessary, to find the macro). To delete the macro, simply select all the statements from Sub TempMacro to End Sub, and then press the Delete key.

With the Relative References button, you can control whether selections are absolute or relative to the current active cell. You can turn the Relative References button on and off as many times as you need while you're recording a macro.

Choose Whether to Save Changes While Closing a File

The statement that closes the database file looks like this:

```
ActiveWorkbook.Close
```

This statement triggers a prompt that asks whether you want to save changes to the file, because you've made changes to it since you opened it. Sometimes when you automate a process, you know that you always will (or won't) want to save changes. The Close method has an optional argument that allows you to specify whether to save changes. For now, while you're testing the macro, set the statement to *not* save the changes.

1. Change the statement that closes the workbook to this:

```
ActiveWorkbook.Close SaveChanges:=False
```

The SaveChanges argument answers the dialog box's question before it even gets asked. While testing, you can have the macro *not* save the workbook. Once you're ready to really use the macro, you can change the argument to True.

2. Save the *Chapter02* workbook. Find a new source worksheet, and then run and test the **AppendData** macro.

3. Once you've finished testing the macro and are ready to use it regularly, change the word *False* to *True*.

   Here's the final version of the AppendData macro:

```
Sub AppendData()
    Range("A1").Select
    Selection.EntireRow.Delete
    Selection.CurrentRegion.Select
    Selection.Copy
    Workbooks.Open Filename:="C:\MSP\ExcelVBA07SBS\Orders.xlsx"
    Selection.End(xlDown).Select
    ActiveCell.Offset(1, 0).Range("A1").Select
    ActiveSheet.Paste
    Application.CutCopyMode = False
    ActiveWorkbook.Close SaveChanges:=True
    Range("A1").Select
End Sub
```

If you want, you can run the macro again now. It will work the same as it did before, but it's also ready for next month, when the database will have more records.

You're almost finished. The only task left is to get rid of the imported worksheet.

Task Five: Deleting the Worksheet

You imported the text file worksheet so that you could fill in the labels and add a column of dates before appending the data to the database. Once the data is safely appended, you don't need the imported worksheet any more. You don't want to delete the *Chapter02* workbook file, because it contains the macros you will need next month. You want to delete only the active worksheet.

Create a Macro to Delete the Active Worksheet

In this section, you'll create a macro that deletes the active sheet. This can be useful in many contexts. While you're developing and testing the DeleteSheet macro, you can use any arbitrary sheet.

1. Activate an expendable worksheet, click the **Record Macro** button, type DeleteSheet as the macro name, and then click **OK**.

2. On the **Home** tab of the Ribbon, click the **Delete** arrow, click **Delete Sheet**, and then click **Delete** when asked to confirm.

3. Click the **Stop Recording** button to turn off the recorder.

4. Edit the **DeleteSheet** macro. The body of the macro contains only one statement:

   ```
   ActiveWindow.SelectedSheets.Delete
   ```

   The statement refers to the "selected sheets of the active window" because it's possible to select and delete multiple sheets at the same time. (Press and hold the Ctrl key as you click several sheet tabs to see how you can select multiple sheets. Then click an unselected sheet without using the Ctrl key to deselect the sheets.) Because you're deleting only one sheet, you could change the statement to ActiveSheet.Delete if you wanted, but that isn't necessary.

The only problem with this macro is that it asks for confirmation each time you run it. When the macro deletes the imported sheet as part of the larger project, you would prefer not to be prompted.

Make the Macro Operate Quietly

The Delete method does not have an optional argument that eliminates the confirmation prompt. You must add a new statement to turn off the warning.

1. In the **DeleteSheet** macro, insert a new line just before the one statement already in the body of the macro, and then enter this statement:

   ```
   Application.DisplayAlerts = False
   ```

   DisplayAlerts is a property of the Excel application. When you set the value of this property to False, any confirmation prompts that you would normally see are treated as if you had selected the default answer. The DisplayAlerts setting lasts only until the macro finishes running, so you don't need to set it back to True. You do, however, need to be careful to never run this macro when the active sheet is something you care about. Naturally, you should also be careful to save your work often and keep backup copies.

   > **Tip** The Auto List Members feature will help you type the words *DisplayAlerts* and *False*. When you select a word in the list, press the Tab key to finish entering the word into the statement.

2. Save the *Chapter02* workbook.

3. Select an expendable worksheet, and run the **DeleteSheet** macro.

Assembling the Pieces

You have all the subordinate task macros ready for carrying out your complex monthly project:

- ImportFile opens and parses the text file.
- FillLabels makes the file look like a database.
- AddDates distinguishes one month from another in the database.
- AppendData adds the new rows to the bottom of the saved database.
- DeleteSheet cleans up the temporary worksheet.

Each piece is prepared and tested. Now you get to put them all together.

Record a Macro That Runs Other Macros

The easiest way to glue macros together is to record a macro that runs other macros.

1. Click the **Record Macro** button, type MonthlyProject as the macro name, and then click **OK**.

2. In the **View** tab of the Ribbon, click the **View Macros** button, click **ImportFile**, and then click **Run**.

3. Select the text file you want to import, and then click **Open**.

4. Click the **View Macros** button, click **FillLabels**, and then click **Run**.

5. Click the **View Macros** button, click **AddDates**, and then click **Run**.

6. Type an appropriate date, and click **OK**.

7. Click the **View Macros** button, click **AppendData**, and then click **Run**.

8. Click the **View Macros** button, click **DeleteSheet**, and then click **Run**.

9. Click the **Stop Recording** button.

10. Now you can look at what you created. Click the **View Macros** button, select the **MonthlyProject** macro, and click **Edit**.

    After deleting the standard comments, here's what the macro to run other macros looks like:

    ```
    Sub MonthlyProject()
        Application.Run "Chapter02.xlsm!ImportFile"
        Application.Run "Chapter02.xlsm!FillLabels"
        Application.Run "Chapter02.xlsm!AddDates"
        Application.Run "Chapter02.xlsm!AppendData"
        Application.Run "Chapter02.xlsm!DeleteSheet"
    End Sub
    ```

The MonthlyProject macro runs each of the subordinate macros in turn. If you think of the MonthlyProject macro as a *routine*, then it makes sense to think of each of the subordinate macros as a *subroutine*. (And this is, in fact, the archaic historical reason each macro begins with the word *Sub:* because it can act as a *subroutine*.)

Simplify the Subroutine Statements

The statement that the macro recorder creates for running a subroutine works, but it is somewhat unwieldy. You can simplify the statement, making it easier to read and faster to run (although you are unlikely to see any difference in speed).

1. Delete everything from each recorded subroutine statement except the name of the macro itself.

    Here's what the macro should look like when you're done:

    ```
    Sub MonthlyProject()
        ImportFile
        FillLabels
        AddDates
        AppendData
        DeleteSheet
    End Sub
    ```

2. Save the *Chapter02* workbook.

3. Press F5 to test the **MonthlyProject** macro. (You might also want to try pressing F8 to step through the main macro and each of the subroutines.)

You now have an automated process for importing each new month's data. You've worked hard and deserve a rest. Take the rest of the day off.

CLOSE the *Chapter02.xlsx* Workbook.

Key Points

- Watch what a macro is doing by reducing the Visual Basic editor window while stepping through the macro.

- Record macros in small pieces. You can always move statements from one macro to another, or run the separate macros as subroutines.

- After recording a macro, watch for ways to generalize it for future use. The CurrentRegion method is a great way to refer to a range that may be a different size each time you run the macro.

- Use GetOpenFilename to prompt for a file name or the InputBox function to get information while running the macro.

- Use variables to store a string or other value so that you can use it later in the macro.

- Switch the recorder to relative mode to record relative movements rather than absolute addresses. This is particularly useful when appending to the bottom of a list.

Chapter at a Glance

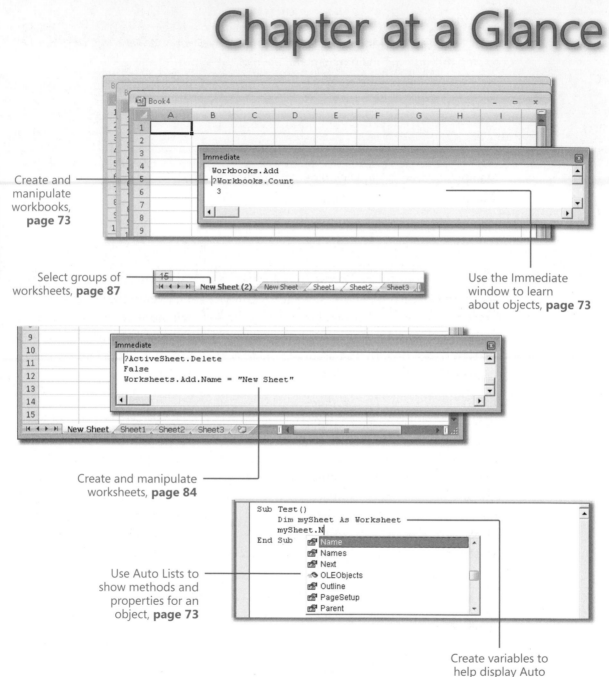

Create and manipulate workbooks, **page 73**

Select groups of worksheets, **page 87**

Use the Immediate window to learn about objects, **page 73**

Create and manipulate worksheets, **page 84**

Use Auto Lists to show methods and properties for an object, **page 73**

Create variables to help display Auto Lists, **page 89**

3 Explore Workbooks and Worksheets

In this chapter, you will learn to:

- ✔ Manipulate collections of workbooks and worksheets.
- ✔ Manipulate individual workbook and worksheet items.
- ✔ Use the Immediate window to execute individual statements.

Think back to your third-grade classroom. Your wooden frame desk, decorated with decades of crudely carved names, was fourth from the front, over in the last row next to the windows. Remember those big stairs down to the main floor, with that magnificent banister you would always watch for a chance to slide down? The main hallway was papered with drawings clustered around each classroom door. Each door led to a classroom, and each classroom was filled with kids.

A Microsoft Office Excel 2007 workbook is a lot like a school. The cells in a worksheet appear in rows and columns like students in a classroom. Worksheets are grouped into workbooks like classrooms in a school. And Excel can have several open workbooks, just as a city can have several schools. Just as you were able to move around freely in the rooms and halls of your old elementary school, you will soon be able to move around freely in Excel objects with your macros. Microsoft Visual Basic interacts with Excel by working with Excel objects. Everything in Excel that Visual Basic can control—workbooks, worksheets, cells, menus, text box controls—are objects. To control Excel from Visual Basic effectively, you must understand what objects are and how they work in Excel.

Important Before you complete this chapter, you need to install the practice files from the book's companion CD to their default locations. See "Using the Book's CD" on page xv for more information.

> **BE SURE TO** close any open workbooks. (To find any hidden workbooks, click Unhide on the View tab of the Ribbon.)
>
> **OPEN** a clean, blank workbook. Restore the workbook window (not the Excel application window) so that it is not maximized. Then right-click the worksheet tab of Sheet1, and click View Code to open the Visual Basic editor.

What Is an Object?

The easiest way to understand objects in Excel is to compare them to objects in the real world. In the real world, cities, schools, classrooms, and students are all objects. A city is dotted with schools, a school is lined with classrooms, a classroom is packed with students—and all the students are arranged in rows of tidy desks, smiling happily and listening attentively to the kind, wise, and firm but patient teacher. Well, maybe not all the desks are tidy.

Objects Come in Collections

Look around you. The world consists of objects in collections, which are in turn objects in other collections: rooms in apartments in buildings in complexes, flowers in beds in yards in neighborhoods, rocks on crags on mountains in ranges, children in households in extended families in clans. Each object—each city, each student, each flower, each mountain, and each family—is an individual item, yet each also belongs to a collection of similar objects, and each collection of objects is itself an individual item within a larger collection.

If you're a city official thinking about the collection of School objects, you might refer to the collection of schools as a group: "All the schools have asbestos problems." Or you might refer to an individual school: "We need to replace the light fixtures at Jefferson Elementary School." When you do refer to an individual school, you might refer to the school by name: "Jefferson Elementary School, as you may know, was named for the esteemed author of the Declaration of Independence." Or you might refer to it by its position in the collection: "The first school built in our city, back in 1887, is the one I attended as a child." Or (if you are conducting a driving tour) you might refer to the individual school by pointing: "Notice the classic architecture of this magnificent school building."

An Excel workbook is like a school. Just as you can have more than one school in a city, you can have more than one workbook open in Excel. Each workbook is individual and unique, yet each is a Workbook object. You can refer to the entire collection of open workbooks as a group ("Close all the open workbooks"), or you can refer to individual workbooks. If you refer to an individual workbook, you can specify the workbook by name ("Open the Chapter 3 workbook"), by position ("What is the first workbook in the list of recently opened files?"), or by pointing ("Save the active workbook").

A worksheet in a workbook is like a classroom in a school, and worksheet cells are like students in a classroom, arranged in neat little rows and columns. Excel also has other collections of objects: menu items in menus in menu bars, columns in a series in a group in a chart, items in fields in rows in a PivotTable. You can refer to each collection, whether in Excel or in the natural world, as a whole or you can refer to a single item within the collection. When you refer to a single item within the collection, you can refer to it by name, by position, or by pointing.

Objects Have Properties

Do you see that little boy in Mrs. Middlefield's class—the one in the third row, in the fourth seat over? He's about 4 feet 7 inches tall. His hair is short. The color of his shirt is blue. His name is Jared. And his eyes are closed.

The boy's height, hair length, shirt color, name, and eye state are *properties* of that one particular Student object. The little girl sitting behind him also has Height, HairLength, ShirtColor, Name, and EyeState properties, but the values of her properties are different. The boy is a different object than the girl, but each is a Student object.

The boy's desk is also an object, a Desk object. A Desk object has a Height property, as does a Student object, but a Desk object does not have a HairLength property. Likewise, a Student object does not have a ManufacturerName property, as a Desk object does. Because the boy and the desk have different lists of properties, they are different types, or classes, of objects. Because the boy and girl share the same list of properties—even though they have different values for the properties—they both belong to the same class of object. They both belong to the Student *object class*. Sharing the same list of properties is what makes two objects belong to the same object class.

Just as Jared is an object—a Student object—Mrs. Middlefield's entire collection of students is also an object—a Students object. The Students object is a collection and has its own set of properties; the properties of the collection are not the same as the properties of the individual objects contained within it. For example, you don't really care about a HairLength property of the entire collection of students. (Would that be total hair length or average hair length?) But a collection object does have properties of its own. For example, the number of students in the collection (the Count) is a property of the Students object. Because Mrs. Middlefield's collection of students has a property list that is different from the property list of the one student Jared. Student and Students are two different object classes. But because Mr. Osgood's collection of students and Mrs. Middlefield's collection of students do both have the same list of properties—even though they might have different values for the properties—both collections belong to the same Students object class. The Students object class is different than the Student object class because the two object classes have different lists of properties.

Some properties are easy to change. You could perhaps change Jared's EyeState property with a good, sharp rap with a ruler on his desk. (And of course, he can change the property right back after you look the other way.) You might even change Jared's name to Gerard temporarily for French language instruction. But changing Jared's height, weight, eye color, or gender probably falls outside the scope of a normal school activity.

Each Excel object class has a list of properties as well, and some of the properties are easy to change and some are not. A workbook has an author. A worksheet has a name. A cell has a width, a height, and a value. A menu has a caption. A collection of worksheets has a count of the worksheets in the collection. Changing the name of a worksheet or the height of a cell is easy. But changing the count of cells on a worksheet probably falls outside the scope of a normal macro activity.

Objects Have Methods

Look, Mrs. Middlefield is telling the class to stand up. She's leading them in a stirring rendition of "Row, Row, Row Your Boat." Student objects can sing songs. Singing a song is an activity. Student objects also do other activities. Student objects eat. Student objects draw pictures. One student might sing, or eat, or draw well; another student might sing, or eat, or draw badly; but they both share the ability to do the action. Desk objects, on the other hand, do not sing, eat, or draw. Desk objects might squeak, whereas Student objects generally don't. In the same way that different classes of objects have different lists of properties, they also have different lists of activities they can do. The activities an object can do are called *methods*. Objects that belong to the same class can all do the same methods.

As with properties, the list of methods that belong to a particular collection object is usually different from the list of methods that belong to the individual items in it. One of the most important methods for most collections is adding a new item to the collection. When a new student joins the class, you are executing the Add method on the Students object, not on an individual Student object. When the construction bond passes and the school gets a new wing, you are executing the Add method on the Classrooms object. You don't add the new classroom to an individual classroom; you add it to the collection of classrooms.

Most Excel collection objects have an Add method for adding a new item to the collection, and they all have an Item property for establishing a link, or a reference, to an individual item in the collection. Excel worksheet objects also have a Calculate method for causing all the cells to recalculate, and Excel charts have a ChartWizard method that quickly changes various attributes of a chart.

VBA has a name for the combined list of methods and properties of an object: *members*. So instead of saying, "What are the methods and properties of a Worksheet object?" you can say "What are the members of a Worksheet object?" The word *members* makes it sound as if an object class is a club, and you have to be a suitable method or property to be able to belong to the club—and in a way, that's exactly how an object class works. The terminology might be a little confusing, because you might think that Jared is a *member* of the Student class. But he's not. The members of the student class are its properties (HairLength and EyeColor) and its methods (FingerPaint and Eat). Jared is an *instance* of the Student class, which means he is a specific example of a student. You could say, "There are too many rules around here; for instance, *they won't let me sleep during class.*" And that means you're giving a specific example of a rule. In the same way, Jared is a specific example of a student. He is an *instance* of a Student. Michael and Rupert and Sachiko and LaDean are all instances of a Student class, so each one has the same list of methods and properties. If you want to really impress people, just casually say, "Yes, but actually each instance has the same list of members as every other instance in the class, don't you think?"

Sometimes the distinction between a method and a property is nothing more than which one the object designer chose to use. When Jared opens his eyes, is he carrying out the OpenEyes method (an action), or is he assigning a new value to his EyeState property? So just thinking of the whole list as the list of members is sometimes convenient. But sometimes it's useful to remember why there are both members and properties. Here are some concepts that might help.

Methods Can Change Properties

Most methods can, and do, change properties. When Jared carries out the Fingerpaint method, the action happens to change his ShirtColor property. When he goes home and carries out the WashClothes method, the ShirtColor property changes back (with perhaps a few residual stains). But the method doesn't remember what it did. After you use the WashClothes method, you still have to use the ShirtColor property to find out what color it is now. Likewise, in Excel, the Add method of the Workbooks object changes the value of the Count property, but the Add method doesn't tell you what the new count is.

Properties Can Involve Actions

Setting a property usually involves some kind of action. When you change the classroom's WallColor property, you do get out the paint rollers and the ladders and start working, but you are more concerned about the finished attribute of the wall than about the action that changed the attribute. Consequently, when you have finished, you can tell your friends that the value of the WallColor property is now BrightYellow. You use the same WallColor property to explain the resulting state that you used to carry out the action. In Excel, hiding a worksheet is an example of setting a property (because the worksheet is still there, and you might want to change the property back, and while it is hidden you can tell people what the current status is). But closing a file is a method because there's no trace of the file left in memory after you're done.

> **Tip** If you are using only recorded macros, you don't need to worry about the difference between properties and methods, because the macro recorder uses the appropriate method or property. But it is useful to know the distinction because of what you do to change the recorded macro: If it's a method, you modify the macro by changing its arguments. If it's a property, you modify the macro by changing what you assign to the property. The same distinction applies, of course, if you are writing the macro from scratch. Excel's online tools and help topics indicate whether something is a method or a property.

In summary, an individual item (a desk or a worksheet) is an instance from one object class, while a collection of those items (a bunch of desks or a bunch of worksheets) is an instance from a different object class. A single instance from one collection can contain an entire collection of other objects. For example, a single instance from the district's collection of schools can contain an entire collection of classrooms, and a single instance from Excel's collection of workbooks can contain an entire collection of worksheets. Each instance belongs to an object class that has a unique list of members (methods and properties). A single object class (the Student object class or the Worksheet object class) can have many different individual instances (Jared or Michiko or Budget2007). In that case, each instance shares the same list of members, while retaining its individual values for the specific properties. In this chapter, you'll learn how to work with many kinds of Excel objects.

Understanding Workbooks

Workbooks are the major structural unit in Excel. You can learn a lot about how objects and collections work in Excel by experimenting with workbooks.

Excel has a powerful tool to help you explore objects, properties, and methods: the Immediate window of the Visual Basic editor. In this window, you can execute VBA statements without actually creating a macro. Everything you do in the Immediate window is lost when you close Excel.

Add a New Workbook

In this section, you'll use a macro statement to create a new workbook. This is equivalent to clicking New on the Microsoft Office Button menu. The macro statement for creating a new workbook is Workbooks.Add. Rather than put that statement in a macro, you can execute it directly in the Immediate window, and rather than type the statement, you can let the Visual Basic editor help you construct it.

1. If the Visual Basic editor is not already open, right-click any worksheet tab, and click **View Code**. Then resize the Visual Basic editor so that you can see the Excel application.

   > **Tip** There are a number of ways to open the Visual Basic editor. If you have a macro in an open workbook, editing the macro opens the editor. The View Code command on the shortcut menu for any worksheet also works. If you have displayed the Developer tab of the Ribbon, it includes a Visual Basic button that also opens the editor. The Alt+F11 shortcut key combination opens the Visual Basic editor as well.

2. On the **View** menu, click **Immediate Window**. If the **Immediate** window is docked within the Visual Basic editor, double click the title bar to undock the window. Then resize the **Immediate** window so that you can see the Excel application.

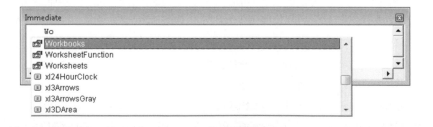

3. With the **Immediate** window active, click the Visual Basic editor **Edit** menu, and then click **Complete Word**.

   A list of methods and properties appears. These are the methods and properties that don't need an explicit object.

4. Type **Wo**—the first two letters of the word *Workbooks*.

   This is enough to select the word in the list. You could also just type a *W* and point to Workbooks or press the Down Arrow key three times.

5. Type a period (.) to display a list of methods and properties suitable for the Workbooks object.

You don't need to type the whole word before typing a period. The list that appears is called an *Auto List*. It contains all the methods and properties that you can use with the preceding object.

6. Type A—the first letter of the word *Add*.

   The first letter is enough to select the appropriate word.

7. Press Enter to add a new workbook on top of the first workbook.

   The Add method added a new workbook to the collection, and you watched it happen.

   In the Immediate window, you can type macro statements and see the effect immediately. The Immediate window is an effective tool for finding out what a statement does. You can use it when planning how to create a new macro or when debugging an existing macro.

8. Press the Up Arrow key to put the insertion point back in the **Workbooks.Add** statement, and then press Enter.

   The Add method adds another Workbook object. Whenever you want to reexecute a statement in the Immediate window, simply put the insertion point anywhere in the line, and press Enter.

The word *Workbooks* refers to the Workbooks object—the collection of workbooks currently open in Excel. The word *Add* is a method of the Workbooks object that adds a new item to the collection. A method follows an object, separated by a single period (object.method). Most collections in Excel have an Add method for adding a new item to the collection.

Dockable Views

The windows in the Visual Basic editor can be confusing. You might find it easier to understand how they work if you compare them to windows in the Excel environment.

In Excel, each workbook you open has its own window. A workbook window can be either maximized to fill Excel's entire work area or resized to have more than one window visible at a time. A workbook window can never move outside the boundary of the Excel application. It's completely owned by the main Excel window. This kind of window is a *child* window.

A task pane such as the Research pane, on the other hand, can be either docked or floating. A task pane can be docked to the left or right side of Excel's main window. To undock a task pane, you drag it away from the docking position. Conversely, to dock a task pane, you drag it close to a docking position. Double-clicking the title bar switches the docked state. You can put a floating task pane anywhere; it doesn't have to remain inside Excel's main window. If you want a task pane to float close to where it would naturally dock, you can prevent it from docking by holding down the Ctrl key as you move it. A task pane is actually a kind of window—a *dockable* window.

The Visual Basic editor has both dockable and child windows. A module window is a child window. It can be minimized, restored, or maximized, but it can never move outside the boundaries of the main Visual Basic window.

The Immediate window is by default a dockable window, similar to a task pane in Excel. You can dock the Immediate window to the top, bottom, left side, or right side of the Visual Basic window, or you can make it float by dragging it away from a docking position. You can also prevent the window from docking by pressing and holding down the Ctrl key as you move the window, just the same as a task pane in Excel.

Visual Basic has six dockable windows: the Locals window, the Immediate window, the Watch window, the Project Explorer window, the Properties window, and the Object Browser window. You can display any of these windows by choosing the appropriate command from the View menu.

To change a Visual Basic dockable window into a child window, right-click the window, and then click the Dockable command to remove the check mark. (Visual Basic windows are different from task panes in this regard: you cannot turn a task pane into a child window.) With the Dockable setting turned off, the window behaves just like any child window; you can minimize, maximize, restore, cascade, or tile it, but you can't move it outside the main window, and it can't float above another active window.

I usually make all windows dockable but undocked. I move, hide, and unhide windows as necessary. I also maximize the module window and keep it relatively small so that I can see the Excel window in the background.

Count the Workbooks

You have now used a method—the Add method—with a Workbooks object. The Workbooks object also has properties. One of the properties—the Count property—tells you how many items are in the collection. The Count property returns a value that you can display in the Immediate window.

1. In the **Immediate** window, type ?Workbooks.Count and press Enter.

   After typing the question mark, you can use the Complete Word command on the Edit menu along with the automatic Auto Lists to help you construct the rest of the statement.

The number 3 (or however many workbooks are currently open) appears. In the Immediate window, when you type a question mark followed by anything that returns a value, that value appears on the next line. Because the Count property returns a number value, you can display that value by using the question mark.

2. Press the Up Arrow key to get back to the **Workbooks.Add** statement, press Enter to add a new workbook, and then press Enter again in the **?Workbooks.Count** statement to see the new count of workbooks.

The count should now be 4 (or one greater than whatever it was before).

The word *Count* is a property. You attach the Count property to its object with a period in the same way that you attach the Add method to the object.

When you execute the Add method, you don't put a question mark in front of it because the Add method does not return a simple value. You can see the effect of the Add method by looking at the Excel application window. When you use the Count property, you want to find out the value of the property. You can't change the number of workbooks by changing the Count property; you must use the Add method to add a new workbook to the collection. A property whose value you can look at but cannot change is called a read-only property.

Close the Workbooks

The Add method of the Workbooks collection object adds one item to the collection. The Workbooks object has an additional method—the Close method—that can close the entire collection.

1. Type Workbooks.Close and press Enter. Click **No** if prompted to save changes.

All the open workbooks disappear. Using the Close method on the Workbooks object closes the entire collection. The Close method closes everything so fast that you might want to see it work again.

2. Reexecute the **Workbooks.Add** statement three or four times to create a few new workbooks.

3. Reexecute the **?Workbooks.Count** statement to see how many workbooks are in the collection.

4. Reexecute the **Workbooks.Close** statement to close all the workbooks.

Doesn't that give you a great sense of power? With one keystroke, all those workbooks are annihilated!

5. Reexecute the **?Workbooks.Count** statement to see how many workbooks are in the collection.

The number 0 appears because you destroyed all the workbooks.

Add and Close are both methods of a Workbooks object. Count is a property of the Workbooks object. The Add and Close methods indirectly change the value of the Count property—they are, in fact, the only ways you can change the read-only Count property.

Refer to a Single Workbook

Closing the entire Workbooks collection all at once is a powerful experience, and might even occasionally be useful. But usually you want more control over which workbooks disappear. To close a single workbook, you need to specify a single item out of the Workbooks collection.

1. Run the **Workbooks.Add** statement at the top of the **Immediate** window several times to create a few new workbooks.

2. Scroll to the bottom of the **Immediate** window. (You can press Ctrl+End to get there quickly.)

3. Type ?Workbooks.Item(1).Name and press Enter.

   The name of the first workbook—the first of the current set of workbooks to be opened (probably something like Book9)—appears. Reading from right to left, you could paraphrase this statement as: "The name of the first item in the Workbooks collection is what?"

- *Name* is a property of a single workbook. Because Name is a property that returns a value, you can display its value by putting a question mark at the beginning of the statement. The Name property is not available for a Workbooks object because a collection of workbooks doesn't have a name.

- *Item* is a property of a collection. Like the teacher establishing a communication link by addressing an individual student, the Item property creates a reference to an individual item in a collection. The Item property requires a single argument: in this case, the position number of the item you want.

- *Workbooks* establishes a reference to the entire collection of workbooks— the Workbooks object. Once you have a reference to the Workbooks object, the word *Item(1)* switches the reference to the specified item within the collection—a *Workbook* object. Once you have a reference to the Workbook object, the Name property returns the name of that object.

> **Tip** Retrieving a single item from a collection is so common that you can leave out the word *Item* (and its accompanying period) and put the parentheses right after the name of the collection. The statement *?Workbooks(1).Name* achieves the same result as *?Workbooks.Item(1).Name*. The macro recorder, Excel's Help files, and most people use the shorter form. However, if you find that you consistently forget to use a plural for the collection method name, you might want to explicitly use the Item property for a while.

4. Type Workbooks(1).Close and press Enter.

The first workbook disappears.

5. Reexecute the **?Workbooks.Item(1).Name** statement.

The name of the first workbook appears. (If the first workbook was Book9 before, the new first workbook is probably Book10.)

6. Reexecute the **Workbooks(1).Close** statement to close the newly promoted first workbook in the collection.

> **See Also** A property that is not preceded by an object is called a *global* property. You will learn more about global properties and methods in the section titled "Refer to a Range by Using an Address" in Chapter 4, "Explore Range Objects."

The word *Workbooks* has two meanings in Excel. On one hand, Workbooks is the name of an object class—the Workbooks object class; it is a noun, a "thing." On the other hand, Workbooks is also the name of a global property that establishes a reference to the collection of open workbooks; it is a verb, an "action." You cannot put the actual Workbooks object (or thing) into your macro. (The Workbooks object is inside Excel; you can see it on your computer screen.) What you put into your macro is the Workbook property that establishes a reference to the Workbooks thing.

Once the Workbooks property establishes a reference to the Workbooks object, you can "talk" to the object using methods and properties from the list that a Workbooks object understands. You can use the Count property to look at the number of items in the collection. You can use the Add method to add a new workbook to the collection. You can use the Close method to close the entire collection of workbooks. *Count*, *Add*, and *Close* are three of the words that a Workbook object can understand.

A Workbooks object can also understand the Item property. The Item property establishes a reference to an individual Workbook thing. Excel doesn't have a Workbook property to link to a single Workbook object. You use the Item property of the Workbooks object (the shortcut form) to establish a reference to an individual object.

Once the Item property establishes a reference to an individual Workbook object, you can talk to the object by using methods and properties that a Workbook object understands. You can use the Name property to look at the workbook's name. And you can use the Close method to close the workbook.

As a general rule, each collection object in Excel shares the same name as the property that establishes a reference to that object. The Workbooks object shares its name with the Workbooks property because the Workbooks property establishes a reference to the Workbooks object. As you learn more about objects, you will see that this pattern holds—the Windows object shares its name with the Windows property, the Charts object shares its name with the Charts property, and so forth.

In Visual Basic code, you never refer to an individual item from a collection by leaving the letter *s* off the name of the collection. For example, you never refer to an individual workbook in a macro by using the word *Workbook*. Every collection object class has an Item property that you use to establish a reference to an individual item in the collection.

You might wonder what the difference is between an item in a collection and an instance of a class. Jared is an instance of a student, but he is an item in Mrs. Middlefield's collection of students. If LaDean is a student in Mr. Gupta's collection of students, she is still an instance of a student, just like Jared. But they are not items of the same collection. In the same way, if you have a Budget2008 workbook and a Budget2007 workbook, they might each have a January worksheet. Both January worksheets are instances of the Worksheet class. In other words, both worksheets are *examples* of worksheets. But they're in different workbooks, so they're in different collections.

Refer to a Workbook by Name

So far when you have used the Item property to establish a reference to an individual workbook, you have specified the workbook you want by number—by indicating its position in the collection. Another way you can refer to an item in a collection is by its name. If you use the name, you must put it in quotation marks. If you use the position number, you do not use quotation marks.

1. If you are running out of workbooks, scroll to the top of the **Immediate** window (press Ctrl+Home), and execute the **Workbooks.Add** statement a few more times.

2. Scroll to the bottom of the **Immediate** window (press Ctrl+End) and pick the name of one of the workbooks, preferably one in the middle of the stack, perhaps a workbook named Book14.

3. Type Workbooks("Book14").Activate and press Enter.

The workbook you specified moves to the top of the stack of workbooks. The word *Activate* is a method that a single Workbook instance understands. Because Book14 is the *name* of the workbook, it appears in quotation marks.

4. Type Workbooks("Book14").Close and press Enter to close the workbook.

5. Reexecute the **Workbooks("Book14").Close** statement.

Excel displays an error message because the workbook with that name no longer exists. When you refer to an item in a collection by name, you always get the same item—as long as it still exists.

Microsoft Visual Basic

⚠ Run-time error '9':

Subscript out of range

OK   Help

6. Click **OK** to remove the error message.

You can use either the name or the position number to refer to an item in a collection. If you use the position number, you might get a different item each time you use the Item property; if you use the name, you'll get an error if the item no longer exists.

Refer to a Workbook by Pointing

Suppose you want to refer to the top workbook on the stack but you don't know its name *or* its position number. Because the top workbook is the active workbook, you can refer to it by pointing.

→ At the bottom of the **Immediate** window, type ActiveWorkbook.Close and press Enter.

The top workbook in the stack disappears.

The word *ActiveWorkbook* in this statement establishes a reference directly to the active workbook, bypassing the Workbooks object. If the first workbook opened happens to be the active workbook, you could substitute Workbooks(1) to establish a reference to the same workbook object as ActiveWorkbook. Once you have a reference to the workbook, you can look up its name or close it. Once you have a reference to an object, the process by which you established that reference is not important.

Change a Workbook Property Value

Both the Count property of the Workbooks object and the Name property of a Workbook object are read-only properties. You can look at the value returned by the property, but you cannot change it. A workbook has other properties, read-write properties, whose values you can change as well as look at.

1. In the **Immediate** window, type **?ActiveWorkbook.Saved** and press Enter.

    The word *True* appears because the workbook hasn't had any changes made to it. When you close a workbook, Excel uses the value of the Saved property to decide whether to prompt you to save changes. If the value of the Saved property is True, Excel does not prompt you; if it is False, Excel does prompt you. Normally, you change the Saved property to False by changing the contents of a cell, and you change the Saved property to True by saving the workbook. You can, however, change the Saved property directly.

2. Type **ActiveWorkbook.Saved = False** and press Enter.

    Nothing seems to happen, but you just changed the value of the property.

3. Reexecute the **?ActiveWorkbook.Saved** statement to see the new value for the property.

    The word *False* appears. Now Excel thinks the workbook has unsaved changes in it.

4. Reexecute the **ActiveWorkbook.Close** statement.

    Because you set the Saved property to False, Excel asks if you want to save changes.

5. Click the **Cancel** button to leave the workbook open.

6. At the bottom of the **Immediate** window, type **ActiveWorkbook.Saved = True** and press Enter.

7. Reexecute the **ActiveWorkbook.Close** statement.

    The workbook closes without a whisper.

If you write a macro that modifies a workbook and you want to close the workbook without saving changes (and without displaying a warning prompt), make the macro change the Saved property of the workbook to True.

The Saved property is a read-write property. You can display its current value, and you can also change its value.

Understanding Worksheets

Worksheets come in collections just as workbooks do. By manipulating worksheets in the Immediate window, you will see some similarities—and some differences—between different collection objects.

Add a New Worksheet

You add a new worksheet to the active workbook the same way you add a new workbook to Excel: by using the Add method.

1. In Excel, close all but one workbook.

   The one workbook should have three sheets, named Sheet1, Sheet2, and Sheet3, with Sheet1 as the active sheet.

2. Switch to the Visual Basic editor. In the **Immediate** window, type Worksheets.Add and press Enter.

   A new worksheet named Sheet4 appears before the original active sheet.

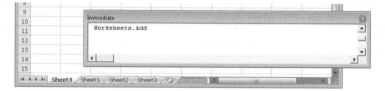

Rename and Delete a Worksheet

A worksheet is an object with properties and methods of its own. You can use those methods and properties to manipulate a worksheet. As you work with worksheets, you will notice that the Auto List of methods and properties will not always appear after you type a period. Later in this chapter, you will learn how to get an Auto List to always appear with a worksheet object.

1. Type ?Worksheets(1).Name and press Enter to display the name of the first worksheet (probably Sheet4).

   In the same way that you use the Item property (in either its long form or its short form) on a Workbooks object to establish a reference to a single Workbook object, you use the Item property on a Worksheets object to establish a reference to a single Worksheet object. Once you have a reference to a Worksheet object, you can use Worksheet object properties, such as Name.

The name of a workbook is a read-only property; you have to save a file to change its name. The name of a worksheet, however, is a read-write property; you can change the name directly.

2. Type Worksheets(1).Name = "Input Values" and press Enter.

   The name of the worksheet changes.

3. Type Worksheets("Sheet1").Activate and press Enter.

   The worksheet named Sheet1 becomes the active sheet.

4. Type ActiveSheet.Delete and press Enter. Click **Delete** when warned that the sheet might contain values.

5. Type Worksheets("Input Values").Activate and press Enter.

As with workbooks, you can refer to a single worksheet by number, by name, or by pointing. With the first worksheet named Input Values and activated, the expressions *Worksheets("Input Values")*, *Worksheets(1)*, and *ActiveSheet* all establish a reference to the same Worksheet object.

Look at the Return Value of the Delete Method

Normally, with a method, you just execute it, but with a property you either retrieve its current value, or you change its value to something new. Methods do, however, return values, and you might want to see the value that a method returns. For example, when you use the Delete method on a worksheet, the action of the method is to close the worksheet, but the method also returns a value to the macro.

1. Type ?ActiveSheet.Delete and press Enter. Click **Delete** when warned that the sheet contains data.

   The active sheet disappears, and the word *True* appears after the statement. When the Delete method succeeds in carrying out its action, it returns the value True. Making the worksheet go away is the action of the method. The word *True* that appears in the Immediate window is the *return value* of the method. A method can have both an action and a return value.

2. Type **?ActiveSheet.Delete** and press Enter. This time, click **Cancel** when warned.

   The word *False* appears after the statement. The Delete method did not complete the action of deleting the worksheet, so it returns the value False.

Many methods follow this pattern of returning True if the action is successful and False if it is not. As you can imagine, this can be useful to know when you write macros.

Look at the Result of the Add Method

The Delete method of the Worksheet object returns either True or False, depending on whether it accomplishes its intended action. The Add method also has an intended action—to create a new item in the collection. But the Add method does not return True or False. Rather, the Add method returns a reference to the newly created object. You can then use that reference the same way you can use the reference created by the Item property or by the ActiveSheet property.

1. In the **Immediate** window, type **Worksheets.Add.Name = "New Sheet"** and press Enter.

   A new worksheet appears in the workbook, with the name New Sheet.

2. Type **Worksheets.Add.Delete** and press Enter. When the confirmation dialog box appears, you can see the new worksheet in Excel. Click **Delete**, and watch the worksheet disappear.

This example is bizarre because it deletes the worksheet as part of the same statement that creates it. It does, however, illustrate how the Add method returns a reference to the newly created object.

The Add method has an action—it creates a new worksheet. In addition, as its return value, it returns a reference to the new object. If you don't use the reference immediately—as part of the same statement—the reference is discarded. If you then want to communicate with the new worksheet, you must establish a new reference using the ActiveSheet property or the Item property. Usually, you don't bother using the reference returned by Worksheets.Add because using ActiveSheet to establish a new reference is as easy as shouting "Jared" to get a slumbering student's attention.

Copy a Worksheet

Another useful method for a worksheet allows you to make a copy of the worksheet. You can copy the worksheet either to a new workbook or to the same workbook.

1. In the **Immediate** window, type Activesheet.Copy and press Enter.

Copying a worksheet without specifying a destination creates a new workbook that includes the copy.

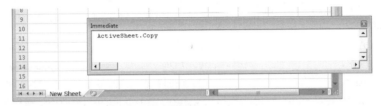

2. Type ActiveWorkbook.Close SaveChanges:=False and press Enter to delete the new workbook.

3. Type Activesheet.Copy Before:=Activesheet and press Enter.

This version of the Copy method tells Excel where to put the new copy: it puts it just before the specified worksheet, which in this case is the original worksheet. If you use the Before argument, you must give it a reference to a worksheet. If you want to copy a worksheet to the end of a workbook, the Copy method has an After argument that you can use instead of the Before argument.

The Copy method is a convenient way to clone a worksheet. The Copy method does not return a reference to the new worksheet (it returns the True or False that indicates successful completion); if you need to refer to the newly created copy, you must use ActiveSheet or some other method or property.

Manipulate Multiple Worksheets

When you work with collections, you typically work either with the entire collection (as when you closed all the workbooks at the same time by using the statement *Workbooks.Close*), or you work with a single item from the collection (as when you closed a single workbook by using the statement *Workbooks(1).Close*). With worksheets, however, you sometimes need to create a subcollection—a new collection that includes some, but not all, the worksheets in the collection.

1. Type **Worksheets(3).Select** and press Enter to select the third worksheet in the workbook.

   The Select method allows you to select a new worksheet within the workbook. When you select a single worksheet, it makes it the active worksheet.

   Excel can have more than one worksheet selected at the same time. This is equivalent to holding down the Ctrl key as you click worksheet tabs.

2. Type **Worksheets(Array(1,3,4)).Select** and press Enter to select the first, third, and fourth worksheets.

   Array is a function that lets you treat multiple values as one. With the Array function, you can select more than one worksheet at the same time. Even though three worksheets are selected, only one is the active worksheet.

3. Type **Worksheets(3).Activate** and press Enter to activate the third worksheet in the workbook, the Sheet1 worksheet, while leaving all three worksheets selected.

   When you select more than one worksheet, one of the worksheets is on top as the active worksheet. All three worksheets are selected, but only one is active. You use the Activate method to specify which worksheet should be the active worksheet. If you activate a worksheet that is not within the currently selected set of worksheets—for example, if only one worksheet is selected—the Select method and the Activate method act the same: they select and activate a single worksheet.

4. Type **Worksheets(2).Activate** and press Enter to select only the second worksheet.

   When you activate a worksheet that is not selected, the selection changes to include only the newly activated worksheet. You can execute methods or assign values to properties for the entire subcollection of worksheets at once.

5. Type **?Worksheets(Array(1,3,4)).Count** and press Enter.

   The number 3 appears. When you select items from a collection with the Array function, the selected items form a new collection.

Not all collections allow you to use the Array function to create sub-collections. For example, you cannot use Array with the Workbooks collection. Generally the object model reflects the user interface. In the user interface, you can select multiple worksheets at the same time, so the object model lets you use the Array function with a Worksheets object. But in the user interface, you cannot select multiple workbooks at the same time, so the object model does not let you use the Array function with a Workbooks object.

Declare Variables to Enable Auto Lists

In a Visual Basic statement, when you type ActiveWorkbook and follow it with a period, an Auto List of methods and properties appropriate for a workbook appear. But when you type ActiveSheet and follow it with a period, no Auto List appears. This is because a workbook can contain different types of sheets: The active sheet could be a chart sheet as well as a worksheet. In the context of a macro, you can get the Auto List to appear by putting the object reference into a specially designated variable.

1. In the Visual Basic editor, close the **Immediate** window, click **Insert**, and click **Module**.

2. In the module, type Sub Test and press Enter to create a new macro.

3. In the body of the macro, type mySheet and then type a period (.).

   No Auto List appears. The word *mySheet* acts as a variable. When you create a new word and use it as a variable, Visual Basic makes it Variant. *Variant* means that you can assign anything you want to the variable, and it will change from Integer to String to Workbook to Range as fast as you can assign different values or objects to it. Visual Basic can't display the Auto List because it really doesn't know what type of value or object will be assigned to the variable at any given moment. You can, however, promise Visual Basic that you'll never, ever assign anything other than a Worksheet object to the mySheet variable.

4. Delete the period you just typed. At the top of the macro, just below the Sub Test statement, enter this statement: Dim mySheet As Worksheet.

   This statement *declares* the variable to Visual Basic—that is, you declare to Visual Basic that mySheet is a variable and that the only thing you'll ever assign to it is a reference to a Worksheet object. (*Dim* is an archaic term. It's short for *Dimension* and has to do with telling the computer how much space you'll need for the variable.)

5. Position the cursor at the end of the statement beginning with mySheet, and type a period (.).

Sure enough, the Auto List appears.

6. Type **N** to select the **Name** property.

```
Sub Test()
    Dim mySheet As Worksheet
    mySheet.N
End Sub        Name
               Names
               Next
               OLEObjects
               Outline
               PageSetup
               Parent
```

7. Press Space, and then type = "Test Sheet".

The final statement should be mySheet.Name = "Test Sheet".

8. Press F5 to run the macro.

You get an error message saying, "Object variable or With block variable not set." Even though you promised that mySheet would contain only a worksheet, you still haven't assigned a worksheet reference to it.

9. Click **End** to close the error message, and then after the Dim statement, add the statement **Set mySheet = ActiveSheet**.

The Set statement assigns a reference to the ActiveSheet object to the mySheet variable.

10. Press F8 repeatedly to run the macro.

The macro first assigns the active sheet object to the variable and then changes the name of that sheet.

You can create a variable "on the fly" simply by assigning a value or an object to it, but if you use Dim to declare how you intend to use the variable, Visual Basic can display Auto Lists that make code much easier to write and less likely to contain errors.

CLOSE Excel.

Key Points

- Use the Immediate window to test statements before you put them in your macro. The Immediate window is particularly useful to step through a macro that just contains variable declarations.

- Make the most of recorded macros that assign values to object properties. You can easily convert those macros into ones that update the existing value of a property.

- Look for additional arguments when the recorder uses a method. There may be interesting capabilities you didn't know were available.

- Watch for objects that are collections. They are very likely to have an Item property (to get one item), a Count property (to find out how many items are in the collection), and an Add method (to create a new item).

- The Add method of most collections returns a reference to the item it creates. Store that item in a variable to make it easy to use later in the macro.

Chapter at a Glance

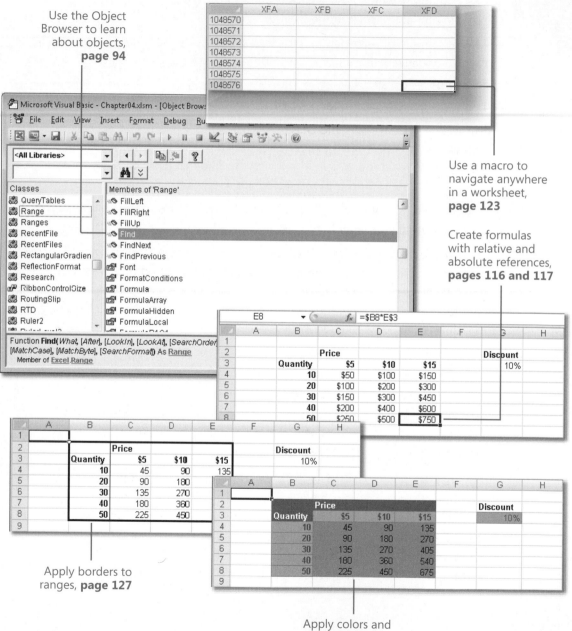

Use the Object Browser to learn about objects, **page 94**

Use a macro to navigate anywhere in a worksheet, **page 123**

Create formulas with relative and absolute references, **pages 116 and 117**

Apply borders to ranges, **page 127**

Apply colors and styles to ranges, **page 131**

4 Explore Range Objects

The world would be much simpler if people were all the same size. You wouldn't need adjustable seats in your car; your head would never get bumped on a door frame; your feet would never dangle from a chair. Of course, you'd have new problems as well: When you went to exchange that hideous outfit you got for your birthday, you wouldn't be able to claim it was the wrong size.

When using Microsoft Visual Basic for Applications (VBA) to write macros for Microsoft Office Excel, you don't need to worry about Range objects as long as all your worksheets and data files are the same size. For example, if you never insert new rows into a budget, if you always put yearly totals in column M, and if every month's transaction file has exactly 12 columns and 120 rows, you can skip this chapter because the macro recorder can take care of dealing with ranges for you.

But in the real-live human world, people are different sizes, and consequently clothes come in different sizes and cars have adjustable seats. And in the real-live worksheet world, models and data files have different—and changing—sizes, and your macros need to fit them. Excel provides many methods and properties for working with Range objects. In this chapter, you'll explore Range objects and in the process learn how you can use the Object Browser to learn about any new, unfamiliar object.

> **Important** Before you complete this chapter, you need to install the practice files from the book's companion CD to their default locations. See "Using the Book's CD" on page xv for more information.

> **USE** the *Ranges.xlsx* workbook. This practice file is located in the *Documents\MSP\ExcelVBA07SBS* folder.
>
> **BE SURE TO** save a macro-enabled copy of the *Ranges.xlsx* workbook as *Chapter4.xlsm* in the trusted folder location you created in Chapter 1.
>
> **OPEN** the *Chapter4.xlsm* workbook.

Referring to a Range

A macro that needs to work with ranges of differing sizes must be flexible. In this section, you'll learn various ways to refer to a range. The examples in this section don't *do* anything except reference ranges within a list, but these are all techniques you'll use many times as you work with ranges. Later in the chapter, you'll use these techniques in more practical contexts.

Refer to a Range by Using an Address

The Range property is a useful and flexible way of retrieving a reference to a range. The Range property allows you to specify the address of the range you want. You can use the Object Browser to see how to use the Range property.

1. In the *Chapter04* workbook, right-click a worksheet tab, and then click **View Code** on the shortcut menu to display the Visual Basic editor.

   Rearrange the Excel and Visual Basic editor windows so that you can see them side by side.

Object Browser

2. In the Visual Basic editor, click the **Object Browser** toolbar button.

   See Also If you want to change the Object Browser into a dockable window, see the sidebar titled "Dockable Views" in Chapter 3, "Explore Workbooks and Worksheets."

The Object Browser appears in the space normally held by the code window. In essence, the Object Browser consists of two lists. The list on the left is a list of object class names. The list on the right is a list of members—methods and properties—available for the currently selected object class. At the top of the list of classes is a special object class named *<globals>*. The <globals> object is not a real object class, but it includes in its list of members all the methods and properties you can use without specifying an object. These are the methods and properties you use to start a statement.

3. In the **Classes** list, select the **<globals>** object, click in the **Members of '<globals>'** list, and press the R key to scroll to the first member that begins with the letter *R*. Then select the **Range** property.

The box at the bottom of the Object Browser displays information about the Range property. This property takes two arguments. The brackets around the second argument indicate that it is optional. The Range property returns a reference to a Range object.

4. Right-click the **Range** property name in the **Members** list, and click **Copy** on the shortcut menu.

5. Click the **View** menu, and click **Immediate Window**.

6. Right-click the **Immediate** window, and click **Paste**.

   This is equivalent to using the Complete Word command to enter the function name.

7. After the **Range** property, type an opening parenthesis (Visual Basic will display the argument list), and then type "B2" followed by a closing parenthesis and a period. Then type Select.

   The complete statement is *Range("B2").Select*. You need the quotation marks around the range definition because this is the *name* of the range, not the item number of a member of a collection.

8. Press Enter to select cell **B2** on the active worksheet.

9. Type Range("B2:H2").Select and press Enter.

   The first argument of the range property can be a multicell range. In fact, it can be anything that Excel recognizes.

10. Type **Range("H14").Select** and press Enter to select the lower-right corner of the list of values. Then type **Range(Selection, "B2").Select** and press Enter.

    This selects the range from cell H14 (the current selection) to cell B2 (the upper left cell of the list). The arguments to the Range property do not have to be strings; they can also be references to range objects. A common use of the two-argument form of the Range property is to select the range that extends from the currently selected range to some fixed point at the top of the worksheet.

11. Type **?Selection.Count** and press Enter.

    The number *91* appears in the Immediate window. There are 91 cells in the currently selected range. If you don't specify otherwise, Excel treats a range object as a collection of cells. If you want to know the number of rows or columns in the range, you can do that by using specialized properties, as you will learn in the section titled "Refer to a Range as a Collection of Rows or Columns," later in this chapter.

> **Tip** As you learned in Chapter 3, typing a question mark before an expression in the Immediate window allows you to display the value of that expression.

The Range property is a flexible way of establishing a link to an arbitrary Range object. You can use either a single text string that contains any valid reference as an argument to the Range property or two arguments that define the end points of a rectangular range. Once you have the resulting reference to a range object, you can use any of the members that appear in Object Browser for the Range class.

Refer to a Range as a Collection of Cells

Multiple worksheets can exist in a workbook, and the Worksheets collection is defined as an object class. A Worksheets object has a list of methods and properties that is separate from a Worksheet object.

Similarly, multiple cells exist on a worksheet. You might expect that Excel would have a Cells collection object. But a collection of cells is more complicated than a collection of worksheets because cells come in two dimensions—rows and columns. For example, you can think of the range A1:B3 as a collection of six cells, as a collection of three rows, or as a collection of two columns.

Excel therefore has three properties that look at a range as a collection. The first of these—the Cells property—returns a collection of cells. However, this is not a separate class. The result of the Cells property is still a Range object, and it can use any of the methods or properties of any other Range object. Because Excel thinks of any range, by default, as a collection of cells, you typically use the Cells property as an alternative to the Range property—using numbers, rather than text strings.

1. In the **Object Browser**, with the **<globals>** object selected in the list of classes, select the **Cells** property from the list of members.

   The description at the bottom of the Object Browser indicates that the Cells property returns a Range object.

2. In the **Immediate** window, type **Cells.Select** and press Enter.

   This selects all the cells on the worksheet. This is equivalent to clicking the box at the upper left corner of the worksheet, between the column A heading and the row 1 heading.

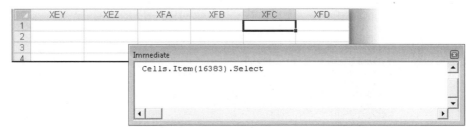

3. Type Cells.Item(5).Select and press Enter.

   This selects cell E1, the fifth cell in the first row. The Cells property returns the range of all the cells on the worksheet as a collection. An individual item in the collection is a cell.

4. Type Cells.Item(16383).Select and press Enter.

   This selects cell XFC1, the next to the last cell in the first row. Excel 2007 now allows 16384 cells in a single row.

5. Type Cells.Item(16385).Select and press Enter.

   This selects cell A2, the first cell in the second row. When you use a single number to select an item in the Cells collection, the number wraps at the end of each row. Since each row of the worksheet contains 16384 cells, cell 16385 is the first cell on the second row.

6. Type Cells.Item(3,2).Select and press Enter.

This selects cell B3, the third row and second column in the worksheet. Unlike most other collections, the Cells collection allows you to specify an item by using both the row and column values.

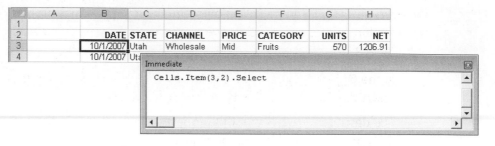

> **Important** In previous versions of Excel, the expression *Cells.Item(257)* referred to cell A2. In Excel 2007, it now refers to cell IW1, the 257th cell in the first row. In order to write macros that work in multiple versions, you should always use the row and column specification in the Cells function. Another consequence of the larger size of the worksheet is that you cannot use the expression *Cells.Count* to retrieve the number of cells on the worksheet, because the number is too big. This is unlikely to ever be a problem, but it illustrates the expanded size of the worksheet grid.

7. Type **Cells.Item(1048576,16384).Select** and press Enter.

This selects cell XFD1048576, the bottom right cell in the worksheet. In case you wonder, these bizarre-looking numbers are really simple powers of 2. You could select the same cell by using the expression *Cells.Item(2^20,2^14)*. You could also use the Range property—*Range("XFD1048576")*.

8. Type **Cells(1).Select** and press Enter to select cell **A1**.

As with other collections, when you use the Cells property to get a collection of cells, you can leave out the Item method, and simply put the argument after the Cells property. The expression *Cells(1)* is equivalent to *Cells.Item(1)*, which is equivalent to *Range("A1")*. All these expressions can be used interchangeably.

Refer to a Range as a Collection of Rows or Columns

In addition to referring to the worksheet range as a collection of cells, you can also think of it as a collection of rows or as a collection of columns. Analogous to the Cells property, the Rows property returns a collection of rows and the Columns property returns a collection of columns. These properties return collections, do not have their own object classes, and return Range objects.

1. In the **Object Browser**, with the **<globals>** object selected in the list of classes, select the **Columns** property in the list of **Members**.

   The description shows that this property, similar to the Range property and the Cells property, returns a Range object.

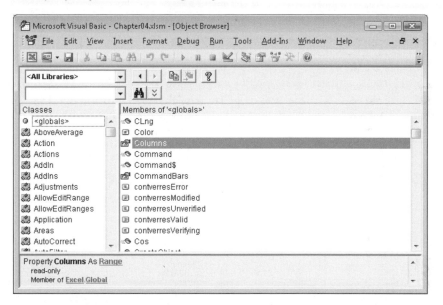

2. In the **Immediate** window, type Columns.Select and press Enter.

   This selects all the cells on the worksheet, exactly the same as Cells.Select. The difference between the two properties appears when you use the Item property to index into a single item in the collection.

3. Type Columns(3).Select and press Enter.

   This selects column C, the third column on the worksheet.

	A	B	C	D	E	F	G	H
1								
2		DATE	STATE	CHANNEL	PRICE	CATEGORY	UNITS	NET
3		10/1/2007	Utah	Wholesale	Mid	Fruits	570	1206.91
4		10/1/2007	Utah	Wholesale	Mid	Books	555	1176.79
5		10/1/2007						
6		10/1/2007						

```
Immediate
    Columns(3).Select
```

4. Type Columns("D").Select and press Enter.

This selects column D. When you specify a column by letter, you are giving the *name* of the item and must enclose it in quotation marks.

	A	B	C	D	E	F	G	H
1								
2		DATE	STATE	CHANNEL	PRICE	CATEGORY	UNITS	NET
3		10/1/2007	Utah	Wholesale	Mid	Fruits	570	1206.91
4		10/1/2007	Utah	Wholesale	Mid	Books	555	1176.79
5		10/1/2007	Utah	Wholesale	Mid	Flowers	285	623.23
6		10/1/200						
7		10/1/200						

```
Immediate
    Columns("D").Select
```

5. Type Columns("B:H").Select and press Enter.

This selects the range of columns from B through H. The only way to specify a range of columns within the collection is by using the column letter names.

	A	B	C	D	E	F	G	H	I
1									
2		DATE	STATE	CHANNEL	PRICE	CATEGORY	UNITS	NET	
3		10/1/2007	Utah	Wholesale	Mid	Fruits	570	1206.91	
4		10/1/2007	Utah	Wholesale	Mid	Books	555	1176.79	
5		10/1/2007							
6		10/1/2007							
7		10/1/2007							

```
Immediate
    Columns("B:H").Select
```

6. Type Rows(2).Select and press Enter.

This selects row 2. With rows, the name of an item is also a number. The expressions *Rows(2)* and *Rows("2")* are functionally equivalent.

	A	B	C	D	E	F	G	H	I
1									
2		**DATE**	**STATE**	**CHANNEL**	**PRICE**	**CATEGORY**	**UNITS**	**NET**	
3		10/1/2007	Utah	Wholesale	Mid	Fruits	570	1206.91	
4		10/1/2007	Utah	Wholesale	Mid	Books	555	1176.79	
5		10/1/2007							

```
Immediate
    Rows(2).Select
```

7. Type **Rows("3:14").Select** and press Enter.

   This selects a range of rows. The only way to specify a range of rows within the collection is by using the row numbers as a name—that is, by enclosing them in quotation marks.

	A	B	C	D	E	F	G	H	I
1									
2		**DATE**	**STATE**	**CHANNEL**	**PRICE**	**CATEGORY**	**UNITS**	**NET**	
3		10/1/2007	Utah	Wholesale	Mid	Fruits	570	1206.91	
4		10/1/2007	Utah	Wholesale	Mid	Books	555	1176.79	
5		10/1/2007	Utah	Wholesale	Mid	Flowers	285	623.23	
6		10/1/2007	Utah	Wholesale	Mid	Herbs	285	622.3	
7		10/1/2007	Utah	Retail	Mid	Fruits	245	856.83	
8		10/1/2007	Utah	Wholesale	Mid	Tools	135	303.75	
9		10/1/2007	Utah	Retail	Mid	Herbs	65	292.5	
10		10/1/2007	Utah	Retail	Mid	Tools	56	252	
11		10/1/2007	Utah	Retail	Mid	Books	40	180	
12		10/1/2007							
13		10/1/2007							
14		10/1/2007							
15									

```
Immediate
    Rows("3:14").Select
```

The \<globals\> object in the Object Browser includes three properties that return all the cells of a worksheet—Cells, Columns, and Rows. In each case, you get a reference to a Range object, but the properties return that object as a collection of cells, columns, or rows, respectively. There are no object classes for Cells, Columns, and Rows. These are simply different ways of representing the same Range object.

Refer to a Range Based on the Active Cell

Many times when writing a macro you want to refer to a range that is somehow related to the active cell or to the current selection. The macro recorder uses the Selection property to refer to the selected range and the ActiveCell property to refer to the one active cell. A Range object has useful properties that can extend the active cell or the selection to include particularly useful ranges.

1. In the **Immediate** window, type Range("B2").Select and press Enter.

   This selects the upper left cell of the sample list.

2. In the **Object Browser**, with the **<globals>** object selected in the **Classes** list, select the **ActiveCell** property.

   The description at the bottom of the Object Browser shows that this property returns a Range object.

3. In the **Immediate** window, click the **Edit** menu, and then click **Complete Word**. In the list of members, click **ActiveCell**.

   > **Tip** When you use the Complete Word command at the beginning of a statement—whether in a macro or in the Immediate window—the Auto List displays all the members of the <globals> object. If you like using the keyboard, you can press Ctrl+Space to display the list of members, type partial words and use arrow keys to select the desired member, and then press the Tab key to insert the member into the statement.

4. Type a period (.). Then type CurrentRegion.Select to create the statement *ActiveCell.CurrentRegion.Select*, and then press Enter.

   This selects the entire sample list. The CurrentRegion property selects a rectangular range that includes the original cell and is surrounded by either blank cells or the edge of the worksheet. It is hard to overstate the usefulness of the CurrentRegion property.

⟋	A	B	C	D	E	F	G	H	I
1									
2		DATE	STATE	CHANNEL	PRICE	CATEGORY	UNITS	NET	
3		10/1/2007	Utah	Wholesale	Mid	Fruits	570	1206.91	
4		10/1/2007	Utah	Wholesale	Mid	Books	555	1176.79	
5		10/1/2007	Utah	Wholesale	Mid	Flowers	285	623.23	
6		10/1/2007	Utah	Wholesale	Mid	Herbs	285	622.3	
7		10/1/2007	Utah	Retail	Mid	Fruits	245	856.83	
8		10/1/2007	Utah	Wholesale	Mid	Tools	135	303.75	
9		10/1/2007	Utah	Retail	Mid	Herbs	65	292.5	
10		10/1/2007	Utah	Retail	Mid	Tools	56	252	
11		10/1/2007	Utah	Retail	Mid	Books	40	180	
12		10/1/2007	Utah	Retail	Mid	Flowers	35	157.5	
13		10/1/2007							
14		10/1/2007							
15									

Immediate

```
Range("B2").Select
ActiveCell.CurrentRegion.Select
```

5. Type ActiveCell.EntireColumn.Select and press Enter.

This selects all of column B because the active cell was cell B2. Because the starting range was the active cell—not the entire selection—the EntireColumn property returned a reference to only one column. Because the initial active cell—B2—is still within the selection, it is still the active cell.

⟋	A	B	C	D	E	F	G	H
1								
2		DATE	STATE	CHANNEL	PRICE	CATEGORY	UNITS	NET
3		10/1/2007	Utah	Wholesale	Mid	Fruits	570	1206.91
4		10/1/2007	Utah	Wholesale	Mid	Books	555	1176.79
5		10/1/2007						
6		10/1/2007						
7		10/1/2007						

Immediate

```
ActiveCell.EntireColumn.Select
```

6. In the **Object Browser**, with the **<globals>** object selected, select the **Selection** property in the list of members.

The description at the bottom indicates that the Selection property returns an *object*, not a Range. The Selection property returns a Range object only when cells are selected. If shapes or parts of a chart are selected, this global property returns a different object type. Because the Selection object can return a different object type at different times, it does not display an Auto List the way the ActiveCell property does.

7. In the **Immediate** window, type Selection.CurrentRegion.Select and press Enter.

   This selects the range B1:H14—the entire sample list plus the one row above it. It's acting the same as if the current selection were only cell B1. When you use the CurrentRegion property with a multicell range as the starting point, it ignores everything except the top-left cell of the range as it calculates the current region.

8. Type Range("A2").Activate and press Enter.

   Because the specified cell is outside of the current selection, the Activate method behaves the same as Select.

9. Type Selection.EntireRow.Select and press Enter.

   This selects all of row 2. Because the selection is a single cell, you would get exactly the same result by using *ActiveCell.EntireRow.Select*.

10. Type Range("B2").Activate and press Enter.

    Because the specified cell is within the selected range, this statement does not change the selection, but it does move the active cell to a new location within the range. If you activate a cell that is not within the current selection, the Activate method behaves the same as Select.

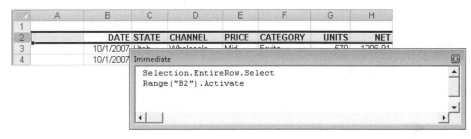

The Selection and ActiveCell properties are useful as starting points for deriving other ranges. The ActiveCell property always returns a reference to a Range object, and therefore displays a convenient Auto List when you are entering a statement. The Selection property returns a reference to a Range object only when a range is actually selected, and thus it does not display an Auto List.

Refer to Subsets of a Range

When you reference a range by using a property from the <globals> object—for example, Range, Cells, Columns, or Rows—you get a range based on the entire active worksheet. These same properties also exist as properties of a Range object. The easiest way to work with properties of a Range object is to declare a variable as a Range. Then the Auto List displays the methods and properties as you type a statement, even if you use the Selection property—which does not display Auto Lists—to assign the range to the variable.

1. In the Visual Basic editor, click **Insert**, and then click **Module**.

2. Type Sub TestRange and press Enter.

   Visual Basic adds parentheses and an *End Sub* statement.

3. Type Dim myRange As Range and press F8 twice to initialize the variable.

4. In the **Immediate** window, type Set myRange = Range("B2") and press Enter. Then type myRange.Select and press Enter again.

This selects cell B2, confirming that the variable contains a reference to that cell.

5. Click the **Object Browser** button. In the list of classes, select the **Range** class. Then in the list of members, select the **Range** property.

This Range property appears very similar to the Range property of the <globals> object. It behaves, however, *relative* to a starting range.

6. In the **Immediate** window, type **myRange.Range("A1:G1").Select** and press Enter.

This does not select the range A1:G1. Rather, it selects the range B2:H2. If you think of cell B2 as the upper left cell of an imaginary worksheet, the range A1:G1 of that imaginary worksheet would correspond to the range B2:H2 of the real worksheet.

	A	B	C	D	E	F	G	H
1								
2		DATE	STATE	CHANNEL	PRICE	CATEGORY	UNITS	NET
3		10/1/2007	Utah	Wholesale	Mid	Fruits	570	1206.91
4		10/1/2007	Utah	Wholesale	Mid	Books	555	1176.79
5		10/1/2007						
6		10/1/2007						
7		10/1/2007						

```
Immediate
Set myRange = Range("B2")
myRange.Range("A1:G1").Select
```

7. Type **Set myRange = myRange.CurrentRegion** and press Enter. Then type **myRange.Select** and press Enter again.

Given that myRange already referred to cell B2, which is inside the sample list, the first statement references the entire sample list, and the second confirms that the variable contains a reference to the appropriate range.

8. Type **myRange.Cells.Item(2,6).Select** and press Enter.

This selects the first data value in the Units column—row 2 and column 6 within the data region.

	A	B	C	D	E	F	G	H	I
1									
2		DATE	STATE	CHANNEL	PRICE	CATEGORY	UNITS	NET	
3		10/1/2007	Utah	Wholesale	Mid	Fruits	570	1206.91	
4		10/1/2007							

```
Immediate
Set myRange = myRange.CurrentRegion
myRange.Select
myRange.Cells.Item(2,6).Select
```

9. Type **myRange.Rows(2).Select** and press Enter.

This selects the second row of values in the list, even though they exist in row 3 of the worksheet. A single row from the collection referenced by the global Rows property includes the entire row of the worksheet; the Rows property of a Range object includes only the cells within the range.

10. Type **myRange.Rows(myRange.Rows.Count).Select** and press Enter.

This selects the last row of the list. Because the Rows property returns a collection, you can use the Count property to find the number of items in the collection. That count can then serve as an index into the same collection.

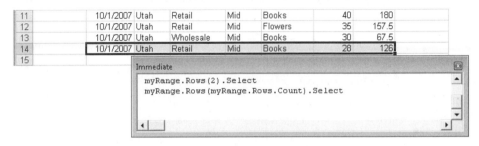

When you use the Range, Cells, Columns, or Rows properties as members of a Range object, the resulting ranges are relative to the upper-left cell of that range. Contrast this to when you use the same functions from the global group—or as members of the Application object or of a Worksheet object. With anything other than a Range object, these functions return ranges that are relative to the upper-left cell of the worksheet.

Refer to a Relative Range

Excel has other properties that can calculate a new range based on one or more existing ranges. Two of these properties do not exist in the list of global members; they exist only as members of a Range object: the Offset property references a range shifted down, up, left, or right from a starting range, and the Resize property references a range with a different number of rows or columns from a starting range. An additional property, the Intersect property, does appear in the list of global members. It is particularly valuable when you need to "trim away" part of a range, such as when you want to remove the header row from the current region.

1. In the **Object Browser**, select **Range** in the **Classes** list. Then, in the **Members** list, select the **Offset** property.

The description indicates that this property has two arguments—RowOffset and ColumnOffset, both of which are optional—and that it returns a Range object.

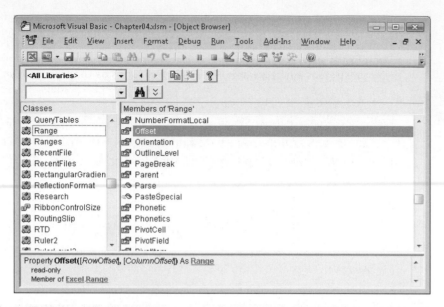

2. In the **Immediate** window, type **myRange.Offset(1).Select** and press Enter.

   This selects a range identical in size and shape to the range stored in the variable, but shifted down by one cell. The first argument to the Offset property indicates the number of rows down to shift the range; the second argument indicates how many columns to the right to shift the range. Omitting an argument is the same as using zero and does not shift the range in that direction.

	A	B	C	D	E	F	G	H	I
1									
2		DATE	STATE	CHANNEL	PRICE	CATEGORY	UNITS	NET	
3		10/1/2007	Utah	Wholesale	Mid	Fruits	570	1206.91	
4		10/1/2007	Utah	Wholesale	Mid	Books	555	1176.79	
5		10/1/2007	Utah	Wholesale	Mid	Flowers	285	623.23	
6		10/1/2007	Utah	Wholesale	Mid	Herbs	285	622.3	
7		10/1/2007	Utah	Retail	Mid	Fruits	245	856.83	
8		10/1/2007	Utah	Wholesale	Mid	Tools	135	303.75	
9		10/1/2007	Utah	Retail	Mid	Herbs	65	292.5	
10		10/1/2007	Utah	Retail	Mid	Tools	56	252	
11		10/1/2007	Utah	Retail	Mid	Books	40	180	
12		10/1/2007	Utah	Retail	Mid	Flowers	35	157.5	
13		10/1/2007	Utah	Wholesale	Mid	Books	30	67.5	
14		10/1/2007							
15									
16									

```
Immediate
    myRange.Offset(1).Select
```

> **Tip** To understand the Offset property, think of yourself as standing on the upper-left cell of the initial range. Face the bottom of the worksheet, and step forward the number of steps specified in the first argument. Zero steps means no movement. Negative steps are backwards. Then face the right side of the worksheet and do the same with the number of steps specified in the second argument. The resulting range is the same size and shape as the original one, but it begins on the cell you end up standing on.

3. In the **Object Browser**, select **Range** in the **Classes** list. Then, in the list of members, select the **Resize** property.

The description indicates that this property has two arguments—RowSize and ColumnSize, both of which are optional—and that it returns a Range object.

4. In the **Immediate** window, type **myRange.Offset(1).Resize(5).Select** and press Enter.

This selects the first five rows of data. The Offset property shifts the range down to omit the heading row. The Resize function changes the size of the resulting range. The first argument to the Resize property is the number of rows for the result range; the second is the number of columns for the result range. Omitting an argument is the same as keeping the size of the original range for that direction.

5. Type **myRange.Offset(1,5).Resize(1,2).Select** and press Enter.

This selects the range G3:H3, which happens to be the numeric values in the first row of the body of the list.

> **Tip** The combined functionality of the Offset and Resize properties is equivalent to that of the OFFSET function available on worksheets.

6. In the **Object Browser**, with the **<globals>** object selected in the list of classes, select the **Intersect** method in the **Members** list.

The description shows that this method returns a Range object, but it also shows that it can take up to *30* arguments! In practice, you usually use two arguments, and you can see that the first two arguments are required. The Object Browser shows that the first two arguments must be range objects, but if you use more than two arguments, they do all need to be ranges. You can use the Intersect method in conjunction with the Offset method to remove headings from the current region.

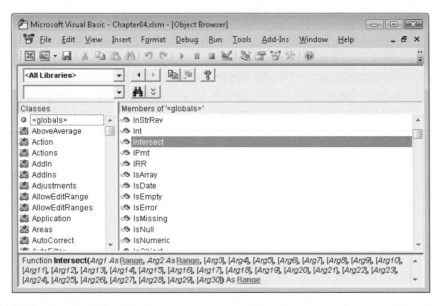

7. In the **Immediate** window, type Intersect(myRange, myRange.Offset(1)).Select and press Enter.

This selects the range B3:H14, which is the entire list except the heading row. You often need to manipulate the body of a list separately from the heading. By using a range as the first argument of the Intersect method, and then an offset version of the range as the second argument, you can trim off portions of the range.

	A	B	C	D	E	F	G	H	I
1									
2		DATE	STATE	CHANNEL	PRICE	CATEGORY	UNITS	NET	
3		10/1/2007	Utah	Wholesale	Mid	Fruits	570	1206.91	
4		10/1/2007	Utah	Wholesale	Mid	Books	555	1176.79	
5		10/1/2007	Utah	Wholesale	Mid	Flowers	285	623.23	
6		10/1/2007	Utah	Wholesale	Mid	Herbs	285	622.3	
7		10/1/2007	Utah	Retail	Mid	Fruits	245	856.83	
8		10/1/2007	Utah	Wholesale	Mid	Tools	135	303.75	
9		10/1/2007	Utah	Retail	Mid	Herbs	65	292.5	
10		10/1/2007	Utah	Retail	Mid	Tools	56	252	
11		10/1/2007	Utah	Retail	Mid	Books	40	180	
12		10/1/2007	Utah	Retail	Mid	Flowers	35	157.5	
13		10/1/2007	Utah	Wholesale	Mid	Books	30	67.5	
14		10/1/2007							
15									

Immediate

```
Intersect(myRange, myRange.Offset(1)).Select
```

8. Press F5 to end the macro.

The Offset and Resize properties, along with the EntireRow, EntireColumn, and CurrentRegion properties and the Intersect method, provide you with flexible tools for calculating new Range objects based on an original starting range. Often, the easiest way to work within a range is to first use the CurrentRegion property to establish the base range, and then use the Offset property and the Intersect method to manipulate the range.

Enhancing Recorded Selections

When you record a macro, the macro recorder dutifully follows all your actions, including selecting ranges before acting on them. You can make a macro do less work—and make it easier to read—by eliminating unnecessary selection changes. A powerful technique for eliminating unnecessary changes to the selection begins with watching for a statement ending in Select followed by one or more statements beginning with Selection or ActiveCell. What you do next depends on whether a single Selection (or ActiveCell) statement follows the Select statement or whether a group of statements follows.

Simplify Select...Selection Pairs

When a single Selection statement follows a Select statement, you can collapse the two statements into one. Record and simplify a macro that puts the names of the months across the top of a worksheet.

1. In Excel, insert a blank worksheet and start recording a macro named **LabelMonths**. Type the labels January, February, and March in the cells **B1**, **C1**, and **D1**.

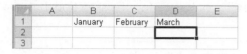

2. Turn off the recorder, and then edit the macro.

   The macro should look similar to the following code. (Your macro might be slightly different, depending on the key you press to enter the values into the cells.)

```
Sub LabelMonths()
    Range("B1").Select
    ActiveCell.FormulaR1C1 = "January"
    Range("C1").Select
    ActiveCell.FormulaR1C1 = "February"
    Range("D1").Select
    ActiveCell.FormulaR1C1 = "March"
    Range("D2").Select
End Sub
```

   For each cell, the word *Select* appears at the end of one statement followed by either the word *Selection* or *ActiveCell* at the beginning of the next statement. You can delete both words, leaving only a single period. If a Select statement is the last one in a macro, you can delete it entirely.

3. Remove the unnecessary selections from the LabelMonths macro by deleting Select and ActiveCell each time they appear.

   The final macro should look like this:

```
Sub LabelMonths()
    Range("B1").FormulaR1C1 = "January"
    Range("C1").FormulaR1C1 = "February"
    Range("D1").FormulaR1C1 = "March"
End Sub
```

4. Insert a new blank worksheet, and test the macro.

   The labels appear in the cells, and the original selection doesn't change.

Why should you get rid of Select...Selection pairs? One reason is that doing so does make the macro run faster. Another reason is that running a macro can seem less disruptive if it doesn't end with different cells selected than when it started. But the most important reason is unquestionably that Select...Selection pairs in a macro are a dead giveaway that you're a beginner who uses the macro recorder to create macros. It's OK to use the macro recorder; you just want to cover your tracks.

Simplify Select Groups

When you eliminate a Select...Selection pair, be sure that only a single statement uses the selection. If you have a single Select statement followed by two or more statements that use the selection, you can still avoid changing the selection, but you must do it in a different way.

1. In Excel, select a sheet with labels in the first row, and start recording a macro named MakeBoldItalic.

2. Click cell **B1**, click the **Bold** button, click the **Italic** button, and then click the **Stop Recording** button.

	A	B	C	D	E
1		*January*	February	March	
2					

3. Edit the macro to look like this:

```
Sub MakeBoldItalic()
    Range("B1").Select
    Selection.Font.Bold = True
    Selection.Font.Italic = True
End Sub
```

Obviously, if you delete the first Select...Selection pair, the macro won't control which cells will become italicized.

4. Edit the macro to assign the range to a variable named *myRange*. Then replace the **Selection** object with the **myRange** object.

The finished macro should look like this:

```
Sub MakeBoldItalic()
    Dim myRange As Range
    Set myRange = Range("B1")
    myRange.Font.Bold = True
    myRange.Font.Italic = True
End Sub
```

5. Change "B1" to "C1" in the macro, and then press F8 repeatedly to step through the macro. Watch how the format of the cell changes without changing which cell is originally selected.

6. Save the *Chapter04* workbook.

Eliminating the selection when there's a group might not seem like much of a simplification. And with only two statements, it probably isn't. But when you have several statements that use the same selection, storing the range in a variable can make the macro much easier to read.

Bold   Italic

Ready

Stop Recording

> **Tip** You could also replace the Select group with a With structure, like this:
>
> ```
> With Range("B1")
>     .Font.Bold = True
>     .Font.Italic = True
> End With
> ```
>
> Secretly in the background, the With structure really just creates a hidden variable, takes the object from the With statement, and assigns that object to the hidden variable. It then puts the hidden variable in front of each "dangling" period. The End With statement discards the hidden variable. An advantage of using an explicit object variable is that you can delare the variable with a specific object type—for example, Dim myRange as Range—and then VBA checks to make sure any methods or properties you use are appropriate. With an explicitly declared variable, VBA also offers Auto Lists to help you modify a macro.

Entering Values and Formulas into a Range

You may have situations where you want to create a macro that dynamically enters formulas into cells. First you should understand how references work in formulas in Excel, and then you can see how to create formulas in a macro.

See Also This section refers to standard Excel formula references. For information about using structured formulas in a table, see the section titled "Record a Macro to Manipulate a Table" in Chapter 5, "Explore Data Objects."

Relative References

Most formulas perform arithmetic operations on values retrieved from other cells. Excel formulas use cell references to retrieve values from cells. Imagine, for example, a list of Retail prices and Wholesale costs.

	A	B	C
1		Retail	Wholesale
2	High	5.50	2.75
3	Mid	4.50	2.25
4	Low	3.50	1.75
5			

Suppose you want to add a column to the list that calculates the *gross margin*—the difference between the Retail price and the Wholesale cost—for each item. You would put the label Margin in cell D1 and then enter the first formula into cell D2. The formula subtracts the first Wholesale cost (cell C2) from the first Retail price (cell B2). So you would enter =B2-C2 into cell D2.

D2		▼	f_x =B2-C2	
A	B	C	D	E
1		Retail	Wholesale	Margin
2 High	5.50	2.75	2.75
3 Mid	4.50	2.25	
4 Low	3.50	1.75	
5			

For each item in the High group, the gross margin is $2.75. Now you need to copy the formula to the other rows. The formula you typed into cell D2 refers explicitly to cells C2 and B2. When you copy the formula to cell D3, you want the formula to automatically adjust to refer to C3 and B3. Fortunately, when you copy the formulas, Excel adjusts the references because, by default, references are relative to the cell that contains the formula. (The Prices worksheet in the *Chapter04* workbook contains these formulas.)

	A	B	C	D	E
1		Retail	Wholesale	Margin	
2	High	5.50	2.75	2.75	
3	Mid	4.50	2.25	2.25	
4	Low	3.50	1.75	1.75	
5					

If the reference =C2 is found in cell D2, it really means "one cell to my left." When you copy the formula to cell D3, it still means "one cell to my left," but now that meaning is represented by the reference =C3.

Absolute References

Sometimes you don't want relative references. Imagine, for example, a worksheet that contains various quantities in column B and prices in row 3. (The Revenue worksheet in the *Chapter04* workbook contains the prices and quantities.)

	A	B	C	D	E	F	G	H
1								
2			Price				Discount	
3		Quantity	$5	$10	$15		10%	
4		10						
5		20						
6		30						
7		40						
8		50						
9								

Suppose you want to add formulas to calculate the revenue for each combination. To calculate the first revenue value (cell C4), you need to multiply the first quantity (cell B4) by the first price (cell C3) . When you type = B4*C3 into cell C4, you get the correct answer: $50.

But if you copy that formula to cell C5, you get the ridiculous answer of $1000. That's because the cell references are relative. In this version of the formula, you're not really referring to cells B4 and C3; you're referring to "one cell to my left" and "one cell above me." When you put the formula into cell C5, "one cell above me" now refers to cell C4, not cell C3.

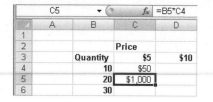

In the Revenue table, you want the Quantity cell references to adjust from row to row , and you want the Price cell references to adjust from column to column, but you always want to reference the Quantity from column B and the Price from row 3. The solution in the user interface is to put a dollar sign ($) in front of the B in the first Quantity reference ($B4), andin front of the 3 in the first Price reference (C$3). The formula that should go into cell C4 is =$B4*C$3. The dollar sign "anchors" that part of the formula, making it absolute. When you copy the formula to the rest of the range C4:E8, you get correct answers. (The RevenueFormulas worksheet in the *Chapter04* workbook contains the correct formulas.)

E8			f_x =$B8*E$3				
A	B	C	D	E	F	G	H
1							
2		Price				Discount	
3		Quantity	$5	$10	$15	10%	
4		10	$50	$100	$150		
5		20	$100	$200	$300		
6		30	$150	$300	$450		
7		40	$200	$400	$600		
8		50	$250	$500	$750		
9							

The relative portion of the formula changes with the row or column of the cell that contains the formula. The absolute portion remains fixed.

If you want to modify the formula so that it also takes into account the discount value from cell G3, you must make both the row and the column of the discount reference absolute. The correct formula would be =$B4*C$3*(1-$G$3). If you assign a name to a cell—for example, if you assign the name Discount to cell G3—then by default, using the name in the formula acts as a completely absolute reference. (The RevenueFormulas worksheet in the *Chapter04* workbook contains these formulas.) Later in this chapter, you will create a macro that will fill the grid with the correct formula, regardless of where it is on the worksheet and how many rows or columns it has.

R1C1 Reference Style

As a default, Excel displays letters for column headings and numbers for row headings. Consequently, the default name for the upper-left cell in the worksheet is cell A1. Referring to cells by letter and number is called *A1 reference style*. In A1 reference style, however, cell references do not really say what they mean. For example, the reference =C4 says "cell C4," but if it's in a formula in cell E4, it really means "two cells to my left," and if it's in a formula in cell C5, it really means "one cell above me." You don't know what the reference really means until you know which cell contains the reference.

Excel has an alternate reference style that uses numbers for both column and row headings. In this alternate reference style, to refer to a cell you use the letter *R* plus the row number and *C* plus the column number. Consequently, the upper-left cell in the worksheet is cell R1C1. Referring to cells by numbers in both rows and columns is called *R1C1 reference style*. In R1C1 reference style, cell references really do say what they mean. Consequently, in macros, when VBA has to understand and use the formulas, it is usually convenient to use R1C1 reference style. When a human has to understand the formula, it is usually easier to use A1 reference style, which is why A1 reference style is the default.

You can, however, change the user interface to use R1C1 reference style if you want to try it out. To turn on R1C1 reference style, click the Microsoft Office Button and then click Excel Options. On the Formulas page, select the R1C1 Reference Style check box, and click OK. (To turn off R1C1 reference style, clear the check box.) The setting in the Excel Options dialog box does not have any effect on macros: a macro can enter formulas using either reference style.

In R1C1 reference style, to specify a relative reference on the same row or column as the cell with the formula, you simply use an *R* or a *C*, without a number. For example, the reference =RC3 means "the cell in column 3 of the same row as me," and the reference =R2C means "the cell in row 2 of the same column as me."

To specify a relative reference in a different row or column, you indicate the amount of the difference, in square brackets, after the *R* or the *C*. For example, the reference =R5C[2] means "two columns to my right in row 5," and the reference =R[-1]C means "one cell above me."

The correct formula for calculating the gross margin on the Prices worksheet was =B2-C2, but only if the formula was entered into cell D2. In R1C1 reference style, the equivalent formula is =RC[-2]-RC[-1] , and it doesn't matter which row contains the formula. The formula to calculate the discounted price on the Revenue worksheet was =$B4*C$3*(1-$G$3), at least for cell C4. In R1C1 reference style, the same formula is =RC2*R3C*(1-R3C7), again, regardless of which cell contains the formula.

> **Important** When you use A1 reference style, the formula changes depending on which range you copy the formula into. When you use R1C1 reference style, the formula is the same, regardless of which cell it goes into. The reference style only makes a difference when you put the same formula into multiple cells.

Put Values and Formulas into a Range

You can explore the properties for putting values and formulas into a range by creating a simple list of incrementing numbers.

1. In the Visual Basic editor, activate the **Immediate** window, type **Worksheets.Add**, and press Enter to create a new, blank worksheet in the active workbook.

2. Type **Range("B2:B6").Select** and press Enter to select a sample starting range of cells.

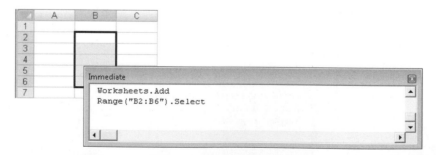

3. Type **Selection.Value = 100** and press Enter to fill all the cells of the selection with the number 100.

Value is a property of the range. When you set the Value property in conjunction with a multicell range, you change all the cells in the range.

> **Tip** When assigning a contant value to a range, the Formula property is equivalent to the Value property, so *Selection.Formula = 100* is the same as *Selection.Value = 100*. The Formula property is equivalent to whatever you see in the formula bar when the cell is selected. The formula bar can contain constants as well as formulas, and so can the Formula property. When you assign a value to a cell, the Formula property and the Value property have the same effect.

4. Type **ActiveCell.Value = 0** and press Enter to change cell **B2** to 0.

Only the active cell changes, not the selected cells. Entering a value in the active cell is equivalent to typing a value and pressing Enter. Entering a value in the selection is equivalent to typing a value and pressing Ctrl+Enter.

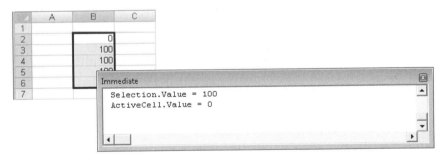

Suppose you want to enter a value in the cell above the active cell, whatever the active cell might be.

5. Type **ActiveCell.Offset(-1).Value = 1** and press Enter to change the value in cell **B1** to 1.

This statement starts with the active cell, uses the Offset property to calculate a new cell one up from that starting cell, and then sets the Value property for the resulting cell.

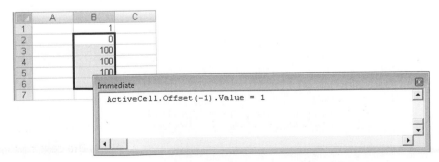

6. Type Selection.FormulaR1C1 = "=R[-1]C*5" and press Enter.

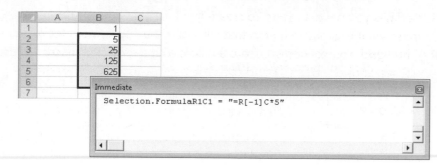

Now each of the selected cells contains a formula, not a constant. The FormulaR1C1 property expects a formula in R1C1 reference style. The reference *R[-1]C* always means "one cell above" regardless of which cell gets the formula.

7. Type ?ActiveCell.Value and press Enter.

This statement displays the value *5* in the Immediate window. The Value property retrieves the result of any formula in a cell. When you retrieve the contents of the cell that contains a formula, the Value property gives you the result of the formula.

8. Type ?ActiveCell.Formula and press Enter.

This statement displays the formula *=B1*5* in the Immediate window. When you retrieve the contents of a cell that contains a formula, the Formula property gives you the formula using A1 reference style. The setting in the Excel Options dialog box is ignored. If you want to retrieve the formula using R1C1 reference style, use the FormulaR1C1 property.

All cells have Formula, FormulaR1C1, and Value properties. The Value property and the Formula property behave the same when you're writing to the cell. When you read the value of a cell, the Value property gives you the value, and the Formula property gives you the formula using A1 reference style. The FormulaR1C1 property is the same as the Formula property, except that it uses R1C1 reference style for all references, whether assigning a formula to the cell or reading the formula from a cell.

> **Tip** The Value property always gives you the unformatted value of the number in a cell. A cell also has a Text property, which returns the formatted value of the cell. The Text property is read-only because it's a combination of the Value property and the NumberFormat property. A range also has a Value2 property. The difference between Value and Value2 has to do with dealing with very large, very precise numbers—as in banking. The Value property uses a data type (double-precision floating point) that can handle either very large numbers or very precise numbers, but not at the same time. The Value2 property uses a data type (currency) that can handle the large-scale precision needed in financial summaries.

Construct Formulas to Fill a Grid

Sometimes you need a macro to create formulas that contain references. For example, suppose want to create a macro that will enter the appropriate formulas into the Revenue grid. You could just record a macro, but a recorded macro will use specific cell addresses. Suppose that the grid could be anywhere on the worksheet—not just starting in cell A1—and that it could be of any size. Your recorded macro can't handle that kind of variation.

If you can make a few simple assumptions, you can create a macro that will find a grid, select the current region to find the size of the grid, and then add the correct formula. You can even have the macro automatically find the location of the Discount cell and assign a name to it so that the formula can reference the cell by name. The assumptions you need to make are very useful for most simple macros:

- Always use the consistent words as labels so you can have the macro search for them.
- Always keep the same number of header columns and rows.
- Separate ranges are separated by at least one empty row or one empty column so that the CurrentRegion method can detect the rectangle.

On the Revenue worksheet, the searchable labels are Price and Discount, the grid has two header rows and one header column, and the ranges are separated by column F. With those simple assumptions, you can create a macro that will automatically create the right formula and put it into the correct range.

1. Make a copy of the Revenue worksheet in the *Chapter04* workbook, with cell **A1** selected.

    Copying the worksheet will give you a chance to test the macro, moving and resizing the revenue grid.

2. In the Visual Basic editor, enter the following macro shell, and press F8 twice to step to the End Sub statement.

```
Sub FillFormulas()
    Dim myOuter as Range
    Dim myInner as Range
    Dim myFormula as String

End Sub()
```

Declaring variables at the top will make it easier to work with different ranges. The myOuter range will refer to the entire current region of the Revenue grid, including the headings. The myInner range will refer to the empy cells in the middle that need formulas. The myFormula string will contain the formula so that you can construct the formula piece by piece in the macro.

3. In the **Object Browser**, select **Range** in the **Classes** list. Then, in the list of members, select the **Find** method.

The description indicates that this property has one required argument—the string you're searching for—and that it returns a reference to a range.

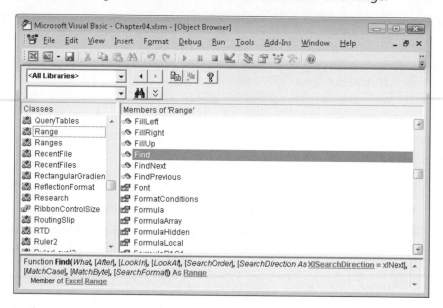

4. In the **Immediate** Window, type **Set myOuter = Cells.Find("Price").CurrentRegion** and then press Enter. When you can confirm the correct range by entering **myOuter.Select**, copy the statement into the macro.

See Also The Intersect and Offset functions are described in the section titled "Refer to a Relative Range" earlier in this chapter.

For the myInner range, you need to remove two header rows at the top and the one header column at the left. You can do that by using the combination of Intersect and Offset.

5. In the **Immediate** window, type
Set myInner = Intersect(myOuter,myOuter.Offset(2,1)) and press Enter. When you can confirm the correct range by entering myOuter.Select, copy the statement into the macro.

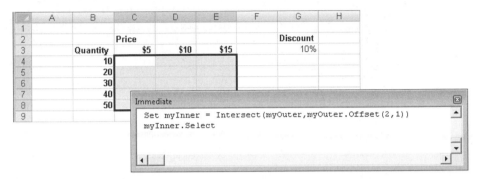

For the Discount range, you can use the label in the top cell to define the name for the lower cell. This creates a name in the worksheet, rather than a variable in Visual Basic. You assign the name by using the CreateNames method. The CreateNames method has four arguments, Top, Bottom, Left, and Right, respectively. These identify which side of the range contains the labels you should use as names. The Discount label is above the discount value, so Top is the only one you need to designate as True. Since Top is the first argument, you can simply omit the others.

6. In the **Immediate** window, type
Cells.Find("Discount").CurrentRegion.CreateNames True and press Enter. When you can confirm the correct range by entering Range("Discount").Select, copy the statement into the macro.

	A	B	C	D	E	F	G	H
1								
2			Price				Discount	
3			Quantity	$5	$10	$15		10%
4			10					
5			20					
6			30					
7			40					
8			50					
9								

```
Immediate
Cells.Find("Discount").CurrentRegion.CreateNames True
Range("Discount").Select
```

For the first part of the formula, you need a reference to the first Price cell, which is currently cell C3. If you think of myOuter as if it were a worksheet, you want cell "B2" of that imaginary worksheet, and you want the address in R1C1 notation, with an absolute row number and a relative column number, from the point of view of the first formula cell. The Address method gives you the address of a cell, with arguments to control what it looks like. Visual Basic prompts you for each of the arguments.

7. In the **Immediate** window, type

   myFormula = myOuter.Range("B2").Address(True,False,xlR1C1,False,myInner)

   and press Enter. Move the mouse pointer over the word *myFormula* to confirm that the address is R3C, and then copy the statement into the macro.

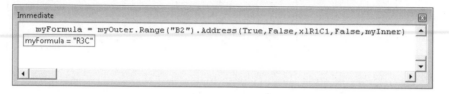

> **Tip** When you use the Range method, Visual Basic shows you tips for the methods and properties that follow. When you use the Cells method, Visual Basic does not show tips. Even though Range("B2") and Cells(2,2) are functionally equivalent, using the Range method makes the statement easier to type. If you find the Cells method easier to understand, you can make the change after you have successfully created the statement.

8. In the **Immediate** window, type myFormula = "=" & myFormula & "*". Move the mouse pointer over the word *myFormula* to confirm that the value is =R3C*, and then copy the statement into the macro.

9. Enter the following three statements into the macro, optionally testing each one first in the **Immediate** window.

   ```
   myFormula = myFormula & _
      myOuter.Range("A3").Address(False, True, xlR1C1, False, myInner)
   myFormula = myFormula & " * ( 1 - Discount ) "
   myInner.FormulaR1C1 = myFormula
   ```

   There is nothing fundamentally new in these statements. The first one appends the quantity address, with relative column and absolute row. The second one adds the Discount portion of the formula. The Discount portion doesn't need to be converted to an address because it's already a name in the worksheet. The third statement assigns the finished formula to the inner range.

10. Create a new copy of the Revenue worksheet, and test the macro. Then make another copy, change the size and location of the revenue grid, and test the macro again.

Quantity	$5	$10	$15	$20	$25
10	45	90	135	180	225
20	90	180	270	360	450
30	135	270	405	540	675
40	180	360	540	720	900
50	225	450	675	900	1125
60	270	540	810	1080	1350
70	315	630	945	1260	1575
80	360	720	1080	1440	1800
90	405	810	1215	1620	2025
100	450	900	1350	1800	2250

(Discount 10%, Price)

Filling ranges of variable sizes with formulas is a powerful technique. You can use the methods and properties of the Range object to create the formula and to find the correct range to fill.

Formatting a Range

Formatting contributes much to the usability of a worksheet. Borders and background colors can emphasize parts of a report, and conditional formatting can highlight exceptions within a range. Cell formatting can be combined into cell styles to make the same formatting combinations easy to reuse.

Add Borders to a Range

Borders help to demarcate regions with a block of cells. Sometimes you want to put borders around every cell within a range. Sometimes you want to put a single border around an entire range of cells. Sometimes you want a different border along one side of a range. A Range object has methods and properties to allow you to completely control whatever type of border you need.

1. In Excel, make a copy of the **RevenueFormulas** worksheet. In the Visual Basic editor, copy the **TestRange** macro, give the new one the name AddBorders, and press F8 twice to initialize the myRange variable.

> **Troubleshooting** If you don't have a TestRange macro, see the first two steps of the "Refer to a Relative Range" section earlier in this chapter.

2. In the **Immediate** window, type Set myRange = Range("B2").CurrentRegion and press Enter to assign the range containing the revenue calculations to the variable.

3. In the **Immediate** window, type **myRange.Borders.LineStyle =**.

   As you type each period in the statement, an Auto List displays the available members. After you type the equal sign, no Auto List appears, but you can use the Object Browser to find the available options.

Search

4. In the **Object Browser**, in the **Search Text** box above the **Classes** list, type **LineStyle**, and click the **Search** button.

5. In the **Search Results** pane that appears, select **XlLineStyle** in the **Class** list.

   The Member list shows all the possible constants you can use for the LineStyle property.

XlLineStyle is not really a class, even though it shows up in the list of classes in the Object Browser. There is no such thing as an XlLineStyle object. It is, rather, an *enumerated list*. An enumerated list is used when a property or argument can accept only certain values. An enumerated list allows the object model designer to give each of those values a special name—for example, *xlContinuous*. Enumerated lists are included in the list of Classes, but with a special icon.

6. In the **Immediate** window, type **xlContinuous** to finish the statement, and then press Enter.

   This adds a continuous border around each cell in the range. When you assign a value to the LineStyle property of the Borders object, the property changes for the border of each cell in the entire range.

7. In the **Immediate** window, type **myRange.Borders.LineStyle = xlNone** and press Enter to remove the borders.

The value xlNone does not appear in the enumeration list for LineStyle because it is a global constant that is used by many Excel objects. You can search for it in the Object Browser if you want to see the complete list of global contants.

The Borders object is actually a collection, and you can select specific borders within that collection. In principle, you could change cell borders one at a time, but because putting a border around an entire range is a common operation, there is a special method just for doing that.

8. In the **Immediate** window, type **myRange.BorderAround Weight:=xlThick** and press Enter.

This changes the edges of the range to a thick border. Because Weight is not the first argument, you have to type its name if you leave out LineStyle. Setting the border weight to Thick implies that the line will be continuous.

Suppose that you want a border on the right side of the quantities. To specify a single border, you can use an enumerated name in conjunction with the Borders collection. Auto Lists can help you with the syntax, but you have to be a little tricky.

9. In the **Immediate** Window, type
   myRange.Borders(xlEdgeRight).LineStyle = xlContinuous, but do *not* press
   Enter. Immediately after **myRange**, type a period (.), type **Columns(1)**, and
   then press Enter.

   Once you use the Columns property in a statement, you don't see any more Auto
   Lists, but if you temporarily leave out the Columns property, you get Auto Lists for
   everything else except the line style. Then, after you get the syntax correct for the
   statement, you can go back and add the Columns property.

	A	B	C	D	E	F	G	H
1								
2		Price					Discount	
3		Quantity	$5	$10	$15		10%	
4		10	45	90	135			
5		20	90	180	270			
6		30	135	270	405			
7		40	180	360	540			
8								
9								

```
Immediate                                                                    ☒
    myRange.Columns(1).Borders(xlEdgeRight).LineStyle = xlContinuous    ▲
                                                                        ▼
```

10. In the **Immediate** window, type
    myRange.Rows(2).Borders(xlEdgeBottom).LineStyle = xlContinuous and press
    Enter. This adds a border under the row of prices.

11. Press F5 to end the macro. Copy the statements from the Immediate window into
    the AddBorders macro, and delete the two statements that fill and remove all the
    borders.

    The finished macro should look like this:

```
Sub SetBorders()
    Dim myRange As Range
    Set myRange = Range("B2").CurrentRegion
    myRange.BorderAround Weight:=xlThick
    myRange.Columns(1).Borders(xlEdgeRight).LineStyle = xlContinuous
    myRange.Rows(2).Borders(xlEdgeBottom).LineStyle = xlContinuous
End Sub
```

12. Create a new copy of RevenueFormulas and test the finished macro.

Borders can emphasize parts of a report. The Borders collection allows you to change all
the borders at one time or choose a particular type of border to modify. The BorderAround
method is a convenient shortcut for assigning a border to all the edges of a multicell range.

Format the Interior of a Range

To enhance the readability of a worksheet, you might want to apply different background colors to various parts. For example, you might apply one format to all the cells that contain values that a user can input, and a different format to all cells that contain formulas.

1. In Excel, create another copy of the **RevenueFormulas** worksheet. In Visual Basic, copy the **TestRange** macro, name the new one **AddColors**, and press F8 twice to initialize the myRange variable.

> **Troubleshooting** If you don't have a TestRange macro, see the first two steps of the "Refer to a Relative Range" section earlier in this chapter.

2. In the **Immediate** window, type **Set myRange = Range("B2").CurrentRegion** and press Enter to assign the range containing the revenue calculations to the variable.

3. In the **Immediate** window, type **myRange.Interior.Color =**.

   As you type each period in the statement, an Auto List displays the available members. After you type the equal sign, however, no Auto List appears. For the Color property, there is no enumerated list. You can enter any number between 0 (which equals black) and 16777215 (which equals white), so there are literally more than 16 million possible values. This is a major change from previous versions of Excel, where colors in a worksheet were limited to a palette of only 56 colors.

   Colors on a computer correspond to the red, green, and blue guns of a cathode ray tube. (Liquid crystal displays use a different technology, but the same component colors.) Visual Basic has an RGB function you can use to specify precise red, green, and blue components, but Excel provides an easier way to specify the color you want: it includes an enumerated list that gives meaningful names to about 140 of the most common colors.

   See Also Excel 2007 also uses theme colors to help you use predefined sets of compatible colors. Theme colors are described in more detail in the section titled "Add a Gradient Fill to a Cell" in Chapter 6, "Explore Graphical Objects."

4. In the **Immediate** window, type **rgbMediumVioletRed** to complete the statement, and press Enter. (Once you get past rgbM, press Ctrl+Space to get to the middle of the rgb color values.)

   The background color of the entire range changes to a medium violet red.

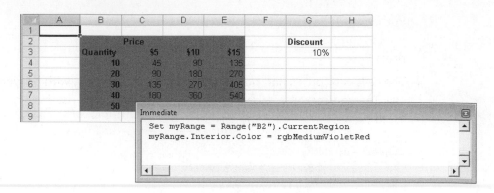

Now that Excel can handle millions of colors, it has a new capability to change how light (the tint) or dark (the shade) a color is without changing the actual color (the hue).

5. In the **Immediate** window, type **myRange.Interior.TintAndShade = -0.2** and press Enter. The color changes to a slightly darker shade of violet red.

A range object has a special method called *SpecialCells* that isolates cells within the range based on various attributes. For example, you can reference all the formula cells within the range.

6. In the **Immediate** window, type **myRange.SpecialCells(xlCellTypeFormulas).Interior.TintAndShade = 0.3** and press Enter.

The block of formulas changes to a lighter tint of violet red. In this range, the formulas form a contiguous block, but SpecialCells can return a range of discontiguous cells as well.

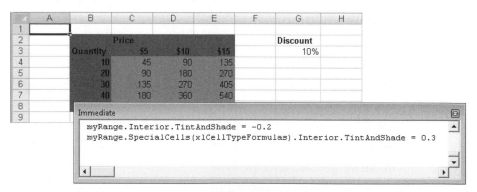

In Excel, you can give a name to a set of formatting characteristics. This is called a *cell style*. There are several built-in styles in a workbook. One of them is named *Input*, so that you can use it to format cells that can accept user input—typically cells that contain constants that are numbers.

7. In the **Immediate** window, type
myRange.SpecialCells(xlCellTypeConstants, xlNumbers).Style = "Input" and
press Enter.

The cells with prices and quantities change to a light tan, with borders around each
cell. The constant xlNumbers doesn't appear in an Auto List, but you can find the
list in the Object Browser by searching for SpecialCells.

You can modify the style format in the same way that you can modify a range
format directly.

8. Enter the following two statements in the **Immediate** window:

```
ActiveWorkbook.Styles("Input").Interior.Color = rgbMediumVioletRed
ActiveWorkbook.Styles("Input").Interior.TintAndShade = 0.5
```

This changes the Input style so that it has a lighter version of the same violet red
shade as the rest of the cells. When applying a style to cells that can take input
values, you may want to search the entire worksheet for the numeric constants.
To do that, you just start with the global Cells property.

9. In the **Immediate** window, type
Cells.SpecialCells(xlCellTypeConstants, xlNumbers).Style = "Input" and press Enter.

This adds the Input style to the Discount cell value. If you had hundreds of input cells
scattered all over the worksheet, this statement would still find them all. The text
labels in the Revenue range are hard to read, with the black text on a dark background. You can use SpecialCells to isolate all the cells that contain text constants.

10. In the **Immediate** window, type
myRange.SpecialCells(xlCellTypeConstants, xlTextValues).Font.Color = rgbWhite
and press Enter.

This changes the font color for the labels to white, but they would look better bold
as well. In fact, all the constants within the formula range would look better if they
were bold.

11. In the **Immediate** window, type
myRange.SpecialCells(xlCellTypeConstants).Font.Bold = True and press Enter.

This changes all the constants within the range store in myRange to bold. By leaving out the second argument to SpecialCells, you get everything that matches the general type. You can also use a special style to clear all the formatting.

	A	B	C	D	E	F	G	H
1								
2			Price				Discount	
3		Quantity	$5	$10	$15		10%	
4		10	45	90	135			
5		20	90	180	270			
6		30	135	270	405			
7		40	180	360	540			
8		50	225	450	675			
9								

12. In the **Immediate** window, type Cells.Style = "Normal" and press Enter.

This clears all the formatting, including the number and formats. When you clear formats from a worksheet, what it really does is apply the Normal style to all the cells. By changing the Normal style, you change the default appearance of cells in the workbook.

	A	B	C	D	E	F	G	H
1								
2			Price				Discount	
3		Quantity	5	10	15		0.1	
4		10	45	90	135			
5		20	90	180	270			
6		30	135	270	405			
7		40	180	360	540			
8		50	225	450	675			
9								

```
Immediate
    Cells.Style = "Normal"
```

13. Press F5 to end the macro. Copy the statements from the **Immediate** window into the **AddColors** macro, and delete the statement that clears all the formatting.

The finished macro, ignoring optional line breaks, should look like this:

```
Sub SetColors()
    Dim myRange As Range
    Set myRange = Range("B2").CurrentRegion

    myRange.Interior.Color = rgbMediumVioletRed
    myRange.Interior.TintAndShade = -0.2
    myRange.SpecialCells(xlCellTypeFormulas). _
        Interior.TintAndShade = 0.3
```

```
    myRange.SpecialCells(xlCellTypeConstants, xlNumbers). _
        Style = "Input"
    ActiveWorkbook.Styles("Input").Interior _
        .Color = rgbMediumVioletRed
    ActiveWorkbook.Styles("Input").Interior _
        .TintAndShade = 0.5
    Cells.SpecialCells(xlCellTypeConstants, xlNumbers) _
        .Style = "Input"

    myRange.SpecialCells(xlCellTypeConstants, xlTextValues) _
        .Font.Color = rgbWhite
    myRange.SpecialCells(xlCellTypeConstants).Font.Bold = True
End Sub
```

14. Create a new copy of **RevenueFormulas** and test the finished macro.

Ranges are powerful objects. They are the essence of Excel. With ranges you can organize information, create formulas, and apply formatting. And you can do all of that with under the control of VBA macros.

> **CLOSE** the *Chapter04.xlsm* workbook.

Key Points

- Use the Object Browser to find out what members—methods and properties—are available for an object, and what each method or property returns.

- Avoid changing the selection during your macros. A macro runs faster and appears more professional if it doesn't have to repaint the screen.

- While debugging, use the Immediate window to test the current reference of a range object.

- Many range-related functions start with one range and return another range. These functions are invaluable for navigating from one range to another. The most important one is CurrentRegion.

- Always use R1C1 references when constructing formulas from macros, and take advantage of the many options—relative, absolute, internal, external—that the Address property gives you.

- Use the Borders collection to simultaneously control the borders of each cell within a range. Use the BorderAround method to treat the range as a single unit.

- Use either the RGB function or the enumerated list of RGB constants to select a color. To create smooth gradations of the shades and tints of a color, take advantage of the TintAndShade property.

Chapter at a Glance

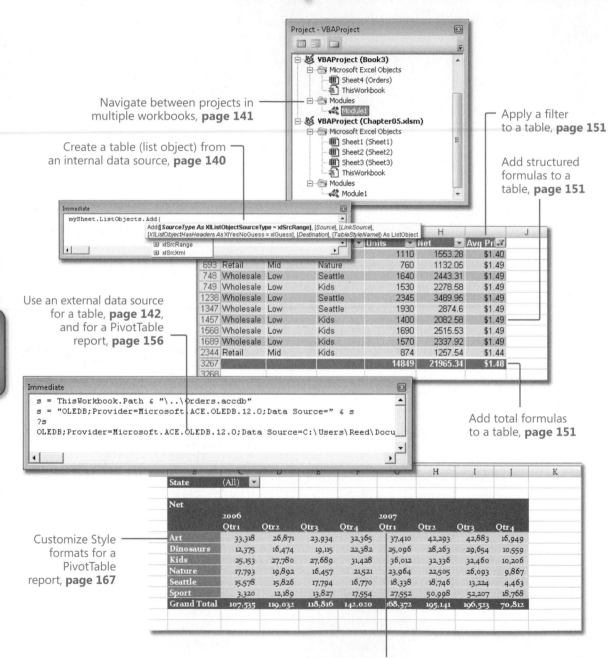

Navigate between projects in
multiple workbooks, **page 141**

Create a table (list object) from
an internal data source, **page 140**

Apply a filter
to a table, **page 151**

Add structured
formulas to a
table, **page 151**

Use an external data source
for a table, **page 142**,
and for a PivotTable
report, **page 156**

Add total formulas
to a table, **page 151**

Customize Style
formats for a
PivotTable
report, **page 167**

Create date groupings in a
PivotTable report, **page 162**

5 Explore Data Objects

In this chapter, you will learn to:

✔ Retrieve data from Excel lists and from external data sources.

✔ Create and format a table object.

✔ Create and format a PivotTable object.

✔ Use the macro recorder to learn about Excel objects.

On May 29, 1913, at the staid Théatre des Champs-Elysées in Paris, a scene of utter chaos occurred. It was the premiere performance of Igor Stravinsky's ballet "The Rite of Spring." The Stravinsky music and Nijinsky choreography was so outrageously original that the audience couldn't comprehend it. Today, "The Rite of Spring" is performed without any commotion, but Igor Stravinsky is still considered to be one of the most inventive composers ever. Stravinsky, however, acknowledged that he was influenced of others. He once said, "Lesser artists borrow, great artists steal." The term *steal* is of course used for dramatic effect, but the point is that when you *borrow*, the item still belongs to the original owner, but when you *steal*, you make it your own.

Some people think of the macro recorder as a tool for beginners—and it is. You can use the macro recorder to build usable macros without having to understand much about how Microsoft Office Excel 2007 objects really work. But the macro recorder is also a powerful reference tool for advanced developers. The secret is in whether you *borrow* from the recorder (leaving it essentially intact) or whether you *steal* (making the code your own).

In this chapter, you'll see how you can use the macro recorder as a reference tool for learning how to work with Excel objects. You'll record actions, but when it's time to write the macros, you won't modify the recorded macros. Instead, you'll create your own macros, taking full advantage of object variables and methods and properties that the recorder doesn't use. In essence, you'll learn how to steal.

> **Important** Before you complete this chapter, you need to install the practice files from the book's companion CD to their default locations. See "Using the Book's CD" on page xv for more information.

> **USE** the *Orders.xlsx* workbook for an internal source, and the *Orders.accdb* database as an external source. These practice files are located in the *Documents\MSP\ExcelVBA07SBS* folder.
>
> **BE SURE TO** save a new empty workbook as a macro-enabled workbook named *Chapter05.xlsm* in the trusted location you created in Chapter 1.
>
> **OPEN** the *Chapter05.xlsm* workbook. Then select the range A1:F5, and apply a red background to the cells. As you create and close multiple workbooks in this chapter, the red cells will remind you which workbook contains the macros so that you don't accidentally close it without saving changes and lose your work.

Working with Excel Tables

An Excel table is basically a list. But it's a powerful list that lets you sort, filter, total, and calculate. Data for an Excel table comes from basically two sources: either you get it from an existing worksheet, or you use some kind of connection to get it from an outside source. You can think of these as *internal* and *external* data sources.

In this section, you will create macros to import data into an Excel table from an Excel worksheet and from an Access database. This will allow you to see the difference between an internal and an external source. Then you'll learn how to use macros to perform basic manipulations on a table.

Create a New File from an Existing Worksheet

The purpose of this first macro is to create a copy of the Orders worksheet from the *Orders.xlsx* file into a new, unsaved file. Excel will not allow you to move the only visible worksheet in a file directly into a new file. You can get around the restriction by first moving the worksheet into the *Chapter05* workbook, and then moving it from there into a new file. First you'll use the macro recorder to create the macro and learn the appropriate methods and properties. Then you'll use clues from the recorded macro to create your own macro, getting additional guidance whenever possible from the Auto Lists feature as you enter each statement. You will add the letter *z* as a prefix for each macro you record, so you can keep the recorded macros separate from the ones you create.

1. Start recording a macro with the name **zOpenOrdersFile**.

Microsoft Office
Button

2. Click the **Microsoft Office Button**, and click **Open**. Navigate to the folder that contains the practice files for this book, select **Orders.xlsx**, and click **Open**.

3. Right-click the **Orders** tab, click **Move Or Copy**, select *Chaper05.xlsm* in the **To book** list, and then click **OK**.

Move or Copy	?	✕
Move selected sheets		
To book:		
Chapter05.xlsm ▾		
Before sheet:		
Sheet1		
Sheet2		
Sheet3		
(move to end)		
☐ Create a copy		
OK		Cancel

4. In the *Chapter05* workbook, right-click the **Orders** tab, click **Move Or Copy**, select **(new book)** in the **To book** list, and click **OK**. Then stop the recorder.

Macros
▾

5. On the **View** tab of the Ribbon, click the **Macros** button, select the **Chapter05.xlsm!zOpenOrderFile** macro, and click **Edit** to review the macro.

> **Important** The exercises in this chapter use shaded code blocks to identify lines from recorded macros. This is so that you can look at the recorded lines as you create the replacement macro without confusing the two. The complete recorded macros—along with the rewritten versions—are included in the *Chapter05.xlsm* file in the *Finished* folder on the companion CD.

```
ChDir "C:\MSP\ExcelVBA07SBS"
Workbooks.Open Filename:= " C:\MSP\ExcelVBA07SBS\Orders.xlsx"
```

The ChDir statement will be in the macro only if you actually had to change folders, but it is redundant anyway, because the Filename argument includes the full path. The problem with including a full path is that if you move the project to a new location, the path will be wrong. A workbook has a Path property that will give you the current full path for that workbook. By prefixing the Path property to the file name, your macro will work even if you move everything to a new location.

Because there are times when the active workbook is not the one that contains the macros, there is a special ThisWorkbook property that returns the macro workbook. Thus, the expression ThisWorkbook.Path returns the full path of the folder that contains the macro workbook, regardless of what the current directory is, or what workbook is currently active. Because the data file is one folder up from the macro workbook, you need to insert a backslash two dots and another backslash (\..\) in front of the file name.

6. In the **Immediate** window, type **Workbooks.Open ThisWorkbook.Path & "\..\ Orders.xlsx"** and press Enter.

This opens the *Orders* workbook, and it will work provided that the macro file is in a subfolder of the data folder—without regard to the current folder or the current location in the file structure.

```
Sheets("Orders").Move Before:=Workbooks("Chapter05.xlsm").Sheets(1)
```

7. In the **Immediate** window, type **ActiveSheet.Move ThisWorkbook.Sheets(1)** and press Enter.

This moves the active sheet to the macro's workbook. It doesn't matter whether it goes before or after the first sheet, because you will move it again anyway.

```
Sheets("Orders").Move
```

8. In the **Immediate** window, type **ActiveSheet.Move** and press Enter to move the Orders sheet to its own workbook.

9. In a Visual Basic module, create a new macro with the name **OpenOrdersFile**. Insert the three statements from the **Immediate** window into the macro. Test the macro by pressing F5 or F8.

This macro gives you a simple data file to use as an internal source, without the risk of damaging your original *Orders.xlsx* workbook. The file is not saved, so you can freely discard it, which is particularly useful while you are creating and testing a macro. You used the macro recorder to learn important syntax clues, but then you made the macro your own.

Create a Table from an Internal Source

Now that you have a worksheet that contains a list of data, you can convert the list into a table. This process is very simple, but you can still generalize and simplify the recorded macro, and you will be able to compare this process to creating a table from an external source. When you record the macro, it will be stored in the new workbook, so if you want to keep it, be sure to copy it into the *Chapter05* workbook module before closing the file.

1. Start with a workbook that contains the Orders sheet. Run the **OpenOrdersFile** macro if necessary.

2. Start recording a macro named zTableFromInternal.

3. On the **Insert** tab of the Ribbon, click **Table**. In the **Create Table** dialog box, leave the default options, and click **OK**.

   This converts the list to an Excel table, as you can tell by the arrows next to each of the column headings.

	A	B	C	D	E	F	G	H
1	Date	State	Channel	Price	Category	Units	Net	
2	January-05	Oregon	Wholesale	High	Art	670	$1,681.65	
3	January-05	Washington	Wholesale	High	Seattle	65	$178.75	
4	January-05	Washington	Wholesale	High	Art	50	$137.50	
5	January-05	Washington	Retail	High	Art	10	$55.00	

4. Stop the recorder, and edit the macro so that you can use it as a reference as you create your own macro.

   The macro you recorded is stored in the new workbook that contains the Orders sheet. When you close that temporary workbook, the recorded macro will be lost. Because this is a temporary macro, losing it does not matter. But when you create your permanent macro, you want to be sure to store it in the permanent *Chapter05* workbook. Visual Basic has a tool to help you navigate macros that are stored in multiple workbooks.

5. On the **Visual Basic View** menu, click **Project Explorer**.

   The Project Explorer shows that the active module is stored in a temporary workbook, but you can also see the Module1 macro sheet in the *Chapter05* workbook.

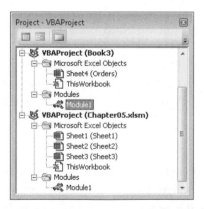

6. In the **Project Explorer**, double-click **Module1** in the *Chapter05* workbook. Then, in the **Immediate** window, type OpenOrdersFile and press Enter to create a new source list file.

7. Create a new macro shell that looks like the following, and press F8 twice to initialize the variable, so that you can get Auto List help with properties of the ActiveSheet.

```
Sub TableFromInternal()
    Dim mySheet As Worksheet
    Set mySheet = ActiveSheet

End Sub
```

Now using the recorded macro as a guide, you can begin to write the new macro.

```
ActiveSheet.ListObjects.Add(xlSrcRange, _
    Range("$A$1:$G$3266"), , xlYes).Name = "Table1"
```

8. In the **Immediate** window, type **mySheet.ListObjects.Add(** and look at the argument list.

All the arguments are optional. The default value for the first argument is xlSourceRange, which is what the recorder inserted. In fact, the default values for all the arguments are suitable.

9. Delete the opening parenthesis. Rename **mySheet** to **ActiveSheet**.

The statement ActiveSheet.ListObjects.Add is all you need in the macro.

10. Press F5 to stop the macro. Then delete the current body of the macro, and copy in the **Add** statement from the **Immediate** window.

11. Run the **OpenOrdersFile** macro, and then test the **TableFromInternal** macro by pressing F5 or F8.

More than anything, this macro shows you how easy it is to create a table from an Excel list. The hardest part was getting the list into a separate file (the OpenOrdersFile macro). Later, you will create macros to manipulate the basic list, but first create a version of the same table by using an external data connection.

Create a Table from an External Source

Excel data lists are very convenient sources for a table, but they are limited to a million rows and cannot retrieve data from a shared database. In this section, you will use Microsoft Office Access as an external data connection, but the same techniques will work with very minor changes for a Microsoft SQL Server database or other supported data source.

1. Start recording a macro with the name zTableFromExternal.

2. Press Ctrl+N to create a new workbook. On the **Data** tab of the Ribbon, click the **From Access** button. Navigate to the folder containing the files for this book, select **Orders.accdb**, and click **Open**. In the **Import Data** dialog box, leave the default options, and click **OK**. Then stop the recorder.

3. Edit the **zTableFromExternal** macro.

This macro looks very convoluted, but most of the complexity is in the connection string, which you can simplify greatly. The other part that makes the macro look imposing is the With structure that surrounds everything. Here's what's happening: The Add method returns an instance of the ListObject that it created. That is not difficult—the Add method for most collections returns the new instance that it creates. Then the recorder uses that reference to access the ListObject's QueryTable property. (The QueryTable object contains the external data link for the ListObject.) But because the QueryTable object has several properties and a method, the recorder puts the QueryTable into a With structure, and the With statement includes the entire Add method. That's a lot to do in a single structure. If you add variables for the ListObject and the QueryTable object, you can separate the parts into separate, more manageable chunks.

4. Clear the contents of the **Immediate** window, create the shell of a macro that looks like the following, and press F8 twice to step to the **End Sub** statement, initializing the variables.

```
Sub TableFromExternal()
    Dim l As ListObject
    Dim q as QueryTable
    Dim s as String

End Sub
```

> **Tip** It is generally a good idea to give descriptive names to variables, but sometimes while developing a macro, short names are convenient. You can use short names while you create the macro and then convert them to descriptive names by using the Replace command from the Edit menu. Be sure to select the Current Procedure, Find Whole Word Only, and Match Case options when doing the replace.

```
Workbooks.Add
```

5. In the **Immediate** window, type **Workbooks.Add** and press Enter.

A new, blank worksheet appears in Excel.

```
With ActiveSheet.ListObjects.Add( _
    SourceType:=0, _
    Source:=Array( _
        "OLEDB;Provider=Microsoft.ACE.OLEDB.12.0;", _
        "Data Source=C:\MSP\ExcelVBA07SBS\Orders.accdb;", _
```

The Source value for the Add method appears very complicated. For an external data source, this string can be quite long, so the Add method allows it to be broken into substrings by using the Array function. The Add method then just concatenates all the pieces from the Array function. The recorder arbitrarily chops the string every 128 characters. Most of the Source string consists of default values—the only parts that are required are data source type, the Provider, and the Data Source. If the whole string is fewer than 128 characters, you don't need an Array function at all.

6. Type (on one line) s = ThisWorkbook.Path & "\..\Orders.accdb" and press Enter. Then put the mouse pointer over the s variable to confirm that the full path name for the database file is correct. For example, if the practice files were in the *C:\Practice Files* folder, the string would be *C:\Practice Files\New\..\Orders.accdb*.

7. Type (on one line) s = "OLEDB;Provider=Microsoft.ACE.OLEDB.12.0;Data Source=" & s and press Enter. This string is too long to show up in a tool tip, so type ?s and press Enter to see the string in the **Immediate** window. Then delete the two rows used to make the confirmation.

8. Type (on one line) Set l = ActiveSheet.ListObjects.Add(xlSrcExternal, s, , xlYes, ActiveCell) and press Enter.

These few lines replace the very long statement from the recorded macro. The next thing the macro does in this long statement is to assign the connection to the list object.

```
    Destination:=Range("$A$1")).QueryTable
    .CommandType = xlCmdTable
    .CommandText = Array("Orders")
    …
    .Refresh BackgroundQuery:=False
End With
```

Most of the property setting for the QueryTable object are optional as well—the only critical properties are the CommandType and CommandText. Even the argument to the Refresh method is the default.

9. Type the following four statements in the **Immediate** window, pressing Enter after each.

```
Set q = l.QueryTable
q.CommandType = xlCmdTable
q.CommandText = "Orders"
q.Refresh
```

Assigning the QueryTable object to a variable takes the place of the With structure in the recorded macro. After you execute the Refresh method, the worksheet fills with data.

10. Press F5 to stop the running macro, and copy the statements from the **Immediate** window into the **TableFromExternal** macro. Then test the **TableFromExternal** macro by pressing F5 or F8.

Surprisingly, this new, short macro has all the essential functionality of the one the recorder created. When dealing with external data sources, the recorder creates macros with huge strings and lots of properties. When you are creating a sophisticated application working with a large, complex, remote, highly-secured corporate database, those options become very valuable. But when you are creating simple macros to access a department database, you can eliminate most of the complexity.

You may notice that when you originally created the table, the Date column was formatted as dates. However, when you run the macro—either the modified version or the original—the dates are not formatted. It appears that Excel does an extra step that isn't included in the macro. Later, you'll learn how to refer to parts of the table so that you can easily add formatting to the Date column.

Record a Macro to Manipulate a Table

A table sits on a worksheet, so it has many properties in common with a range, but it also has special behaviors of its own. For example, the way you refer to regions within the table is unique to a table. And the way you create formulas that refer to other cells within the table is unique. Tables also allow you to add structured totals, and you can filter the table based on the values in the columns. Recording a macro can help you learn about how to manipulate a table, but if you apply your understanding of typical collections objects—and make a few trial-and-error guesses—you can significantly simplify and improve a macro that manipulates a table.

1. Run the **OpenOrdersFile** and the **TableFromInternal** macros to get a fresh simple table. Then start recording a macro named zTableManipulate.

   One thing you can do with a table is to insert a new column into the middle of it. For example, suppose that you want to insert a column named *Year* that contains just the year of the order date. Ideally, the new column should be adjacent to the Date column.

2. Right-click cell **B1**, point to **Insert**, and click **Table Columns To The Left**. In cell **B1**, replace **Column1** with Year.

3. In cell **B2**, type =Year(, click cell **A2**, type), and press Enter to fill the column with years.

	A	B	C	D	E	F	G	H	I
	B2	▾	f_x	=YEAR(Table1[[#This Row],[Date]])					
1	Date	Year	State	Channel	Price	Category	Units	Net	
2	January 2005	June 1905	Oregon	Wholesale	High	Art		670	1681.65
3	January 2005	June 1905	Washington	Wholesale	High	Seattle		65	178.75
4	January 2005	June 1905	Washington	Wholesale	High	Art		50	137.5
5	January 2005	June 1905	Washington	Retail	High	Art		10	55

4. Move the mouse over the top of the **Year** label until the pointer turns into a solid black downward arrow, and click to select the cells in the body of the column. Right click cell **B2** and click **Format Cells**. On the **Number** tab, select **Number** with no decimal places and no thousands separator, and click **OK**. Press Ctrl+A to select the entire table.

   This recorded statement will serve as a marker in the macro that you've finished a section.

5. In cell **I1**—just to the right of the column headings—type Avg Price and press Enter.

In the new Avg Price column, you need a formula that divides the Net column by the Units column. If you just point at the cells to create the formula, you get the formula =*Table_ExternalData_1[[#This Row],[Net]]/Table_ExternalData_1[[#This Row],[Units]]*. The only essential part of the formula is =*[Net]/[Units]*. As you type the short version of the formula into the cell, note that Excel helps you with the name of the columns. As with the Auto Lists in Visual Basic, you can select a column name and press Tab to insert the name into the formula.

6. In cell **I2**, type =**[Net]/[Units]** and press Enter.

7. Move the mouse pointer over the **Avg Price** label until the pointer turns into a solid black downward arrow, and then click to select the cells in the body of the column. Right-click any cell in the column, and click **Format Cells**. On the **Number Format** tab, select **Currency**, and click **OK**. Press Ctrl+A to select the entire table and insert a marker into the macro.

8. On the **Table Tools Design** tab of the Ribbon, click the **Total Row** check box.

9. Click the **Total** cell at the bottom of the **Units** column, click the arrow, and select **Sum**. Repeat for the **Net** column.

10. In the **Total** cell for the **Avg Price** column, type an equal sign, click the total cell for **Net**, type a division sign (/), click the total cell for **Units**, and then press Enter. Press Ctrl+A to select the current region.

This inserts a marker into the macro so that you can easily differentiate separate sections of the macro.

11. Click the **Avg Price** header cell arrow, point to **Number Filters**, and click **Top 10**. Select **Bottom** from the first list, and click **OK**.

This selects the 10 rows with the lowest average price.

	D	E	F	G	H	I	J
1	Channel	Price	Category	Units	Net	Avg Pri	
612	Retail	Mid	Nature	1110	1553.28	$1.40	
693	Retail	Mid	Nature	760	1132.05	$1.49	
748	Wholesale	Low	Seattle	1640	2443.31	$1.49	
749	Wholesale	Low	Kids	1530	2278.58	$1.49	
1238	Wholesale	Low	Seattle	2345	3489.95	$1.49	
1347	Wholesale	Low	Seattle	1930	2874.6	$1.49	
1457	Wholesale	Low	Kids	1400	2082.58	$1.49	
1568	Wholesale	Low	Kids	1690	2515.53	$1.49	
1689	Wholesale	Low	Kids	1570	2337.92	$1.49	
2344	Retail	Mid	Kids	874	1257.54	$1.44	
3267				14849	21965.34	$1.48	
3268							

12. Select the **Avg Price** header cell. Then on the **Home** tab of the Ribbon, click **Sort & Filter**, and then click **Clear**.

13. Stop the recorder, and edit the recorded macro.

Every time you see Range("Table1").Select followed by a statement to activate a cell, delete the two statements and replace them with a blank line. These breaks help you see the major sections of the recorded macro.

> **Tip** The complete recorded macro is available in the *Chapter05* macro workbook in the *Finished* folder.

Now you're ready to convert the recorded macro into a more elegant one. You can use clues from the recorded macro, but don't limit yourself to methods and properties that are actually found there.

Manipulate Table Columns

You are already familiar with the ListObject for a table. Assigning the table to a variable will simplify the statements and give you Auto List assistance. The recorded macro also frequently manipulates columns within the table. You can use a ListColumn object as well.

1. In the Visual Basic **Project Explorer**, double-click **Module1** in the *Chapter05* workbook if it's not already active. Then, run the **OpenOrdersFile** and **TableFromInternal** macros. Then, create the shell of a macro that looks like this, and press F8 three times to initialize the variables:

```
Sub TableManipulate()
    Dim l as ListObject
    Dim lc as ListColumn
    Set l = ActiveCell.ListObject
End Sub
```

You're now ready to start entering the statements for the body of the macro.

```
Selection.ListObject.ListColumns.Add Position:=2
```

2. In the **Immediate** window, type **Set lc = l.ListColumns.Add(2)** and press Enter.

The recorder uses the ListColumns collection to create a new column, but it doesn't store the new ListColumn object in a variable. By storing the created object in a variable, you can take advantage of Auto List help.

```
ActiveCell.FormulaR1C1 = "Year"
```

3. Type **lc.Name = "Year"** and press Enter.

The macro recorder simply puts the label into the active cell. By using a property of the ListColumn object, you don't have to worry about where the active cell happens to be when the macro runs.

```
ActiveCell.FormulaR1C1 = "=YEAR(Table1[[#This Row],[Date]])"
```

4. Type **lc.DataBodyRange="=Year([Date])"** and press Enter.

The recorder puts a complete structured reference into the formula. If the cell that contains the formula is inside the same table—and is on the same row—all you really need is the column identifier. Note that a table uses square brackets to identify named regions within the table. This is to avoid confusion with Excel named ranges.

```
Range("Table1[Year]").Select
Selection.NumberFormat = "0"
```

5. Type **lc.DataBodyRange.NumberFormat = "0"** and press Enter.

The recorder uses a string expression to reference the Year column, but if you create a table with a different name, the recorded macro will break. By using the Auto List to look at the methods and properties available for a ListColumn object, you can find DataBodyRange, which is a more robust way to access the same range.

> **Tip** In the earlier section titled "Create a Table from an External Source," you saw that the date formats are not imported from an external data source. To apply the number format for the Date column, you can use the statement l.ListColumns("Date")). DataBodyRange.NumberFormat = "mmm-yy".

```
ActiveCell.FormulaR1C1 = "Avg Price"
```

6. Type Set lc = l.ListColumns.Add and press Enter.

   This assigns a different ListColumn object to the same object variable, replacing the old one. The recorder created a new column by putting a label adjacent to the table. But in your macro, you don't want to be dependent on specific cell addresses. You've already seen that you can use the Add method of the ListColumns collection to insert a column. By using the Auto List help as you type the statement, you can see that the Position argument to the Add method is optional. Leaving it out adds a new column to the right side of the table. This approach is easy to read and can be used multiple times to add multiple columns.

7. Type lc.Name = "Avg Price" and press Enter.

   This adds the caption to the column. When you recorded the macro, you typed the label, which created a list column. When you build your own macro, you create the column and then add the caption to the object.

```
ActiveCell.FormulaR1C1 = "=[Net]/[Units]"
```

8. Type lc.DataBodyRange = "=[Net]/[Units]" and press Enter.

   By carefully crafting the formula in the user interface, you were able to get a simple formula in the recorded macro. If you had simply pointed at the referenced cells, the formula would include the table name and [#This Row] as qualifiers. Even if you recorded the macro with the complex names, you could simplify the formula when you create your own macro.

```
Range("Table1[Avg Price]").Select
Selection.NumberFormat = "$#,##0.00"
```

9. Type lc.DataBodyRange.NumberFormat = "$#,##0.00" and press Enter.

   When you use the object model, you don't have to go through the step of selecting the range.

A ListObject—that is, an Excel table—has an extensive object model, with great collections for the columns and the rows. Even though the macro recorder doesn't take advantage of those collections, if you understand how collections typically work, you can make effective guesses about how the collections in a ListObject work. As you type statements, the Auto List gives you excellent clues about what methods and properties are available.

Manipulate Table Totals and Filters

When you recorded the macro, you also recorded statements to modify the totals and filters of the Excel table. For the most part, converting these statements into your own consists of straightforward simplifications. Sometimes—as in the case of putting a formula into the Total row—you may need to do some trial-and-error experiments to find out what will work and what won't.

> **Important** Before executing each step in this procedure, you should have stepped through the declaration statements of the TableManipulate macro from the preceding procedure and you should refer to statements from the recorded macro in the earlier section titled "Record a Macro to Manipulate a Table."

```
ActiveSheet.ListObjects("Table1").ShowTotals = True
```

1. In the **Immediate** window, type l.ShowTotals = True and press Enter.

A Total row appears at the bottom of the table, but you can't see it yet. This statement simply converts the recorded statement to use the object reference variable.

```
Range("Table1[[#Totals],[Units]]").Select
```

2. Type l.TotalsRowRange.Select and press Enter.

This statement makes it possible to see the total row. You can omit it from the final macro if you want.

```
ActiveSheet.ListObjects("Table1").ListColumns("Units") _
    .TotalsCalculation = xlTotalsCalculationSum
Range("Table1[[#Totals],[Net]]").Select
ActiveSheet.ListObjects("Table1").ListColumns("Net") _
    .TotalsCalculation = xlTotalsCalculationSum
```

3. Type the following two statements, pressing Enter after each one.

```
l.ListColumns("Units").TotalsCalculation = xlTotalsCalculationSum
l.ListColumns("Net").TotalsCalculation = xlTotalsCalculationSum
```

These two statements are essentially identical to the recorded statements. They add Sum as the total to the respective columns. Note that they use the TotalsCalculation property. This property puts a formula into the total cell, but the formula must be one of the predefined formulas from the list.

```
Range("Table1[[#Totals],[Avg Price]]").Select
ActiveCell.FormulaR1C1 = _
    "=Table1[[#Totals],[Net]]/Table1[[#Totals],[Units]]"
```

4. Type l.ListColumns("Avg Price").Total.Formula = "=[[#Totals],[Net]]/ [[#Totals],[Units]]" and press Enter.

When you refer to cells in the body of the table, you can use just the column name. When you need to refer to cells in the total row, you must add the special keyword *[#Total]*. In the reference [[#Totals],[Net]], the [#Totals] part identifies the row and the [Net] part identifies the column. You separate them by a comma, and then you have to include the whole reference in another pair of brackets. The recorder added the table name as well. Because the reference is inside the table, you don't need the table name part. This structured reference is logical, if a little cumbersome. But it will work regardless of where the table may be on the worksheet, and it automatically adjusts when you add or remove rows from the table.

5. Type l.HeaderRowRange.Select and press Enter.

This statement just gets you to the top of the table without having to switch back to Excel. You can leave it out of the final macro if you want.

```
ActiveSheet.ListObjects("Table1").Range.AutoFilter _
    Field:=9, Criteria1:="10", Operator:=xlBottom10Items
```

6. Type l.Range.AutoFilter l.ListColumns("Avg Price").Index, 10, xlBottom10Items and press Enter.

The recorder refers to the column by number. You would prefer to use the column name, but the argument requires the number. Many items from a collection have an Index property that tells the position of the item within the collection. You can use the Index property to convert the name to the required number. The macro recorder included the argument names. You can include them or omit them as you wish.

```
ActiveSheet.ShowAllData
```

7. Type l.AutoFilter.ShowAllData and press Enter.

The recorder used a ShowAllData method from the active sheet. Because you used the AutoFilter property to create the filter, you can look to see if the AutoFilter has its own ShowAllData method. It does. By using the ShowAllData method from the

AutoFilter object rather than the sheet, you can have different filter states for different tables on the same worksheet.

8. Press F5 to stop the macro. Copy the statements from the **Immediate** window into the **TableManipulate** macro. Run the **OpenOrdersFile** and **TableFromInternal** macros, and then run the **TableManipulate** macro to test it.

Sometimes converting information from a recorded macro into your own macro requires some trial and error. For example, when looking at the total formula that the recorder generated for the Avg Price column, you might try converting it to =[Net]/[Units], because that simple version worked for the other rows. But it doesn't work. So you need to try adding back a little more of the recorded formula until it does work. Of course, you could just leave the formula the way the recorder created it, but then the macro would break if you ran it on a table that happened to have a different table name. If you do leave the table name in a reference in a macro, you should explicitly set the table name earlier in the macro.

Working with PivotTable Reports

An Excel table is like an X-ray photograph. It's an image, but it's a static image. If the rows and columns aren't properly defined, the person reviewing the report might miss important relationships. A PivotTable report, in contrast, is like a CAT scan. It's a multi-dimensional view of the data that enables you to find the most meaningful perspective. PivotTable reports are particularly useful for analytical reporting.

See Also The macros from this PivotTable report section were used when I created the Enterprise Information System (EIS) application described in the Appendix.

Create a PivotTable Report from an Internal Source

As with a table, you can make a PivotTable report retrieve its data from either an Excel list or from an external data source. Retrieving data from a list is relatively simple, but a PivotTable report manages the data somewhat differently than a table does.

1. Close other workbooks so that the *Chapter05* workbook is active. Then run the **OpenOrdersFile** macro to get a new orders list file.

> **Troubleshooting** If you don't have an OpenOrdersFile macro, see the section titled "Create a New File from an Existing Worksheet," earlier in this chapter.

2. Start recording a macro named zPivotFromInternal.

3. On the **Insert** tab of the Ribbon, click **PivotTable**, and click **OK** to accept the default options.

   By default, a new PivotTable report displays an empty placeholder on the work-sheet, and the PivotTable Field List appears on the right.

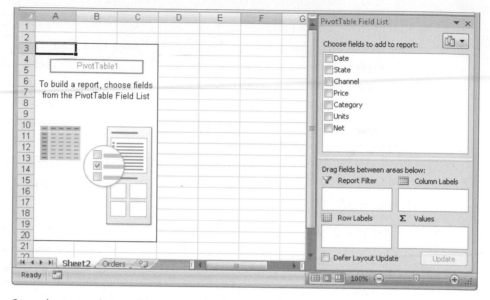

4. Stop the recorder, and look at the macro in Visual Basic.

5. In the **Project Explorer**, double-click **Module1** in the *Chapter05* workbook. Then, in the **Immediate** window, type **OpenOrdersFile** and press Enter.

   A new copy of the *Orders* file opens. You can run a macro from Visual Basic by simply stating the macro name.

6. Clear the contents of the **Immediate** window, create the shell of a macro that looks like the following, and press F8 twice to step to the **End Sub** statement.

```
Sub PivotFromInternal()
    Dim pc As PivotCache

End Sub
```

   You're now ready to start entering the statements for the body of the macro.

```
ActiveWorkbook.PivotCaches.Create(SourceType:=xlDatabase, _
    SourceData:= "Orders!R1C1:R3266C7", _
    Version:=xlPivotTableVersion12).CreatePivotTable _
```

   Ignoring the statement that creates a new sheet, the recorded macro's next statement—which extends onto multiple lines—actually has two parts. It first adds a new item to the PivotCaches collection, using the word *Create* instead of the typical *Add*. Notice the opening parenthesis after the Create method. Then look for the corresponding closing parenthesis (just following the word *xlPivotTableVersion12*). After the closing parenthesis, there's a CreatePivotTable method, which has its own arguments.

7. Type (on one line) **Set pc = ActiveWorkbook.PivotCaches.Create(xlDatabase, Range("A1").CurrentRegion)** and press Enter.

   Nothing appears to happen, but you now have a memory cache loaded and ready to create a PivotTable report. Rather than using an explicit range address for the source as the recorded macro did, you use the current region surrounding cell A1.

   A PivotTable report has a memory cache to store the data. This is different from a table. For a table, all the data is right there in the table—there is nothing hidden. For a PivotTable report, the data is actually stored in the memory cache. The name *cache* is appropriate, because it means "a hidden storage place." You can create multiple PivotTable reports that use the same memory cache.

8. Type **Worksheets.Add** and press Enter.

   This creates a new, blank worksheet. In the recorded macro, adding a new worksheet came at the beginning, but you don't need it to create the memory cache, so you can move it lower in your macro.

   ```
       Version:=xlPivotTableVersion12).CreatePivotTable _
       TableDestination:="Sheet2!R3C1", _
       TableName:="PivotTable1", _
       DefaultVersion:=xlPivotTableVersion12
   ```

9. Type **pc.CreatePivotTable ActiveCell** and press Enter.

   This creates the shell of the PivotTable report. The only required argument for the CreatePivotTable method is the TableDestination. Because you can create multiple PivotTable reports from a single cache, you need to specify a location for each one.

10. In the **Immediate** window, execute the **Worksheets.Add** and **pc.CreatePivotTable ActiveCell** statements a second time.

    You end up with two different worksheets, each of which contains the shell of a PivotTable report. They're both connected to the same memory cache.

11. Press F5 to end the current macro. Then copy the statements from the **Immediate** window into the macro, and press F5 to test the macro.

One of the powerful features of a PivotTable report is the ability to create multiple views of the same data—without needing multiple copies of the data.

Create a PivotTable Report from an External Source

Creating a PivotTable report based on an external source is similar to creating a table based on an external source. With a table, however, you assign the source connection string to the ListObject and the table name to the QueryObject that belongs to it. With a PivotTable report, you assign both the source connection string and the table name to the PivotCache object.

1. In Excel, close other workbooks so that the *Chapter05* workbook is active.

2. Start recording a new macro named **zPivotFromExternal**.

3. Press Ctrl+N to open a new workbook. On the **Data** tab of the Ribbon, click **From Access**, navigate to the folder containing the practice files for this book, select **Orders.accdb**, and click **Open**. In the **Import Data** dialog box, select the **PivotTable Report** option, and click **OK**.

4. Stop the recorder, and look at the macro.

   The top part of the macro has an array similar to the one in the macro where you created a table from an external data source, but this time, it is part of creating a PivotCache object. In addition to creating a memory cache for the PivotTable, this macro also adds an item to the workbook's Connections collection. The name for a single item in the Connections collection is not *Connection*, as you might expect, but rather *WorkbookConnection*. As usual, if you assign the objects to variables, you can make the macro easier to read.

5. Clear the contents of the **Immediate** window, create the shell of a macro that looks like the following, and press F8 twice to step to the End Sub statement.

```
Sub PivotFromExternal()
    Dim wc As WorkbookConnection
    Dim pc As PivotCache
    Dim s As String
End Sub
```

You're now ready to start entering the statements for the body of the macro.

```
Workbooks.Add
```

6. In the **Immediate** window, type **Workbooks.Add** and press Enter.

```
Workbooks("Book2").Connections.Add "Orders", "", Array( _
    ...
    "Support Complex Data=False"), Array("Orders"), 3
```

7. Type the following two statements, and press Enter after each one.

```
s = ThisWorkbook.Path & "\..\Orders.accdb"
s = "OLEDB;Provider= Microsoft.ACE.OLEDB.12.0;Data Source=" & s
```

These statements are exactly the same as the ones that set the source string in the TableFromExternal macro earlier in this chapter. Notice that in the recorded macro, some of the arguments for the Add method come before the array and some come after the array. By putting the data source into a string, it's easier to see the whole structure of the Add method.

8. Type (on one line) **Set wc = ActiveWorkbook.Connections.Add("", "", s,"Orders", 3)** and press Enter.

The first argument of the Add method is the Name argument. It is required, and the recorder inserted "Orders" as the name. But if you use an empty string for the argument, Add will generate a default name—automatically generating a new unique name if you create multiple connections in the same workbook. The arguments after the source string are the same as in the recorded statement.

> **Tip** Creating an explicit connection in the macro is one way that a PivotTable report is different from a table. When you create a table from an external connection, the QueryTable object actually does create a new WorkbookConnection, but it creates it implicitly, without putting it in the macro. When you create a PivotTable report from an external connection, the macro explicitly creates a WorkbookConnection object and then links the PivotCache to it.

```
ActiveWorkbook.PivotCaches.Create( _
    SourceType:=xlExternal, _
    SourceData:=ActiveWorkbook.Connections("Orders"), _
    Version:=xlPivotTableVersion12).CreatePivotTable
```

9. Type (on one line) **Set pc = ActiveWorkbook.PivotCaches.Create(xlExternal, wc)** and press Enter.

As with the Create method for creating a memory cache from an internal source, most of the arguments are optional. From an external source, you use the reference to the workbook connection as the source. By assigning the memory cache to a variable, you can split the CreatePivotTable method into a new statement.

```
Version:=xlPivotTableVersion12).CreatePivotTable _
TableDestination:="Sheet1!R1C1", _
TableName:="PivotTable4", _
DefaultVersion:=xlPivotTableVersion12
```

10. Type the following two statements, pressing Enter after each one.

```
Worksheets.Add
pc.CreatePivotTable ActiveCell
```

Creating a PivotTable from an external connection is exactly the same as creating one from an internal connection—it's the memory cache that is different when you access an external source.

11. Press F5 to end the current macro. Then copy the statements from the **Immediate** window into the macro, and press F5 to test the macro.

Multiple PivotTable reports can access the same memory cache, and thus the same workbook connection. If you need to change the source for the connection, just change the one connection object and all the dependent PivotTable reports will change appropriately.

Record a Macro to Set the PivotTable Structure

When you first create a PivotTable report, you get an empty shell on the worksheet, along with a Field List task pane to help you create the layout. You can use the macro recorder to help you learn the methods and properties for defining the PivotTable structure.

1. Run the **PivotFromExternal** macro to create a new workbook with the shell of a PivotTable report.

2. Start recording a macro with the name zPivotSetStructure.

3. In the **PivotTable Field List**, select the **Net** check box.

Because the field is numeric, it generates a data field in the Values list named *Sum of Net*. The name *Sum of Net* also appears in cell A1, along with the grand total in cell A2. You can change the name of the data field by simply typing over it.

4. In cell **A1**, type **Net** plus a trailing space, and then press Enter.

You can rename a field by typing the new name on the report, but you cannot give a data field the same name as any of the database fields. By adding a space after the name, you can make the name appear to be the same as the field name.

	A	B	C
1	**Net**		
2	1363877.46		
3			

5. In the field list, select the **Category** check box.

   The category names appear in column A. Because the field is text, it defaults to the Row Labels area.

6. In the field list, drag the **State** field to the **Report Filter** area.

   The state field moves above the report, and the rest of the report shifts down to make room. If you want a text field to go somewhere other than the Row Labels area, you need to explicity drag it.

7. In the field list, drag the **Date** field to the **Column Labels** area.

   The dates appear across the top of the report. A PivotTable report recognizes dates and allows you to create automatic groupings for them.

8. Right-click any of the date column labels and click **Group**. Clear **Months**, select **Quarters** and **Years**, and click **OK**.

   Note that there are seven possible grouping levels, and you selected the bottom two.

9. On the **PivotTable Tools Options** tab of the Ribbon, click **Select**, and then click **Entire PivotTable**. Click **Select** again, and click **Values**. Then, on the **Home** tab of the Ribbon, click **Cell Styles** and click **Comma [0]**.

   This applies a basic number format with no decimals to just the data area of the PivotTable report.

10. Stop the recorder, and look at the macro.

You can now create a new macro by using information gleaned from the recorded macro.

Set the PivotTable Structure

The ability to control the structure of a PivotTable report from a macro is a powerful skill—particularly if you want to automate analytical reports. The recorder shows how you can manipulate the PivotTable report, but as usual, it does not always make the changes in the simplest way.

1. Run the **PivotFromExternal** macro. Then clear the **Immediate** window, create the shell of a macro that looks like this, and press F8 three times to initialize the variable.

```
Sub PivotSetStructure()
    Dim pt as PivotTable
    Set pt = ActiveCell.PivotTable

End Sub
```

You're now ready to create the statements for the body of the macro.

```
ActiveSheet.PivotTables("PivotTable1").AddDataField _
    ActiveSheet.PivotTables("PivotTable1"). _
    PivotFields("Net"), "Sum of Net", xlSum
```

2. In the **Immediate** window, type **pt.PivotFields("Net").Orientation = xlDataField** and press Enter.

The recorded macro uses AddDataField to convert the Net field into a data field. But simply assigning xlDataField to the Orientation property—by analogy with the other fields—works just as well and keeps the macro statements consistent.

```
ActiveSheet.PivotTables("PivotTable1"). _
    DataPivotField.PivotItems("Sum of Net").Caption = "Net "
```

3. Type **pt.DataFields(1).Caption = "Net "** and press Enter.

Rather than refer to the data field as a PivotItem from the DataPivotField object, you can simply refer to it directly as a field in the DataFields collection. The simpler option makes the macro easier to read.

```
With ActiveSheet.PivotTables("PivotTable1").PivotFields("State")
    .Orientation = xlPageField
    .Position = 1
End With
```

4. Type the following three statements, pressing Enter after each one.

```
pt.PivotFields("Category").Orientation = xlRowField
pt.PivotFields("State").Orientation = xlPageField
pt.PivotFields("Date").Orientation = xlColumnField
```

The recorded macro uses three different With structures to move the fields to the appropriate locations. Because there is only one field on each axis, it is not necessary to specify the Position property, so it's not necessary to use a With structure or a variable.

```
Range("B4").Select
Selection.Group Start:=True, End:=True, _
    Periods:=Array(False, False, False, False, False, True, True)
```

5. Type **pt.ColumnFields("Date").DataRange.Cells(1).Group Periods:=Array(False, False, False, False, False, True, True)** and press Enter.

The Year and Quarter groups appear. The array corresponds to the seven levels of summary in the grouping dialog box. You want the last two items—quarter and year—which is why those two elements of the array are true. The recorder uses the cell address to find the column field, but that is a fragile way to write the macro. Using the Date field directly is much more robust.

```
ActiveSheet.PivotTables("PivotTable1").PivotSelect "", xlDataOnly, True
Selection.Style = "Comma [0]"
```

6. Type **pt.DataBodyRange.Style = "Comma [0]"** and press Enter.

The recorded macro gets to the data range by using the PivotSelect method. You have already used a DataBodyRange property for the ListObject of an Excel table. With the assistance of Auto Lists, you can quickly determine that a PivotTable also has a DataBodyRange property, which, because it is a Range object, has a Style property.

7. Press F5 to stop the macro. Then copy the statements from the **Immediate** window into the **PivotSetStructure** macro. Run the **PivotFromExternal** macro, and then run the **PivotSetStructure** macro to test it.

The recorded macro didn't use the Orientation property for the data field, but because it used it for the other fields, you were able to check the enumeration list for the Orientation property to see if there was an option for the data field. Sometimes recording one action can give you a clue that helps simplify the way you write other statements.

Record a Macro to Customize a PivotTable Layout

By default, a PivotTable report automatically adjusts itself based on the specific data it contains—it automatically adjusts column widths and automatically hides rows and columns that don't contain data. But sometimes you want a report that always has the same layout, regardless of what data it contains. For example, maintaining a consistent layout can make it easier to compare results when you switch the report from one state to another.

> **Troubleshooting** If you don't have a current version of a PivotTable report, run the PivotFromExternal and PivotSetStructure macros.

1. Start recording a macro with the name zPivotSetLayout.

2. Click the **State** report filter arrow in cell **B2**, select **Idaho**, and then click **OK**.

   Lucerne Publishing started selling products in Idaho only recently, so only some of the categories and dates have values. By selecting a state with limited data, you can make sure that the report shows the same grid regardless of the state.

	A	B	C	D	E
1	State	Idaho ⟱			
2					
3	**Net**	Column Labels ▾			
4		⊟2007		Grand Total	
5	Row Labels ▾	Qtr3	Qtr4		
6	Art	695	773	1,468	
7	Dinosaurs	533	443	975	
8	Kids	474	442	915	
9	Nature	398	318	715	
10	Sport	1,665	1,733	3,398	
11	**Grand Total**	3,763	3,707	7,470	
12					

3. Right-click any of the row labels—say, Dinosaur—and click **Field Settings**. Click the **Layout & Print** tab, select **Show items with no data**, and click **OK**.

   The Seattle category now appears—even though there is no data in the row.

4. Right-click the **2007** column label, and click **Field Settings**. Click the **Layout & Print** tab, select **Show items with no data**, and click **OK**.

All the available years now appear. You never want to show the less-than and greater-than options that date grouping automatically generates, and for the current reporting purposes, you want to see only the most recent two years.

	A	B	C	D	E	F	G	H	I	J	K	L	M	N	O	P	Q
1	State	Idaho															
2																	
3	Net	Column Labels															
4		⊟<1/1/2005		⊟2005				⊟2006				⊟2007			⊟>10/2/2007	Grand Total	
5	Row Labels	<1/1/2005	Qtr1	Qtr2	Qtr3	Qtr4	Qtr1	Qtr2	Qtr3	Qtr4	Qtr1	Qtr2	Qtr3	Qtr4	>10/2/2007		
6	Art											695	773			1,468	
7	Dinosaurs											533	443			975	
8	Kids											474	442			915	
9	Nature											398	318			715	
10	Seattle																
11	Sport											1,665	1,733			3,398	
12	Grand Total											3,763	3,707			7,470	
13																	

5. Click the **Column Labels** arrow, and clear **<1/1/2005, 2005,** and **>10/2/2007**. In other words, clear all the boxes except the final two full years.

6. On the **PivotTable Tools Design** tab of the Ribbon, click **Grand Totals**, and then click **On For Columns Only**.

The totals to the right of 2007 disappear. The total for just those two years is not a meaningful number.

The PivotTable report typically autofits all the columns in the report. This avoids the possibility of seeing hash marks where the number is too big, but it is disruptive when you switch from one state to another. By setting all the columns just wider than the widest column, you can keep them all consistently at the same width.

7. Click the **State** report filter arrow in cell **B2**, and then click **All**. Then select the columns from **B** to **I**, and double-click the border between column **C** and column **D** to autofit all the columns. Drag the border between column **C** and column **D** slightly to the right to set all the columns to the same size—slightly larger than the minimum that autofit detected.

	A	B	C	D	E	F	G	H	I	J
1	State	(All)								
2										
3	Net	Column								
4		2006				2007				
5	Row Labels	Qtr1	Qtr2	Qtr3	Qtr4	Qtr1	Qtr2	Qtr3	Qtr4	
6	Art	33,318	26,871	23,934	32,365	37,410	42,293	42,883	16,949	
7	Dinosaurs	12,375	16,474	19,115	22,382	25,096	28,263	29,654	10,559	
8	Kids	25,153	27,780	27,689	31,428	36,012	32,336	32,460	10,206	
9	Nature	17,793	19,892	16,457	21,521	23,964	22,505	26,093	9,867	
10	Seattle	15,578	15,826	17,794	16,770	18,338	18,746	13,224	4,463	
11	Sport	3,320	12,189	13,827	17,554	27,552	50,998	52,207	18,768	
12	Grand Total	107,535	119,032	118,816	142,020	168,372	195,141	196,523	70,812	
13										

8. Right-click any cell in the PivotTable report, and click **PivotTable Options**. On the **Layout & Format** tab, clear both the **Autofit column widths on update** and the **Preserve cell formatting on update** check boxes, and then click **OK**.

   If you don't clear the Autofit option for column widths, the widths will automatically adjust again each time you change the state.

9. On the **PivotTable Tools Options** tab of the Ribbon, click **+/- Buttons** to turn off the buttons, and click **Field Headers** to turn off the headers.

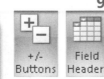

+/- Buttons   Field Headers

   When you have limited navigation for a report, you don't need the extra user interface features offered by a PivotTable report.

10. Turn off the recorder, and edit the **zPivotSetLayout** macro.

You can now use information you learned in the recorded macro to create one of your own that refines the layout of a PivotTable report.

Customize a PivotTable Layout

When working with a PivotTable report layout, the macro recorder does a good job. You will, of course, want to use an object variable for the PivotTable object. This macro uses pivot fields in several places, so it will be helpful to create a variable for a PivotField object. Rather than use range references—which may not always be the same—you can use reference points from within the PivotTable object.

1. Run the **PivotFromExternal** and **PivotSetStructure** macros. Then in Visual Basic, create the shell of a macro that looks like the following, and press F8 four times to initialize the variables.

```
Sub PivotSetLayout()
    Dim pt As PivotTable
    Dim pf as PivotField
    Set pt = ActiveCell.PivotTable
    Set pf = pt.ColumnFields("Years")

End Sub
```

You're now ready to create the statements for the body of the macro.

```
ActiveSheet.PivotTables("PivotTable1").PivotFields("State"). _
    ClearAllFilters
    ActiveSheet.PivotTables("PivotTable1").PivotFields("State"). _
    CurrentPage = "Idaho"
```

2. Type **pt.PageFields("State").CurrentPage = "Idaho"** and press Enter.

This allows you to see the collapsed report so that you can verify the subsequent statements. You can leave it out of the final macro if you want.

```
ActiveSheet.PivotTables("PivotTable1"). _
    PivotFields("Category").ShowAllItems = True
ActiveSheet.PivotTables("PivotTable1")._
    PivotFields("Years").ShowAllItems = True
```

3. Type the following two statements, following each with Enter.

```
pt.RowFields("Category").ShowAllItems = True
pf.ShowAllItems = True
```

These statements are essentially the same. They show all the items for the row and column fields, and they differ from the recorded macro in that they use object variables.

```
With ActiveSheet.PivotTables("PivotTable1").PivotFields("Years")
    .PivotItems("<1/1/2005").Visible = False
    .PivotItems("2005").Visible = False
    .PivotItems(">10/2/2007").Visible = False
End With
```

4. Type the following three statements, following each with Enter.

```
pf.PivotItems(1).Visible = False
pf.PivotItems(2).Visible = False
pf.PivotItems(pf.PivotItems.Count).Visible = False
```

These hide the first two items and the last item in the Year field, leaving the last two full years. By using the Count of the number of PivotItems to find the last one, the macro will adapt more gracefully if the data set includes more than three years.

```
ActiveSheet.PivotTables("PivotTable1").RowGrand = False
ActiveSheet.PivotTables("PivotTable1").HasAutoFormat = False
```

5. Type the following two statements, following each with Enter.

```
pt.RowGrand = False
pt.HasAutoFormat = False
```

These are straightforward property assignments. The only change from the recorded macro is using the object variable.

```
ActiveSheet.PivotTables("PivotTable1").PivotFields("State")._
    ClearAllFilters
ActiveSheet.PivotTables("PivotTable1").PivotFields("State").CurrentPage _
    = "(All)"
```

6. Type **pt.PageFields("State").CurrentPage = "(All)"** and press Enter.

This statement ensures that the values in the report are as large as possible. This statement is an important part of the macro because you don't want to accidentally set the column width based on a filter with very small values. The recorder adds an extra statement to clear the existing filters, but that is not necessary.

```
Columns("B:I").Select
Columns("B:I").EntireColumn.AutoFit
```

7. Type **pt.DataBodyRange.Columns(2).AutoFit** and press Enter.

The whole purpose of this statement is to find the width you should use for all the columns. The macro recorder changed all the columns, but you need to resize only the one you will use in the next statement, and you don't need to change the selection to do it.

```
Selection.ColumnWidth = 9.43
```

8. Type (on one line) **pt.DataBodyRange.ColumnWidth = pt.DataBodyRange. Columns(2).ColumnWidth + 1** and press Enter.

This adjusts all the columns of the data body range to be slightly wider than the one column you automatically adjusted in the previous step. You don't want to use an absolute width; you want to use a width based on the AutoFit from the previous statement.

```
ActiveSheet.PivotTables("PivotTable1").DisplayFieldCaptions = False
ActiveSheet.PivotTables("PivotTable1").ShowDrillIndicators = False
```

9. Type the following two statements, pressing Enter after each one.

```
pt.DisplayFieldCaptions = False
pt.ShowDrillIndicators = False
```

These statements differ from the recorded macro only in the use of the object variable.

10. Press F5 to stop the macro. Then copy the statements from the **Immediate** window into the **PivotSetLayout** macro. Run the **PivotFromExternal** and **PivotSetStructure** macros, and then run the **PivotSetLayout** macro to test it.

11. After running the macro, switch between different values in the **State** list to see that the report maintains its layout.

Making the columns consistently visible and consistently sized makes it easier for users to compare information between states.

Record a Macro to Customize a PivotTable Style

Excel 2007 has a powerful tool for applying a consistent style to an Excel table or a PivotTable report. You can select from 60 built-in styles for a table or from 84 built-in styles for a PivotTable report. You can also create new styles, with different formatting for different structured portions of the table or the PivotTable report. Table styles are also integrated with workbook themes, which means that once you apply a style, you can change the appearance dramatically but consistently simply by selecting a new theme.

1. Start recording a macro with the name zPivotSetStyle.

2. On the **PivotTable Tools Design** tab of the Ribbon, click the **More** arrow for **PivotTable Styles**.

3. Without clicking, move the mouse pointer over **Pivot Style Medium 23** (second column of the bottom row of the **Medium** section) and then over **Pivot Style Dark 2** (second column of the top row of the **Dark** section).

The medium style highlights the first column but not the total row. The dark style highlights the total row but not the first column You want both. The solution is to create a duplicate of the dark style and then modify it to highlight the first column

4. Right-click **Pivot Style Dark 2**, and then click **Duplicate**. Type NewPivotStyle as the name for the duplicated style, and click **OK**.

This creates the duplicate of the style, but does not apply it to the report. You must explicitly apply the style to the report.

5. Click the **More** arrow for **PivotTable Styles** again, and then click **NewPivotStyle**.

Now you're ready to modify the custom style.

6. Right-click the **NewPivotStyle** and click **Modify**. In the **Table Element** list, select **First Column**.

7. Click the **Format** button, and on the **Fill** tab, click the color swatch in the fourth row and fifth column of the main block of colors.

In this palette, tool tips don't appear, but in a standard color palette, the tool tip for this swatch says *Blue, Accent 1, Darker 25%*.

This changes the first column to a darker color, but it also makes the font hard to read.

8. On the **Font** tab, in the **Font Style** list, click **Bold**, and in the **Color** list, click **White**. Then click **OK** twice.

This changes the font to white and bold so that it's visible against the dark background.

The styles are aligned with the Office themes. By switching from one theme to another on the Page Layout tab of the Ribbon, you can change the entire look and feel of the report. The font, however, does not change with the theme. The style uses the Normal cell style to define the font, and by default, the Normal style uses Arial. By changing the Normal cell style to use a theme font, you can completely synchronize your PivotTable report with the current theme.

9. On the **Home** tab of the Ribbon, click the **Cell Styles** arrow, right-click **Normal**, and then click **Modify**. Click **Format**, and on the **Font** tab, in the **Font** list, select **Calibri (Body)**. Then click **OK** twice.

   Even though the font name says Calibri (if you're using the default Office theme), you're really setting the font to the *body* font of the current theme, and that will change as you change themes.

10. Stop the recorder.

11. Before editing the macro, try out the report with various themes. Insert a new column **A** and give it a width of about **45** so that you can see the PivotTable report behind the theme list. Then on the **Page Layout** tab of the Ribbon, click the **Themes** button, and move the mouse pointer over the various themes to see the PivotTable change styles.

12. Edit the **zPivotSetTheme** macro.

You can now use information you learned in the recorded macro to create one of your own that changes the style for a PivotTable report.

Customize a PivotTable Style

The biggest enhancement you can make to the code produced by the macro recorder to modify a style is to eliminate statements that redefine properties that you didn't change. Simplifying a macro so that it includes only the properties you actually change not only makes the macro much shorter, but it also clarifies the purpose of the macro: you don't have to wonder which of the hundreds of properties was important to the macro.

1. Run the **PivotFromExternal** and **PivotSetStructure** macros. (Running the PivotSetLayout macro is not essential before creating a macro that customizes the style, but doing so would not hurt anything.) Then clear the **Immediate** window, create the shell of a macro that looks like the folowing, and press F8 three times to initialize the variables.

```
Sub PivotSetStyle()
    Dim pt As PivotTable
    Dim ts As TableStyle
    Set pt = ActiveCell.PivotTable

End Sub
```

You are now ready to start entering the statement in the Immediate window to create the body of the macro.

```
ActiveWorkbook.TableStyles("PivotStyleDark2").Duplicate ("NewPivotStyle")
```

2. In the **Immediate** window, type (on one line) **Set ts = ActiveWorkbook. TableStyles("PivotStyleDark2").Duplicate("NewPivotStyle")** and press Enter.

This is no different from the recorded statement except that you assign the resulting style to a variable for future convenience.

The recorded macro next includes about 26 With blocks that recreate all the elements of the duplicated style. You can ignore all the statements down to the one that assigns the NewPivotStyle to the current PivotTable report.

```
ActiveSheet.PivotTables("PivotTable1").TableStyle2 = "NewPivotStyle"
```

3. Type **pt.TableStyle2 = ts.Name** and press Enter.

This uses the objects instead of the longer reference. By using the Name property of the table style stored in the TableStyle variable, the macro will continue to work even if you change your mind about what name to use in the first statement of the macro.

```
With ActiveWorkbook.TableStyles("NewPivotStyle").TableStyleElements( _
    xlFirstColumn).Font
    .FontStyle = "Bold"
    .TintAndShade = 0
    .ThemeColor = xlThemeColorDark1
End With
```

4. Type the following two statements (each on a single line), pressing Enter after each one.

```
ts.TableStyleElements(xlFirstColumn).Font.FontStyle = "Bold"
ts.TableStyleElements(xlFirstColumn).Font.ThemeColor = xlThemeColorDark1
```

These just set the font style to Bold and the color to white. One advantage of the Immediate window over the user interface is that you can see each change as you make it, without having to wait to close the dialog box.

> **Tip** It's ironic that the name for the *white* theme color is *xlThemeColorDark1*.
> The reason has to do with the fact that theme colors were developed primarily for Microsoft Office PowerPoint 2007. In PowerPoint, light colors on a dark background are common, so in a typical PowerPoint theme, this color would actually be dark.

```
With ActiveWorkbook.TableStyles("NewPivotStyle").TableStyleElements( _
    xlFirstColumn).Interior
    .ThemeColor = xlThemeColorAccent1
    .TintAndShade = -0.249946592608417
End With
```

5. Type the following two statements (each on a single line), pressing Enter after each one.

```
ts.TableStyleElements(xlFirstColumn).Interior.ThemeColor = _
    xlThemeColorAccent1
ts.TableStyleElements(xlFirstColumn).Interior.TintAndShade = -0.25
```

It takes two statements to implement a single color swatch from the theme colors palette. This is because the colors in a column of the palette are really just tints and shades of the accent color at the top. The implication is that from a macro, you are not limited to the five tint and shade variations in the theme palette. You can set the TintAndShade property to any level between -1 and 1, and the color will still shift appropriately when the workbook theme changes.

6. Type **ActiveWorkbook.Styles("Normal").Font.ThemeFont = xlThemeFontMinor** and press Enter.

   The recorded macro includes almost two dozen statements just to set the theme font. In the Cell Style dialog box, you specified Calibri (Body) as the font, but the identifier for the font in the object model is the generic term *xlThemeFontMinor*. This is what enables the font to change to whatever specific font is defined in the current theme.

7. Press F5 to stop the macro. Then copy the statements from the **Immediate** window into the **PivotSetStyle** macro. Run the **PivotFromExternal**, **PivotSetStructure**, and **PivotSetLayout** macros, and then run the **PivotSetStructure** macro to test it.

   After testing the macro, be sure to try out switching themes to make sure the colors and fonts change appropriately.

Excel tables and PivotTable reports are powerful tools for exploring and analyzing data, from both internal and external sources. The ability to use VBA macros to create and manipulate tables and PivotTables will enable you to develop stunning—and stunningly useful—tables for your own use and for the use of others.

CLOSE the *Chapter05.xlsm* workbook.

Key Points

- When you want to quickly find the methods and properties that accomplish a simple task, record a macro and the use the output of the Macro Recorder as a quick help reference.

- Whenever you have a list that you need to sort or filter, consider turning it into a table. Use the worksheets ListObjects collection to create or access a table.

- Use ThisWorkbook.Path as a basis to help you open files that will always be close to the macro workbook.

- The recorder is great for determining the connection string for an external reference, such as a database. Many of the parameters in a recorded connection string are default values, so you can omit them from your macro if you choose.

- Creating formulas that refer to cells in a table results in structured references. If the formula is inside the table, you can often simplify the default formula to get just what is essential for your needs.

- When you create a PivotTable report, you first create a memory cache to store the data. You can create many PivotTable reports that share the same memory cache. To access the memory cache, use the PivotCache property of a PivotTable object.

- To modify the style for a PivotTable report or for a regular table, you first duplicate an existing style. Use the TableStyleElements collection to find and select the part you want to change.

Chapter at a Glance

Use Help topics to learn about objects, **page 176**

Range Object Members

Represents a cell, a row, a column, a selection of cells containing one or more contiguous blocks of cells, or a 3-D range.

Methods

	Name	Description
	Activate	Activates a single cell, which must be inside the current selection. To select a range of cells, use the Select method.
	AddComment	Adds a comment to the range.
	AdvancedFilter	Filters or copies data from a list based on a criteria range. If the initial selection is a single cell, that cell's current region is used.
	ApplyNames	Applies names to the cells in the specified range.
	ApplyOutlineStyles	Applies outlining styles to the specified range.
	AutoComplete	Returns an AutoComplete match from the list. If there's no AutoComplete match ... this me...
	AutoFill	Perform...

Use a macro to apply advanced formatting to shapes and text, **page 189**

Use a macro to create graphical buttons that can launch macros, **page 196**

Apply enhanced formatting to chart regions, **page 206**

Automatically synchronize the scale of separate charts, **page 203**

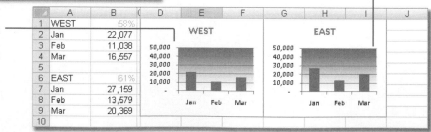

6 Explore Graphical Objects

In this chapter, you will learn to:

✔ Manipulate advanced fills in worksheet cells.

✔ Manipulate graphical shapes on a worksheet.

✔ Manipulate chart objects.

✔ Use help as a reference tool.

A few weeks ago, I invited a friend to join me for lunch at a restaurant near my house. About a half-hour after our scheduled meeting time at my place, I got a call from her. She was in a completely different part of town. The problem was that I had given her *directions* to my house. What she really needed was my *address* so that she could enter it into her car's Global Positioning System (GPS) navigation system, which would then provide her with directions as she was driving to my house. I have heard that a GPS navigation system can be a godsend. It doesn't drive the car for you, but it does give you the information you need while you are driving. However, if you are in a remote, unmapped region where a satelite connection is unavailable, or if you are driving a rental car or a borrowed car that doesn't have a navigation system, it's a good idea to know how to read a regular map and understand street signs even if you typically use a GPS navigation system.

The macro recorder in Microsoft Office Excel 2007 is like a GPS navigation system. It can give you invaluable information about how to steer the macros you write. But there are times when the macro recorder may not be available, so it's important to know how to take advantage of other navigational aids, such as the Object Browser, Auto Lists, and Help, so that you can get to your desired destination even if the macro recorder is not there to help you.

In this chapter, you're going to use Microsoft Visual Basic for Applications to work with various graphical objects in Excel 2007. Graphical objects include shapes, WordArt, charts, and even the new fancy formatting—such as gradient fills—that is available for ordinary cells. You'll use the macro recorder for reference, but you'll also learn how to work without the recorder for those times when it is not available.

Important Before you complete this chapter, you need to install the practice files from the book's companion CD to their default locations. See "Using the Book's CD" on page xv for more information.

USE the *Graphics.xlsx* practice file located in the *Documents\MSP\ExcelVBA07SBS* folder.

BE SURE TO save the *Graphics.xlsx* practice file as a macro-enabled workbook called *Chapter06.xlsm* in the trusted location that you created in Chapter 1.

OPEN the *Chapter06.xlsm* workbook.

Exploring Graphical Objects

Graphical objects float on a layer above the worksheet grid. The graphical capabilities of Excel have always been very good, and with Excel 2007 they verge on phenomenal. You could practically use Excel as a full-fledged graphics program. Unfortunately, the macro recorder does not yet work with these newly enhanced shape objects, so this section will be a good exercise for your navigational skills. Fortunately, the macro recorder does work with some of the enhanced worksheet cell formatting and can provide clues that you can use in the uncharted territory.

Use Worksheet Cells as a Drawing Grid

Many graphics programs have a "snap to grid" feature to help the designer align objects optimally, and typically it is possible to adjust the scale of the grid. Excel also has a snap-to-grid feature—it's the grid of cells on the worksheet. When working with graphics, it's useful to be able to control the size of the grid and to use the grid to align objects.

1. In Excel, activate the **Shapes** tab of the *Chapter06* workbook, and then in the Visual Basic **Immediate** window, type **Cells.RowHeight** = 72 and press Enter.

   The height of all the rows on the worksheet changes to 1 inch tall. You specify the height of a row by using *points*, and there are 72 points in 1 inch.

2. Type Cells.ColumnWidth = 13 and press Enter.

The width of all the columns on the active sheet changes to 1 inch wide. You specify the width of a column by using the average width of the zero (0) character in the standard 10-point Arial font—the font used by the Normal cell style. It just so happens that in this font, 13 zero (0) characters fit into 1 inch.

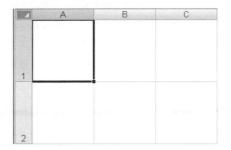

3. Place the insertion point in the word **ColumnWidth**, and press the F1 key.

The Help topic for the ColumnWidth property of a Range object appears. The Help topic explains the unique qualities of the property. Because ColumnWidth is a property of a Range object, at the bottom of the page there is a link to the complete list of members for the Range object.

Excel Developer Reference

Range.ColumnWidth Property

Returns or sets the width of all columns in the specified range. Read/write **Variant**.

Syntax

expression.**ColumnWidth**

expression   A variable that represents a **Range** object.

Remarks

One unit of column width is equal to the width of one character in the Normal style. For proportional fonts, the width of the character 0 (zero) is used.

Use the **Width** property to return the width of a column in points.

If all columns in the range have the same width, the **ColumnWidth** property returns the width. If columns in the range have different widths, this property returns **null**.

Example

This example doubles the width of column A on Sheet1.

Visual Basic for Applications

```
With Worksheets("Sheet1").Columns("A")
    .ColumnWidth = .ColumnWidth * 2
End With
```

See Also

- Range Object
- Range Object Members
- RowHeight Property

4. Click the **Range Object Members** link.

A page appears with descriptions and links for all the methods and properties available for a Range object. Each object in the Excel object model has a similar page of members.

Range Object Members

Represents a cell, a row, a column, a selection of cells containing one or more contiguous blocks of cells, or a 3-D range.

Methods

	Name	Description
◈	Activate	Activates a single cell, which must be inside the current selection. To select a range of cells, use the Select method.
◈	AddComment	Adds a comment to the range.
◈	AdvancedFilter	Filters or copies data from a list based on a criteria range. If the initial selection is a single cell, that cell's current region is used.
◈	ApplyNames	Applies names to the cells in the specified range.
◈	ApplyOutlineStyles	Applies outlining styles to the specified range.
◈	AutoComplete	Returns an AutoComplete match from the list. If there's no AutoComplete match or if more than one entry in the list matches the string to complete, this method returns an empty string.
◈	AutoFill	Performs an autofill on the cells in the specified range.

Help is an important tool, particularly when navigating in unfamiliar territory. One particularly valuable feature of Help is the annotated list of members for an object. Auto Lists or the Object Browser can give you the list of members, but it is easier to scan for a new method or property by using Help.

Add a Gradient Fill to a Cell

Traditionally, Excel cells have contained solid colors. Excel 2007 allows you to add gradient fills and other special formatting to cells. The ability to control extended cell formatting from a macro is useful in its own right, but recording and creating cell gradients can also help you understand how to add gradients to other shapes.

1. In Excel, start recording a macro named rCellGradient. Right-click cell **B1**, and click **Format Cells**. On the **Fill** tab, click **Fill Effects**. Under **Shading Styles**, select **Vertical**. Leave the first **Variant** selected, and then click **OK** twice.

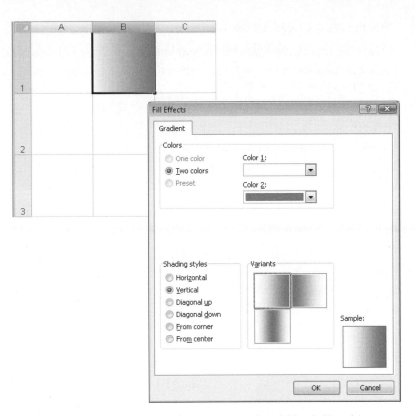

2. Stop the recorder, and edit the macro. It should look like this:

```
Sub rCellGradient()
    Range("B1").Select
    With Selection.Interior
        .Pattern = xlPatternLinearGradient
        .Gradient.Degree = 0
        .Gradient.ColorStops.Clear
    End With
    With Selection.Interior.Gradient.ColorStops.Add(0)
        .ThemeColor = xlThemeColorDark1
        .TintAndShade = 0
    End With
    With Selection.Interior.Gradient.ColorStops.Add(1)
        .ThemeColor = xlThemeColorAccent1
        .TintAndShade = 0
    End With
End Sub
```

The critical part of this macro is setting the Pattern property. You can accomplish the same effect in a single step.

See Also For more details about theme colors, see the section titled "Record a Macro to Customize a PivotTable Style" in Chapter 5, "Explore Data Objects."

3. Select cell **B2**. Then in Visual Basic, create the following macro shell, and press F8 three times to initialize the variable.

```
Sub CellGradient()
    Dim myInterior as Interior
    Set myInterior = Selection.Interior

End Sub
```

When you declare an object variable, you can set it at the most useful level. If you'll be working mostly with cells, you can create a Range object variable. If you'll be working mostly with a subordinate object, you can make the rest of the macro simpler by creating an object variable specifically for the lower-level object.

4. In the **Immediate** window, type **myInterior.Pattern = xlPatternLinearGradient** and press Enter.

Cell B2 changes to have the same gradient fill as cell B1. The recorder includes many statements that simply set default properties. But, fortunately, those extra statements show you a lot about how a gradient works. One of the extra statements includes a property called GradientStops. As with most collections, you can specify a single item from the collection.

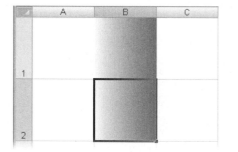

5. Type **myInterior.Gradient.ColorStops(1).ThemeColor = xlThemeColorAccent6** and press Enter.

The left side of the gradient changes from white to orange. The Fill Effects dialog box allows you to choose only a two-color gradient, but ColorStops is a collection that you can add to.

6. Type **myInterior.Gradient.ColorStops.Add 0.75** and press Enter.

A new, white stripe appears in the gradient, about three quarters of the way to the right within the cell. There are now three items in the ColorStops collection. When you add a new item to the ColorsStops collection, you must give the new item a position between 0 and 1. The items in the collection are then sorted by position, so to access the new item, you use 2 as the index, not 3.

7. Type **MyInterior.Gradient.ColorStops(2).Position = 0.25** and press Enter.

The white stripe moves to approximately one quarter of the way to the right within the cell.

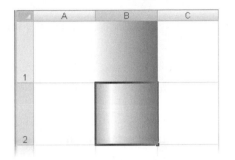

8. Press F5 to end the macro. Copy the contents of the **Immediate** window and paste it into the **CellGradient** macro. In Excel, select cell **B3**, and then in Visual Basic, press F8 repeatedly to test the macro.

9. In Excel, select the range **C1:E2**, and then in Visual Basic, press F5 to test the macro.

Each cell is formatted individually. In Excel, formats such as gradients are applied one cell at a time.

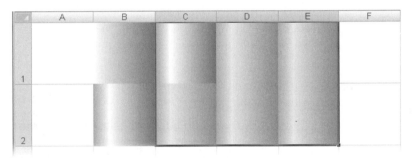

The finished macro should look like this:

```
Sub CellGradient()
    Dim myInterior As Interior
    Set myInterior = Selection.Interior

    myInterior.Pattern = xlPatternLinearGradient
    myInterior.Gradient.ColorStops(1).ThemeColor = xlThemeColorAccent6
    myInterior.Gradient.ColorStops.Add (0.75)
    myInterior.Gradient.ColorStops(2).Position = 0.25
End Sub
```

The macro recorder can help you start to understand the methods and properties for dealing with cell gradients. However, you can do many things from a macro statement that you cannot do in the user interface, so those things will never appear in a recorded macro. For example, in the user interface, you cannot create multiple color stops in the gradient for a cell, and you can't adjust the position of a color stop within the gradient. You can do both in a macro.

> **Tip** In Excel 2007, conditional formatting works very much the same as gradients. Each conditional format is part of a collection that you can manipulate. By applying a conditional format while recording a macro, you can see the critical property names.

Add a Gradient-Filled Shape

Cells are rigidly rectangular, and when you apply a gradient fill to a range of cells, a separate gradient fills each cell. By using shapes, you can create graphics with much more flexibility. The methods and properties for creating and formatting a Shape object are not quite the same as those for a Range object, but there are enough similarities that you can use Help and other techniques to navigate through the details. By using macro statements to create a rectangular Shape object and then apply the same format you gave the worksheet cell, you can compare the way a gradient works with a shape with the way it works with a range.

1. Create the following shell of a macro, and press F8 twice to initialize the variables.

```
Sub ShapeGradient()
    Dim myShapes as Shape
    Dim myFill as FillFormat

End Sub
```

2. In the **Immediate** window, type
Set myShape = Sheet1.Shapes.AddShape(msoShapeRectangle, 0, 0, 72, 72) and press Enter.

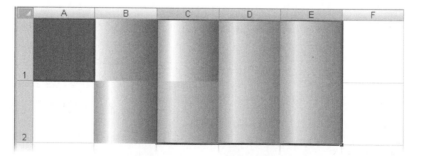

A rectangle appears, exactly filling cell A1. The name *Sheet1* happens to be the code name for the Shapes worksheet. By using the code name, you can get Auto List Help as you construct the statement. If you want the macro to create a shape on any worksheet, replace the code name with *ActiveSheet* after you finish testing the macro. The top, left, height, and width values for a shape are all specified in points—with 72 points to 1 inch.

> **Tip** To identify the code name for the active worksheet, in the Immediate window, type *?ActiveSheet.CodeName* and press Enter.

3. Type **Set myFill = myShape.Fill** and press Enter.

The name of an object sometimes differs from the name of the property that returns the object. In this case, the Fill property returns a FillFormat object. The FillFormat of a shape is analogous to the Interior object of a range.

> **Tip** You can find the object returned by a property in several ways. To use Help, click the property name—in a statement or in the Object Browser—and press F1 to see the topic for the property. The property topic contains a link to the object it returns, and the object topic contains a link to the annotated list of members for that object. (If a link in Help is broken, try typing the object name in the Search box.) In addition, you can type the TypeName function along with the expression that uses the property in the Immediate window. For example, to find the name of the object for the Fill property of a shape named *myShape*, you could type *?TypeName(myShape.Fill)*.

4. Type **myFill.TwoColorGradient msoGradientVertical,1** and press Enter.

The shape becomes filled with a vertical gradient similar to that of the worksheet cell, but the colors are reversed. With a range, you add a gradient by assigning a value to the Pattern property. With a shape, you execute a method to get the same effect.

5. Type **myFill.GradientStops(1).Color.ObjectThemeColor = msoThemeColorAccent6** and press Enter.

The left side of the rectangle changes to the same color as the left side of the cell—orange in the default theme. With a range, you use the ColorStops property to specify the parts of the gradient. The name of this property is similar enough to GradientStops that simply by using Auto Lists, you should be able to discover the new property. With a shape, you also split Color out into a separate object and use ObjectThemeColor instead of simply ThemeColor.

6. Type **myFill.GradientStops(2).Color.ObjectThemeColor = msoThemeColorAccent1** and press Enter.

The right side of the rectangle changes to the same color as the right side of the cell—blue in the default theme.

7. Type **myFill.GradientStops.Insert rgbWhite,0.75** and press Enter.

A white band appears three-quarters of the way to the right of the rectangle. With a cell, you use the Add method to add a new value to the ColorStops collection. With a shape, you use the Insert method to add a new value to the GradientStops collection.

8. Type **myFill.GradientStops(3).Position = 0.25** and press Enter.

The white stripe moves to the left. With a cell, color stops are sorted by the position within the gradient. With a shape, gradient stops are sorted in the order that you add them to the collection.

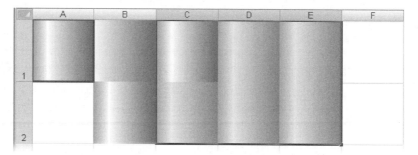

The gradient in the rectangle now looks very similar to the gradient in the cell, but because it is a shape, you can completely change its look.

9. Type **myShape.AutoShapeType = msoShapeRightArrow** and press Enter to change the rectangle into a right-pointing arrow.

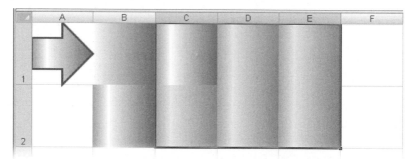

There are almost 200 possible shape types to choose from! You can use shapes on your worksheet for anything from adding interest, to focusing attention on a cell value, to providing snazzy buttons to run macros, to creating a sophisticated company logo.

> **Tip** When you create a new shape on the worksheet, Excel gives it a default name—usually something like *Rectangle 2* or *Oval 5*. You can see the name of the shape in the Name Box to the left of the Formula Bar. You can also use the Name Box to type a new name for the shape. When you refer to the shape from a macro, you can make your macros easier to read and less likely to contain errors if you change the shape names to something meaningful.

Reference a Selected Shape

The earliest versions of Excel did not have shapes. Instead, they had something called *drawing objects*. Shapes were developed as graphical objects that could be used across all Microsoft Office applications, and they are much more powerful than the old drawing objects. Shapes in the 2007 release of Microsoft Office are even more powerful than in earlier versions.

Drawing objects had their own extensive set of objects. To maintain backward compatibility, Excel didn't remove the old DrawingObjects; they're still there, but they're hidden. Occasionally, you might see vestiges of these old drawing objects. One place that you encounter them is when working with the Selection property to refer to the currenly selected object. When you're comfortable with how to assign the currently selected object to a Shape object variable, you don't have to think much about the old drawing objects.

1. In Excel, select a shape—the shape you created in the previous section will do fine. Then create the following macro shell in Visual Basic, and press F8 twice to initialize the variable.

    ```
    Sub SelectionShape()
        Dim s As Shape

    End Sub
    ```

2. In the **Immediate** window, type Set s = Selection and press Enter.

    You get an error message that says "Type mismatch." When you created the object, you assigned it to a Shape variable, so why can't you assign it to a similar variable now?

3. Type ?TypeName(Selection) and press Enter.

    The word *Rectangle* appears. (All the AutoShapeTypes—with the exception of a few of the basic shape types—belong to the Rectangle object class.) However, if you search for a Rectangle class in the Object Browser, you won't find one. If you place the insertion point in the word *Rectangle* and press F1, you get a generic message, but nothing relevant to a Rectangle.

4. Place the insertion point in the word **Shape** (in the variable declaration), and press F1. When prompted for clarification, leave **Shape (Object)** selected, and click Help.

> **Troubleshooting** If you're not connected to the Internet, you can still access help on your computer. In Excel Help, click the Search button arrow and click Developer Reference at the bottom of the list (in the Content From This Computer section).

The Help topic explains that if you want to work with shapes within the selection, you should use a ShapeRange collection.

Excel Developer Reference
Shape Object

Represents an object in the drawing layer, such as an AutoShape, freeform, OLE object, or picture.

Remarks

The **Shape** object is a member of the **Shapes** collection. The **Shapes** collection contains all the shapes in a workbook.

> ☑ **Note**
>
> There are three objects that represent shapes: the **Shapes** collection, which represents all the shapes on a workbook; the **ShapeRange** collection, which represents a specified subset of the shapes on a workbook (for example, a **ShapeRange** object could represent shapes one and four in the workbook, or it could represent all the selected shapes in the workbook); and the **Shape** object, which represents a single shape on a worksheet. If you want to work with several shapes at the same time or with shapes within the selection, use a **ShapeRange** collection.

Using the Shape Object

The following sections describes how to:

---

5. Scroll to the bottom of the topic, and click the link to the **ShapeRange Object** Help topic. Scroll to the bottom to the **Returning All or Some of the Selected Shapes on a Document** subheading.

This section gives an example of using ShapeRange with the selection. The ActiveWindow object at the beginning has no effect.

Returning All or Some of the Selected Shapes on a Document

Use the **ShapeRange** property of the **Selection** object to return all the shapes in the selection. The following example sets the fill foreground color for all the shapes in the selection in window one, assuming that there's at least one shape in the selection.

Visual Basic for Applications

```
Windows(1).Selection.ShapeRange.Fill.ForeColor.RGB = _
    RGB(255, 0, 255)
```

The explanation says to use the ShapeRange property of the Selection object. But there is no such thing as a Selection object. Selection is a property that returns whatever kind of object happens to be currently selected. The Help topic explanation is simply masking over the existence of the Rectangle object.

6. In Visual Basic, press F2 to display the Object Browser. Right-click in the list of classes, and click **Show Hidden Members**. Then select the **Rectangle** class on the left and the **ShapeRange** property on the right.

![Object Browser window showing Classes list with Rectangle selected and Members of 'Rectangle' with ShapeRange highlighted]

7. In the **Immediate** window, type Set s = Selection.ShapeRange(1) and press Enter.

This is essentially the same expression as is in the Help topic, and it does work. If you pretend that Selection is an object, as the Help topic suggests, then you can think of ShapeRange as a property of that imaginary object.

8. Type s.AutoShapeType = msoShapePentagon and press Enter to confirm that the selected shape really is properly assigned to the variable.

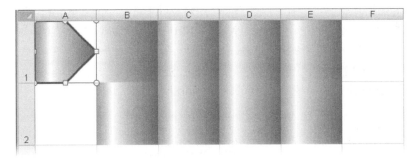

9. Press F5 to stop the macro.

The only reason you need to know about the hidden objects is that selecting an object in the user interface and then typing *?TypeName(Selection)* in the Immediate window is a very useful way to find out the appropriate object class for a variable. Knowing about the hidden objects can also make the result less confusing.

Shape-Related Object Classes

The three (visible) object classes that relate to shapes are easily confused.

The *Shapes object* is a collection of all the Shape objects on a worksheet. To refer to the Shapes object, you use the Shapes property of a worksheet. As with most collections, you can specify a single item from the collection by using the name or number of the item. A single item from the Shapes collection is a Shape (singular) object.

A *Shape object* is the primary mechanism of interacting with a shape on a worksheet. You can move it, resize it, name it, apply formatting to it, and even delete it.

A *ShapeRange object* is like a Shape object, except that a shape range can include more than one shape. In other words, it is a collection. To create a shape range from a Shapes object, you use the Range property, combined with the Array function from Visual Basic. (This is the same syntax as selecting multiple worksheets by using an Array function combined with the Worksheets property.) The Array function turns a list of items into the single argument required by the Range property.

See Also   For information about using the Array function with worksheets, see the section titled "Manipulate Multiple Worksheets" in Chapter 3, "Explore Workbooks and Worksheets."

When you want to modify multiple shapes, use a shape range. When you want to modify a single shape, it's easier to just use a shape, even though a shape range can consist of only one shape. A few of the properties available for a single shape don't work with a shape range. For example, it doesn't make sense to give a name to an arbitrary set of shapes, so the Name property returns an error message if you use it with a shape range that contains more than one shape.

Shapes allow you to create extremely powerful graphical effects. But keeping the different types of objects straight can be a bit confusing at first. Here's a summary:

- *Shapes collection object.* Use the Shapes collection object for selecting all the shapes on a worksheet, for accesing a single shape, or for adding a new shape. You can apply only limited formatting to the entire Shapes collection.
- *Shape object.* Use the Shape object for manipulating a single shape.
- *ShapeRange collection object.* Use the ShapeRange object for manipulating multiple shapes at the same time.

Use an AutoShape to Create a Logo

Excel has a very large collection of shapes that you can insert into a worksheet. But what makes them remarkable is the degree to which you can enhance and modify the shapes. You can even add text to the shapes and format the text with the same flexibility as the shape itself.

> **Tip** The MakeLogo macro is available in the *MakeLogo.txt* file in the folder with practice files, so you can copy it into a module and step through it if you want. But Auto Lists makes typing the statements relatively easy and will help you understand how the objects work. At any time while executing the statements, you can switch to the user interface and look at the corresponding properties there.

1. In Excel, activate the **Logo** worksheet—which is blank. Then in Visual Basic, create the following macro shell, and press F8 twice to initialize the variables.

```
Sub MakeLogo()
    Dim s As Shape
    Dim tf As TextFrame2
    Dim tr As TextRange2
    Dim sf As ShadowFormat

End Sub
```

Some of the object classes may seem unfamiliar, but they are simply subobjects for detailed parts of the shape's format. The reason TextFrame2 and TextRange2 have a 2 at the end is because these are new, improved versions of previously existing objects. Old macros that access the (now hidden) TextFrame or TextRange objects will continue to run, but new macros can take advantage of the new capabilities.

2. Enter the following statements into the **Immediate** window.

```
Set s = Main.Shapes.AddShape(msoShapeUpArrowCallout, 0; 0, 72, 72)
s.Select
Set tf = s.TextFrame2
Set tr = tf.TextRange
Set sf = tr.Font.Shadow
s.Name = "Logo"
```

The first statement creates a new shape, similar to the way you created a new rectangle earlier in this chapter. The size and location are unimportant because you will align them to cell boundaries in separate statements later. The Select statement simply makes it easier to see the shape you're modifying; you don't need it in the finished macro. The other statements assign references to sub-objects that pertain to formatting. The final statement simply gives a name to the object in case you ever want to refer to it in a different macro.

3. Enter the following statements into the **Immediate** window.

```
s.Left = Range("C6").Left
s.Top = Range("C6").Top
s.Width = Range("C:F").Width
s.Height = Range("6:15").Height
```

These statements show how easy it is to align a shape with the worksheet grid. Note that the Left, Top, Width, and Height properties of a range are all read-only—you have to use different properties or methods to change their values—but they are very helpful in aligning shapes.

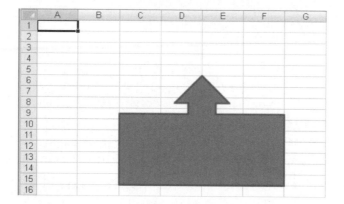

You now have a basic shape on the worksheet. Before you continue, you may want to explore the shape in Excel. The shape has four yellow triangles called *adjustment handles*. These allow you to adjust the relative size of different portions of the shape, effectively turning the hundreds of available shapes into millions. If you move the adjustment handles in Excel, you'll understand better what the following macro statements are doing.

4. Enter the following statements into the **Immediate** window.

```
s.Adjustments(1) = 1.2
s.Adjustments(2) = 0.6
s.Adjustments(3) = 0.15
s.Adjustments(4) = 0.7
```

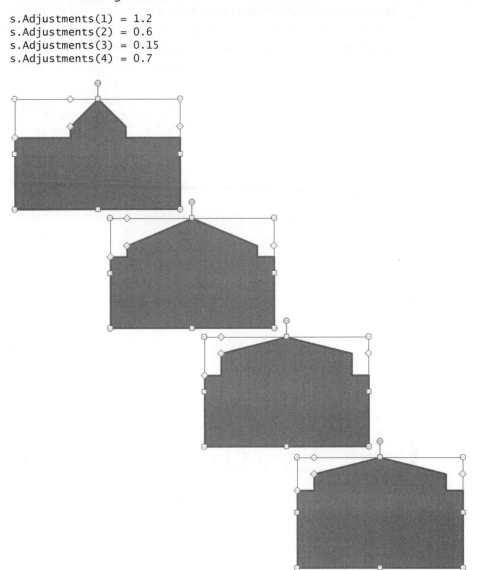

An Up Arrow Callout shape has four adjustment handles: the first adjusts the width of the arrow shaft, the second adjusts the width of the arrow head, the third adjusts the height of the arrow head, and the fourth adjusts the height of the main rectangular body. Different shapes have different adjustments. The best way to determine the appropriate values is simply to experiment.

5. In Excel, right-click the shape, and click **Format Shape**. Then enter the following statements in the **Immediate** window.

```
s.Line.Visible = msoFalse
s.Fill.ForeColor.ObjectThemeColor = msoThemeColorAccent2
s.Fill.ForeColor.TintAndShade = -0.3
s.Fill.Transparency = 0.25
```

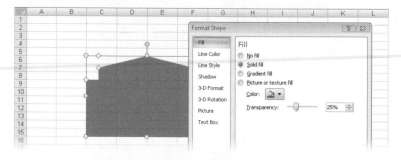

These statements remove the border and change the fill color. Transparency greater than 0 allows the worksheet grid to show through the shape. The Format Shape dialog box can stay visible as you execute macro statements, so you can immediately see the effect of the statement.

6. Enter the following statements into the **Immediate** window.

```
tr = "Lucerne" & vbCrLf & "Publishing"
tr.Font.Size = 28
tr.Font.Bold = msoTrue
```

These statements add the company name to the shape and make the name large and bold. vbCrLf is a special constant in Visual Basic that means *Carriage Return Line Feed* which was the description of a new line when Visual Basic was first invented. The ampersand characters join parts of the name together, allowing you to insert the new line into the middle of the name.

7. In Excel, right-click in the middle of the text, and click **Format Text Effects**. Then enter the following statements into the **Immediate** window.

```
tr.Font.Spacing = 2
tf.VerticalAnchor = msoAnchorBottom
tf.MarginBottom = 20
```

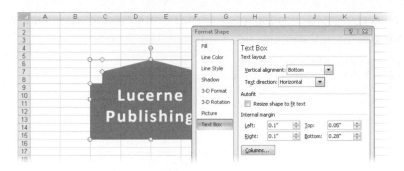

Font spacing is part of the Font dialog box, which can't stay open while you're executing macro statements. The default spacing value is 0, which is neither expanded nor condensed. Alignment appears in the Format Text Effects dialog box, which can stay open as you execute statements. To center text in an irregular shape, the best approach is to pick an appropriate side to anchor the text to and then adjust the margin as needed to get a centered look. In this case, the bottom is a good reference point. In the macro, you use points to specify sizes, but the dialog box displays sizes in inches.

8. In Excel, click the **Text Outline** page of the **Format Text Effects** dialog box. Then enter the following statements into the **Immediate** window.

```
tr.Font.Fill.ForeColor.ObjectThemeColor = msoThemeColorAccent2
tr.Font.Fill.ForeColor.TintAndShade = -0.6
tr.Font.Line.Visible = msoTrue
tr.Font.Line.ForeColor.ObjectThemeColor = msoThemeColorAccent2
tr.Font.Line.ForeColor.TintAndShade = 0.3
```

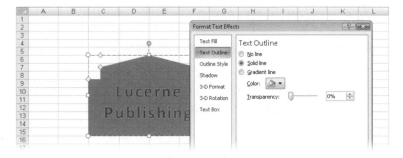

These statements give you a taste of the kind of formatting you can apply to a font—separately from the container shape. Because the Font Format object is separate from the Shape Format object, it can use the same Fill and Line properties as the shape itself. As a result, you can apply most of the things you learned about formatting the shape to formatting the font.

9. In Excel, click the **Shadow** page of the **Format Text Effects** dialog box. Then enter the following statements into the **Immediate** window.

```
sf.Style = msoShadowStyleOuterShadow
sf.ForeColor.ObjectThemeColor = msoThemeColorLight1
sf.OffsetX = 5
sf.OffsetY = 5
sf.Blur = 8
```

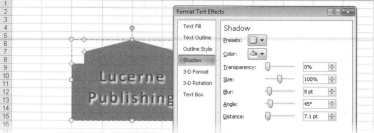

These statements show you what you can do with a font shadow. You need to create the shadow, then give it a color, and then shift it horizontally and vertically. Adding a blur effect makes the shadow look more natural.

10. In Excel, right-click the shape, click **Format Shape**, and click **3-D Format**. Then enter the following statements into the **Immediate** window.

```
s.ThreeD.BevelTopDepth = 12
s.ThreeD.BevelTopInset = 24
s.ThreeD.BevelTopType = msoBevelSoftRound
s.ThreeD.PresetMaterial = msoMaterialMetal2
s.ThreeD.PresetLighting = msoLightRigFlood
```

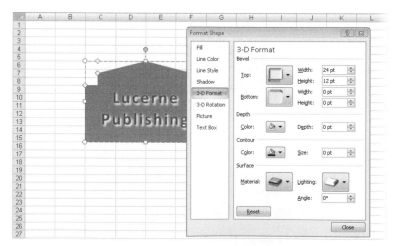

These statements give you a taste of 3-D formatting. Even without using the macro recorder, by experimenting with formatting in the user interface, you can see the possibilities. You can apply 3-D formatting either to the shape (the Format Shape dialog box) or to the text (the Format Text Effects dialog box). After you add 3-D effects to a shape, you can add lighting and transparency options that, just a few years ago, were available only on specialized graphics devices.

11. In Excel, click the **3-D Rotation** page of the **Format Shape** dialog box, type s.ThreeD.RotationX = 40 in the **Immediate** window, and then press Enter to see the look of the logo with a different 3-D orientation.

You can also rotate the shape around Y or Z axes.

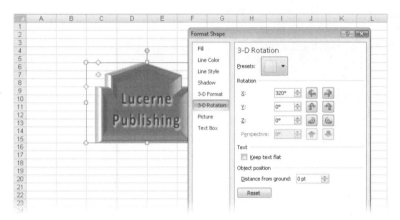

12. Press F5 to stop the macro. Then copy the contents of the **Immediate** window into the macro, replace **Sheet3** with **ActiveSheet**, create a new worksheet in Excel, and test the macro.

This logo should give you a good sense of the range of formatting that you can apply to a shape—and how to create the statements in a macro. The properties in the object model correspond very closely to the options in the user interface. You may even discover properties in the object model that help you learn about options you hadn't noticed in the user interface.

See Also The MakeLogo macro was used to create the animated logo used in the Enterprise Information System (EIS) application included in the Appendix.

Use Grouped Shapes to Create Macro Buttons

Multiple shapes can be combined into a single group. For example, on the Map page of the *Chapter06* workbook, there is a map that shows the states in the western United States where Lucerne Publishing sells products.

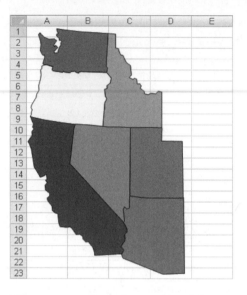

The map consists of a group of shapes—one for each state. From a macro, you can refer to each individual component of the group. You can even make each state into a button that runs a macro.

> **Tip** The MakeMapButtons macro is available in the same folder as *MakeMap.txt*, so you could copy it into a module and step through it if you want, but Auto Lists makes typing the statements relatively easy and will help you understand how the objects work. This macro was used to help create the user interface in the Enterprise Information System (EIS) application in the Appendix.

1. In Excel, drag the **Map** worksheet tab to the right, and as you release the mouse, press the Ctrl key to create a copy of the worksheet.

2. In Visual Basic, create the following placeholder macro.

```
Sub StateButton()
    MsgBox "Hello"
End Sub
```

You'll make a state shape run this macro.

3. Create the following macro shell, and press F8 twice to initialize the variable.

```
Sub MakeMapButtons()
    Dim s As Shape

End Sub
```

4. Enter the following statements into the **Immediate** window.

```
myNumber = 4
myName = "Washington"
myCaption = "WA"
myColor = 6
```

These attributes are unique for the state of Washington. Washington is the fourth item in the group. (Trial-and-error is the best approach to determine the order of a shape within a group.) Once you've written the macro, you can change these values and run the same macro to apply the appropriate formatting to a different state.

5. Enter the following statements into the **Immediate** window.

```
Set s = ActiveSheet.Shapes(1).GroupItems(myNumber)
s.Select
s.Name = myName
```

The map of Washington state is selected, and the name in the Name Box changes from the default name to *Washington*.

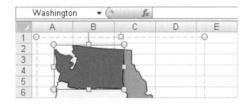

A Shape object has a GroupItems property that returns a collection of all the shapes in the group. You can use a number to reference a single shape from the collection. The grouped item is not part of the worksheet's Shapes collection, but it is part of the GroupItems collection for the shape that forms the group. The Select statement enables you to see which state you are referencing. You can leave that out of the final macro. There is no requirement to assign a name to the individual shape, but if you do, it will make it easier to reference the state from a different macro later. If you do change the name, you can see it in the Name Box in Excel.

6. Enter the following statements into the **Immediate** window.

```
s.Fill.ForeColor.ObjectThemeColor = myColor
s.ThreeD.BevelTopDepth = 6
```

Washington state changes color and takes on a three-dimensional look—like a button.

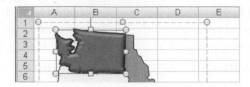

You can change the color and 3-D properties of a grouped shape, just as you can a non-grouped shape. Shapes have a ThreeD property that allows you to access a large number of three-dimensional formatting effects, including BevelTopDepth. Setting the BevelTopDepth of the shape makes it look more like a button.

7. Enter the following statements into the **Immediate** window.

```
s.TextFrame2.TextRange = myCaption
s.TextFrame2.HorizontalAnchor = msoAnchorCenter
s.TextFrame2.VerticalAnchor = msoAnchorMiddle
```

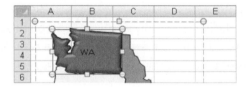

When you first add text to a shape, the text is attached to the top-left corner. The HorizontalAnchor and VerticalAnchor properties allow you to center the text within the shape. The Washington shape is basically rectangular, so centering the text works fine. For some states, you may need to manually adjust the location of the text so that it appears centered.

8. Enter the following statements into the **Immediate** window.

```
s.TextFrame2.TextRange.Font.Size = 20
s.TextFrame2.TextRange.Font.Bold = msoTrue
s.TextFrame2.TextRange.Font.Fill.ForeColor.ObjectThemeColor = _
    msoThemeColorLight1
s.Fill.OneColorGradient msoGradientHorizontal, 1, 0
s.TextFrame2.TextRange.Font.Reflection.Type = msoReflectionType5
```

The first three statements simply make the text easier to read. Adding a gradient to the shape and a reflection to the text gives the button a classy effect.

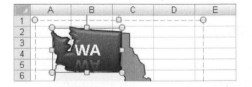

A shape has an OnAction property that allows you to link the shape to a macro. In principle, you should be able to assign the OnAction property to any shape—including one that is part of a group. But in fact, you can only use the OnAction property of a top-level shape. Fortunately, it is easy to ungroup and regroup the shapes.

9. Enter the following statements into the **Immediate** window.

```
s.Parent.Parent.Ungroup
s.OnAction = "StateButton"
s.DrawingObject.ShapeRange.Regroup
```

The Ungroup property of a shape works only if the shape contains grouped items. The Parent of the individual grouped shape is not a shape, but is a GroupShapes object. The parent of the grouped shapes is the shape you really need. There is no "grandparent" property, so you simply use the Parent property twice. Regroup is a method of a shape range, not of a shape—although it considers only the first item in the collection when deciding what to regroup. A shape does not have a ShapeRange property. But to get from a shape—such as the current Washington state shape—to its shape range, you can take a shortcut through the hidden DrawingObject property.

> **Tip** If you don't want to use the hidden DrawingObject property and you have given a name to the shape, you can access the shape range from the Shapes collection. For example, to regroup a shape named *Washington*, you can use the statement *ActiveSheet.Shapes.Range("Washington").Regroup*.

10. Press F5 to stop the **MakeMapButtons** macro, and then copy the statements from the **Immediate** window into it.

11. Delete the statement that selects the shape from the macro, and then select any cell on the worksheet (to deselect the map). Change the constants at the top to the following, and press F5 to test the macro.

```
myNumber = 3
myName = "Oregon"
myCaption = "OR"
myColor = 9
```

The macro should format the shape for Oregon without changing the selection.

See Also In the section titled "Creating Custom Functions" in Chapter 8, "Extend Excel and Visual Basic," you will learn how to create and use arguments for macros that you write, allowing you to make them even more reusable.

12. In Excel, try clicking the formatted states.

You should see the placeholder message.

Grouped shapes are almost as easy to work with as simple shapes. Assigning a macro to the OnAction property is one of the few reasons you need to explicitly ungroup a shape before you can use it. Notice also that by using explicit variables at the top of a macro to store values that can vary, you can make the macro easier to reuse: you just change the variable values all in one place.

See Also The MakeMapButtons macro was used to create the map interface for the Enterprise Information System (EIS) application included in the Appendix.

Selecting Multiple Items

Grouped shapes can be very convenient to work with from a macro. To create your own group in the user interface, you need to select multiple items. One way to select multiple items is to hold down the Ctrl key as you click. Another is to drag a rectangle around the objects. But when you drag a rectangle on a worksheet, you simply select a range of cells.

Excel has a special mode that allows you to drag a rectangle to select multiple objects. On the Home tab of the Ribbon, in the Editing Group, click the Find & Select arrow, and then click Select Objects. While Select Objects is turned on, clicking or dragging on the worksheet does not select cells.

If you forget to turn off Select Objects, the behavior of Excel can be disconcerting. If you use Select Objects frequently, you may want to add the button to the Quick Access Toolbar so that you always see the current state and can turn it on and off easily.

Exploring Chart Objects

Embedded charts are shapes in Excel. You add, manipulate, and delete Chart objects in much the same way you do rectangles. Chart objects, of course, have additional properties that are unique to charts. The macro recorder works for creating or modifying the basic structure of a chart, but it does not capture new advanced formatting. You can take advantage of the recorder where it is useful and use what you have learned with other shapes for enhanced chart formatting.

Create a Chart

The ChartData worksheet in the *Chapter06* workbook has enough data to create a simple chart. In this section, you start by recording a macro and then create your own macro to create the chart.

1. Activate the **ChartData** worksheet in the *Chapter06* workbook, and select cell **A1**.

2. Start recording a macro named rMakeChart.

3. On the **Insert** tab of the Ribbon, in the **Charts** group, click the **Column** arrow, and select the top-left chart from the list (**Clustered Column**).

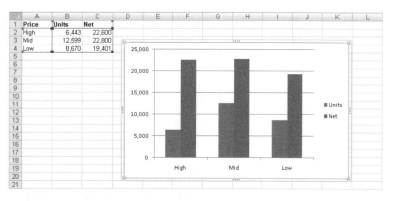

4. Stop the macro recorder, delete the chart, and then edit the recorded macro.

    The macro should look similar to the following:

    ```
    Sub rMakeChart()
        ActiveSheet.Shapes.AddChart.Select
        ActiveChart.SetSourceData Source:=Range("ChartData!$A$1:$C$4")
        ActiveChart.ChartType = xlColumnClustered
    End Sub
    ```

    Once you've recorded the macro to create a chart, you can create your own macro to create the type of chart you want.

5. In Excel, select cell **A1**.

6. In Visual Basic, create the following macro shell, and press F8 twice to initialize the variable.

```
Sub MakeChart()
    Dim myChart As Chart

End Sub
```

7. In the **Immediate** window, type **Set myChart = ActiveSheet.Shapes.AddChart.Chart** and press Enter.

This creates a default chart using data from the current region of the active cell. If the active cell is in the correct data region, you don't need the SetSourceData method.

8. Type **myChart.ChartType = xlCylinderColStacked** and press Enter.

After you type the equal sign, the Auto List displays the entire list of possible chart types, so you can just select the one you want. However, the row and column orientation, is not right: it doesn't make sense to stack dollars on top of units.

9. Type **myChart.PlotBy = xlRows** and press Enter to make the column headings into the category labels.

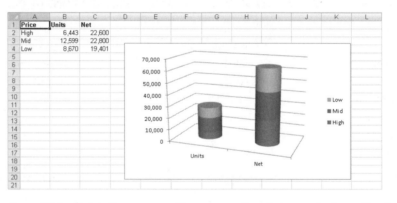

10. Press F5 to finish the macro. Then copy the statements from the **Immediate** window into the **CreateChart** macro, and press F8 to step through the macro to test it.

Here's what your finished macro looks like:

```
Sub MakeChart()
    Dim myChart As Chart
    Set myChart = ActiveSheet.Shapes.AddChart.Chart
    myChart.ChartType = xlCylinderColStacked
    myChart.PlotBy = xlRows
End Sub
```

Creating a new chart on a worksheet—without going through the recorder's selection process—is not difficult, but you must remember to use the AddChart method of the Shapes collection, and then explicitly reference the Chart from the resulting Shape object.

The Current Selection and Charts

With most shapes, it's easy to refer to an object in the Shapes collection but harder to refer to the currently selected object. (In the section titled "Reference a Selected Shape" earlier in this chapter, you learned how to refer to a selected shape.) With charts, you have the opposite issue. When you click a chart, you don't actually select the chart, or even the old-style ChartObject drawing object that contains it. Rather, you select one of the objects within the chart. Regardless of what is selected within the chart, the ActiveChart property returns the Chart object. But from a macro, you often want to manipulate an object without having to select it first.

To get to the chart without first selecting it, you need to navigate to the Chart object. You can do that in one of two ways. One way is to use the old-style ChartObjects collection (which is what the recorder does). The other way is to use the new-style Shapes collection. Both object classes—ChartObject and Shapes—have a Chart property that returns the actual chart object you want. So, assuming that there's only one shape on the worksheet, you can assign either *ActiveSheet.ChartObjects(1).Chart* or *ActiveSheet.Shapes(1).Chart* to a variable declared as a Chart object.

One side effect of never selecting the chart's ChartObject or Shape directly is that it is virtually impossible to use the user interface to rename the active chart the way you can with other shapes. With most shapes, you simply select the object, type the name in the Name Box to the left of the Formula Bar, and press Enter. With a chart, that technique doesn't work. From a macro statement, however, you can give the name *My Chart* to the active chart by using the statement *ActiveChart.Parent.Name = "My Chart"*. This renames the shape so that you can then refer to it with the expression *ActiveSheet.Shapes("My Chart")*.

Synchronize Two Charts

The TwoCharts worksheet in the *Chapter06* workbook contains two charts that show total orders for two different regions. The one on the left is named *West* and the one on the right is named *East*.

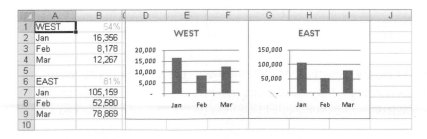

Based on a quick glance at the charts, you might conclude that the performance of the two regions is roughly equal. But that conclusion would be wrong. The East region's performance is substantially lower than the West region's, but Excel automatically scales the axes to fit the data. You want to create a macro that will change the value axis on the East chart to match the axis on the West chart.

1. Activate the **TwoCharts** sheet, and press F9 a couple of times.

   The data values for the charts come from formulas that automatically randomly adjust the scale so that the relative scale of the two charts will change. The macro should make the upper scale of both charts match the automatic scale of whichever one has bigger values.

2. Start recording a macro named **rSetChartAxis**. Right-click the value axis of the **West** chart, and click **Format Axis**. Under **Axis Options**, for the **Maximum**, click the **Fixed** option, and click the **Auto** option. Then turn off the recorder, and edit the macro.

   The macro should look something like this, although the maximum value might be different:

   ```
   Sub rSetChartAxis()
       ActiveSheet.ChartObjects("ChartWest").Activate
       ActiveChart.Axes(xlValue).Select
       ActiveChart.Axes(xlValue).MaximumScale = 20000
       ActiveChart.Axes(xlValue).MaximumScaleIsAuto = True
   End Sub
   ```

3. In Visual Basic, clear the **Immediate** window, create the following shell of a macro, and press F8 three times to initialize the variables and recalculate the chart values.

   ```
   Sub SynchronizeCharts
       Dim myWest As Axis
       Dim myEast As Axis
       Application.Calculate

   End Sub
   ```

   The macro uses the ChartObjects collection to get to a ChartObject of the active sheet. You can use the Shapes collection just as well. By using the code name for the active sheet—*Sheet3* in this case—you can get Auto List Help as you type the statements.

4. Clear the **Immediate** window, and then type the following two statements, pressing Enter after each.

   ```
   Set myWest = Sheet3.Shapes("ChartWest").Chart.Axes(xlValue)
   Set myEast = Sheet3.Shapes("ChartEast").Chart.Axes(xlValue)
   ```

   These statements assign the relevant axes to the object variables.

5. Type the following two statements to make sure that the value axis on each chart is set to automatic.

```
myWest.MaximumScaleIsAuto = True
myEast.MaximumScaleIsAuto = True
```

The MaximumScaleIsAuto property was in the recorded macro.

6. Type (on one line) **myMax = WorksheetFunction.Max(myWest.MaximumScale, myEast.MaximumScale)** and press Enter to calculate the larger of the two axis maximum values.

Most worksheet functions are available in a macro. The ones that are available are grouped under the WorksheetFunction object. Even if the maximum scale of an axis is set to automatic, you still can read the current value from the MaximumScale property.

7. Type the following two statements to set both axes to the same maximum value.

```
myEast.MaximumScale = myMax
myWest.MaximumScale = myMax
```

This sets the two charts to have the same maximum value. Setting the value of the MaximumScale property automatically changes the MaximumScaleIsAuto property to False.

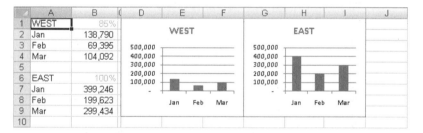

8. Press F5 to finish the macro. Then copy the contents of the **Immediate** window into the macro, and press F8 or F5 to test the macro.

9. In Excel, right-click the **West** chart, and click **Assign Macro**. Select **SynchronizeCharts** from the list, and click **OK**.

10. Press Esc to deselect the chart, and then click the chart multiple times to see the macro synchronize the charts at multiple scales.

The difference between the two regions is much more obvious now. Both charts share the same maximum scale, regardless of which one has larger values. You could add other synchronization tasks to this macro as well. For example, you could make the minimum value for each axis the same.

Format the Plot Area of a Chart

As with all the new formatting capabilities, you can't record a macro to learn how the formatting object model works. But with Excel 2007, charts use exactly the same formatting subobjects as shapes, so you can readily apply what you learned about formatting shapes to formatting charts. All you need to understand is how to navigate from the chart to the object you want to format. In this section, you'll gain that understanding by applying a gradient format to the plot area of the charts on the TwoCharts sheet.

1. Create the following macro shell, and press F8 twice to initialize the variables.

```
Sub FormatPlotArea()
    Dim myPlot As PlotArea
    Dim myFormat as FillFormat

End Sub
```

2. Clear the contents of the **Immediate** window, type
   Set myPlot = Sheet3.Shapes("ChartEast").Chart.PlotArea and press Enter.

   By using the code name for the active sheet, you get Auto List Help. If you want to make a macro work with any sheet, replace the code name with ActiveSheet after you have tested the macro. Notice that you use the Chart property to navigate from the shape to the chart that it contains. From there, Auto List helps you find all the component subobjects within a chart.

3. Type **Set myFormat = myPlot.Format.Fill** and press Enter.

   You declared the myFormat variable as a FillFormat object. This is exactly the same class that you used when creating a shape in the section titled "Add a Gradient-Filled Shape" earlier in this chapter. Once you have a reference to the FillFormat object, formatting a component within a chart is identical to working with any other shape. To get to the FillFormat object, you must first go through the Format property. There is actually a hidden Fill property for the plot area itself, but that returns an old-style ChartFillFormat object, and you don't want to use that one.

4. Type **myFormat.OneColorGradient msoGradientHorizontal, 2, 0** and press Enter.

   This statement applies a gradient format, the same as it would with a shape.

5. Type
   myFormat.GradientStops(2).Color.ObjectThemeColor = msoThemeColorAccent1
   and press Enter.

   This changes the color of the gradient to a standard theme color.

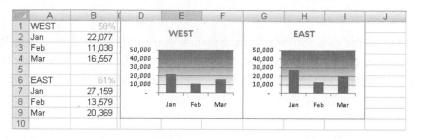

6. Press F5 to stop the macro. Then copy the contents of the **Immediate** window into the macro, change **West** to **East** in the obect name, and test the macro.

Even though you can't record the steps for formatting a chart, everything you learn about formatting a shape applies to formatting a chart, and vice versa.

The new shape formatting capabilities in Excel 2007 really are amazing. Even though you cannot use the macro recorder, you can learn to navigate your way around the objects so that you can format them. Fortunately, the formatting capabilities of the user interface and the object model correspond very closely, and you can sometimes even use the object model to discover new features that you never noticed in the user interface.

✕ CLOSE the *Chapter06.xlsm* workbook.

Key Points

- Use Help to find annotated lists of all the members for an object. Even if you're not on-line, there is offline help available on your computer.

- Add new items to the ColorStops collection of a cells gradient format to get multiple colors that are not available in the user interface.

- Take advantage of the Adjustments for shapes to multiply the number of available shapes available.

- When a shape contains grouped objects, you can use the GroupShapes collection to access the subordinate shapes without ungrouping and regrouping the shape.

- When the macro recorder doesn't show you the methods and properties for an object, look at the user interface for clues.

Chapter at a Glance

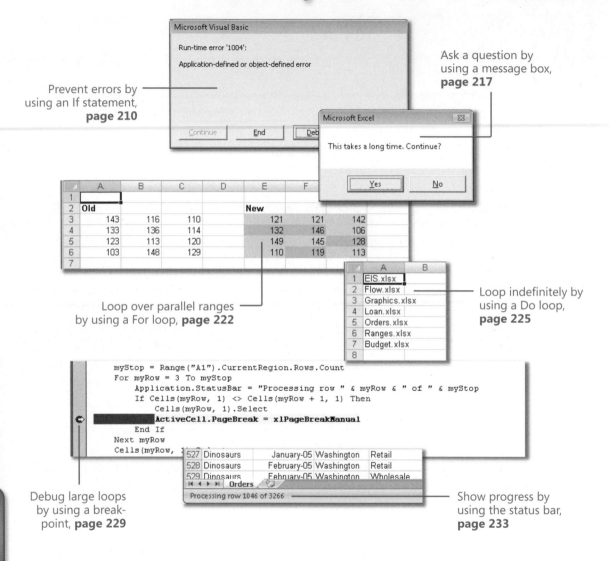

Prevent errors by using an If statement, **page 210**

Ask a question by using a message box, **page 217**

Loop over parallel ranges by using a For loop, **page 222**

Loop indefinitely by using a Do loop, **page 225**

Debug large loops by using a breakpoint, **page 229**

Show progress by using the status bar, **page 233**

7 Control Visual Basic

In this chapter, you will learn to:

✔ Use conditional statements.

✔ Create loops using three different blocks.

✔ Retrieve the names of files in a folder.

✔ Create breakpoints to debug long loops.

✔ Show progress while a macro executes a loop.

The first successful underwater tunnel ever built was begun in 1825. It is the Thames Tunnel. It was a financial disaster at the time, but amazingly it is still in use as part of the London Underground system. The genius behind the the tunnel's engineering was a man named Marc Brunel. Twenty years before launching the Thames Tunnel, Brunel made a name for himself by devising a way of inexpensively producing the pulley blocks needed to build ships for the British shipping industry. Brunel's technique later came to be known as an "assembly line," and Henry Ford turned the invention into an industry, supplying America with Model T cars that cost only $3,500 in today's dollars.

Repetition can have a dramatic effect on efficiency. Computer programs—including macros that you write—become more powerful when you add a multiplier effect. In this chapter, you'll learn how to add loops to your macros. And to make those loops more effective, you'll learn how to create conditional expressions that let the macro make decisions.

Important Before you complete this chapter, you need to install the practice files from the book's companion CD to their default locations. See "Using the Book's CD" on page xv for more information.

> **USE** the *Flow.xlsx* workbook, the *Flow.txt* text file, and the *Orders.xlsx* workbook. These practice files are located in the *Documents\MSP\ExcelVBA07SBS* folder. The *Flow* text file contains some initial macros that you will copy into your workbook and modify during this chapter. The initial macros are stored in a simple text file so that you can be certain there is no malicious code before you put the code into a trusted location.
>
> **BE SURE TO** save the *Flow.xlsx* workbook as a macro-enabled workbook named *Chapter07.xlsm* in the trusted location you created in Chapter 1.
>
> **OPEN** the *Flow* text file. Then open the *Chapter07* workbook, right-click any sheet tab, and click View Code to open the Microsoft Visual Basic editor. In the Visual Basic editor, from the Insert menu, click Module to create a new module for your macros, and then save the file. Arrange the Microsoft Office Excel 2007 and Visual Basic editor windows so that you can see both of them side by side.

Using Conditionals

Recorded macros are not very smart. They can repeat what you did when you recorded the macro, but they can't behave differently in different circumstances. They can't make decisions. The only way that you can make your macros "smart" is to add the decision-making ability yourself.

Make a Decision

The *Flow* text file contains a macro named *MoveRight*, which looks like this:

```
Sub MoveRight()
    ActiveCell.Offset(0, 1).Select
End Sub
```

This macro selects the cell to the right of the active cell and works fine—most of the time.

1. Copy the **MoveRight** macro from the text file, and paste it into a VBA module in the *Chapter07* workbook.

2. With cell **A1** selected in the workbook, activate the Visual Basic editor, click in the **MoveRight** macro, and press F5.

   The macro selects cell B1 in the workbook.

3. In Excel, press Ctrl+Right Arrow to select cell **XFD1**, the rightmost cell on the first row.

4. In the Visual Basic editor, press F5.

   Visual Basic displays an error.

You can't select the cell to the right of the rightmost cell. If your macro can't move to the right, you'd rather have it do nothing than display an error message.

5. In the error message box, click the **Debug** button to jump to the macro, and then click the **Reset** button to stop the macro.

6. Insert the statement If ActiveCell.Column < Columns.Count Then after the **Sub** statement. Indent the statement that changes the selection, and then insert the statement **End If** before the end of the macro.

Be sure to indent each statement in such a way as to make it clear which statement is governed by the If statement. Visual Basic doesn't require proper indentation, but indentation is critical to help you (or someone following after you) interpret the macro the same way that Visual Basic does.

The revised macro should look like this:

```
Sub MoveRight()
    If ActiveCell.Column < Columns.Count Then
        ActiveCell.Offset(0, 1).Select
    End If
End Sub
```

An If statement (a statement that begins with the word If) pairs with an End If statement. The group of statements from the If to the End If is called an If block.

Visual Basic looks at the expression immediately after the word *If* and determines whether it evaluates to True or False. This true-or-false expression is called a conditional expression. In a simple If block such as this example, if the value of the expression is True then Visual Basic executes all the statements between the If statement and the End If statement. If the expression is False, Visual Basic jumps directly to the End If statement. You must always put the word *Then* at the end of the If statement. In this case, the conditional expression tests for whether the current column is less than the total number of columns in the worksheet. You could also compare to a constant—such as 16384 or 2^14—but using object properties allows the macro to work with older versions of Excel (with 256 columns) and also with Excel 2007 (with 16384 columns).

7. Switch back to Excel, select cell **XFA1**, activate Visual Basic, and then press F5 four or five times.

The macro moves the active cell to the right until it gets to the last cell. After that it does nothing, precisely according to your instructions.

XEZ	XFA	XFB	XFC	XFD	

The macro recorder will never create an If block. This kind of decision is pure Visual Basic, and you must add it yourself. Fortunately, adding an If block is easy.

1. Figure out a question that has a "yes" or "no" answer. In this example, the question is, "Is the column number of the active cell less than 256?" You can turn this question into the true-or-false conditional expression in an If statement.

2. Put the word *If* in front of the conditional expression, and put the word *Then* after it.

3. Figure out how many statements you want to execute if the conditional expression returns a True value.

4. Put an *End If* statement after the last statement that you want controlled by the If block.

By using If blocks, you can add intelligence to your macros.

Make a Double Decision

Sometimes—such as when you're preventing an error—you want your macro to execute only if the conditional expression is True. Other times, you want the macro to behave one way if the expression is True and a different way if the condition is False.

For example, suppose that you want a macro that moves the active cell to the right, but only within the first five columns of the worksheet. When the active cell gets to the fifth column, you want it to move back to the first cell of the next row. In this case, you want the macro to carry out one action if the cell column is less than five (move to the right) and a different action if it isn't (move down and back). You can make the macro choose between two options by adding a second part to the If block.

1. Switch to the Visual Basic editor, and copy the **MoveRight** macro. Change the name of the new copy to FiveColumnWrap.

2. In the **FiveColumnWrap** macro, change the expression **Columns.Count** to 5 in the If statement.

3. Add the statement **Else** before the **End If** statement, and press Enter.

4. Press Tab, and add the statement **Cells(ActiveCell.Row + 1, 1).Select** after the **Else** statement.

The revised macro should look like this:

```
Sub FiveColumnWrap
    If ActiveCell.Column < 5 Then
        ActiveCell.Offset(0, 1).Select
    Else
        Cells(ActiveCell.Row + 1, 1).Select
    End If
End Sub
```

The Else statement simply tells Visual Basic which statement or statements to execute if the conditional expression is False.

Tip Several different statements would select the first cell of the next row. For example, here are a few alternatives:

```
Rows(ActiveCell.Row + 1).Cells(1).Select
```

```
ActiveCell.EntireRow.Cells(2, 1).Select
```

```
ActiveCell.Offset(1, 0).EntireRow.Cells(1).Select.
```

They all get from the same starting point (the ActiveCell) to the same destination. When you write macros, you often have multiple alternatives. You simply choose the one that is easiest to understand.

---

5. Press F5 repeatedly to execute the macro.

You see the selection move to the right and then scroll back to column A, much as a word processor wraps to the next line.

An If block can contain a single part, executing statements only when the conditional expression is True, or it can have two or more parts, executing one set of statements when the conditional expression is True and a different set when it's False.

Tip In most cases, If and Else are sufficient. There is also a way to use an If block to create multiple conditions by adding an ElseIf statement. To find out more about If blocks, highlight the word If in the macro and then press F1.

Ask Yourself a Question

In Chapter 2, "Make a Macro Do Complex Tasks," you created a macro that asked you to enter a date. You used the Visual Basic InputBox function to do that. The InputBox function is excellent for asking a question, but you must be careful about what happens when you click the Cancel button.

The *Flow* text file contains a macro named *TestInput* that prompts for the date. The code in this macro should look familiar.

```
Sub TestInput()
    Dim myDate As String
    myDate = InputBox("Enter Month in MMM-YYYY format")
    MsgBox "Continue the macro"
End Sub
```

The macro prompts for a date. It then displays a simple message box indicating that it's running the rest of the macro.

1. Copy the **TestInput** macro from the text file, and paste it into a module in the *Chapter07* workbook in the Visual Basic editor.

2. Click in the **TestInput** macro. Press F5 to run the macro, type Nov-2007 for the date, and then click **OK**.

   The message box appears, simulating the rest of the macro.

3. Click **OK** to close the message box.

4. Press F5 to run the macro again, but this time click **Cancel** when prompted to enter the date.

   The message box still appears, even though your normal expectation when you click Cancel is that you'll actually cancel what you started.

5. Click **OK** to close the message box.

You need a conditional expression where a True result means that you want the macro to continue. An appropriate question is, "Did the user enter anything in the box?" since clicking Cancel is the same as leaving the box empty: Whether you click Cancel or leave the box empty, the InputBox function returns an empty string (equivalent to two quotation marks with nothing between them). The operator <> (a less-than sign followed by a greater-than sign) means "not equal;" it's the opposite of an equal sign.

6. Before the **MsgBox** statement, enter the statement If myDate <> "" Then. Before the **End Sub** statement, enter End If. Indent the statement inside the **If** block.

The revised macro should look like this:

```
Sub TestInput()
    Dim myDate As String
    myDate = InputBox("Enter Month in MMM-YYYY format")
    If myDate <> "" Then
        MsgBox "Continue the macro"
    End If
End Sub
```

7. Press F5 and test to make sure the macro properly handles an input value. Type a date, and click **OK**.

The macro "continues."

8. Click **OK** to close the message box.

9. Now run the macro again, but this time click **Cancel** when prompted for a date.

The macro stops quietly.

Whenever you allow user input in a macro, you must be sure to check whether the user took the opportunity to cancel the macro entirely.

Test for a Valid Entry

Testing for an empty string checks to see whether the user clicked the Cancel button, but it does not help you determine whether the value entered into the box is valid. You can add a second test to check the input value.

1. Run the **TestInput** macro again, but this time type hippopotamus in the input box, and click **OK**.

The macro continues—the same as it would have if you had entered a date.

2. Click **OK** to close the message box.

   This behavior could be a problem. You need to check whether the box is empty, but you also need to check for a valid date. Visual Basic has an IsDate function that will tell you whether Visual Basic can interpret a value as a date. However, you want to check for a date only if the user didn't click Cancel. This calls for nested If blocks.

3. Change the macro to look like this:

```
Sub TestInput()
    Dim myDate As String
    myDate = InputBox("Enter Month in MMM-YYYY format")
    If myDate <> "" Then
        If IsDate(myDate) Then
            MsgBox "Continue the macro"
        Else
            MsgBox "You didn't enter a date"
        End If
    End If
End Sub
```

   Be sure to indent each statement in such a way as to make it clear which statement is governed by which If or Else statement.

4. Run the macro at least three times. Test it with a valid date, with an invalid entry, and by clicking **Cancel**.

   The valid and invalid entries should display the appropriate messages. Clicking Cancel or leaving the box empty should display no message.

Tip Visual Basic can interpret several different formats as dates. Try different date formats, such as 11/07, to see which ones Visual Basic interprets as dates.

Using the InputBox function can be a valuable way of making a macro useful across a wide range of circumstances. You must be careful, however, to check the result of the InputBox before you continue the macro. Typically, you need to check for three possibilities: valid input, invalid input, and Cancel. An If block—and sometimes a nested If block—can make your macro smart enough to respond to all the possible options.

Ask with a Message

The Visual Basic MsgBox function is handy for displaying simple messages. As its name implies, this function displays a message box. The MsgBox function can do much more than that, however. It can ask questions, too. Many times, when a macro asks a question, all it needs is a simple "yes" or "no" answer. The MsgBox function is perfect for yes-or-no questions.

Suppose that you have two macros. One is a long, slow macro named *PrintMonth*, and the other is a short, quick macro named *ProcessMonth*. You find that you often acciden-tally run the slow one when you intend to run the quick one. One solution might be to add a message box to the beginning of the slow macro that asks you to confirm that you intended to run the slow one.

The *Flow* text file includes a macro named *CheckRun*. You'll enhance this macro to see how to use a MsgBox function to ask a question. The macro looks like this before you start:

```
Sub CheckRun()
    MsgBox "This takes a long time. Continue?"
    MsgBox "Continue with slow macro..."
End Sub
```

1. Copy the **CheckRun** macro from the text file into a module in the *Chapter07* workbook.

2. Click in the **CheckRun** macro, and press F5 to run it. Click **OK** twice to close each message box.

   The first message box appears to ask a question, but it has only a single button. To ask a question, you must add more buttons.

3. Move the cursor to the end of the first **MsgBox** statement. Immediately after the closing quotation mark, type a comma.

As soon as you type the comma, Visual Basic displays the Quick Info for the MsgBox function. The first argument is named *Prompt*. That's the one in which you enter the message you want to display. The second argument is named *Buttons*. This is an enumerated list of values. The default value for Buttons is vbOKOnly, which is why you saw only a single OK button when you ran the macro before.

```
Sub CheckRun()
    MsgBox "This takes a long time. Continue?",|
    MsgBox(Prompt, [Buttons As VbMsgBoxStyle = vbOKOnly], [Title], [HelpFile], [Context]) As VbMsgBoxResult
End Sub
                                      ▣ vbApplicationModal
                                      ▣ vbCritical
                                      ▣ vbDefaultButton1
                                      ▣ vbDefaultButton2
                                      ▣ vbDefaultButton3
                                      ▣ vbDefaultButton4
```

Along with the Quick Info box, Visual Basic also displays the Auto List of possible values for the Buttons argument. You want the buttons to ask the question in terms of yes or no.

4. Scroll nearly to the bottom of the list, select **vbYesNo**, press Tab, and then press F5 to run the macro.

   The first message box now has two buttons.

   ```
   Microsoft Excel                    ☒

   This takes a long time. Continue?


        [   Yes   ]        No
   ```

5. Click **Yes** to close the first message box, and then click **OK** to close the second one.

   The message box asks a question, but it totally ignores your answer. You need to get the answer from the MsgBox function and use that answer to control the way the macro runs.

6. Type the statement Dim myCheck As VbMsgBoxResult at the beginning of the macro.

   When you know a variable will contain only the value from an enumerated list, you can use the name of the list when you declare the variable. When you later write a statement to test the value of the variable, Visual Basic will display the list of possible values for you.

7. At the beginning of the first **MsgBox** statement, type myCheck = and then put parentheses around the argument list of the **MsgBox** function.

The revised statement should look like this:

```
myCheck = MsgBox("This takes a long time. Continue?", vbYesNo)
```

> **Important** When you use the return value of a function such as MsgBox, you must put parentheses around the argument list. When you don't use the return value, you must not use parentheses.

8. Insert these three statements before the second **MsgBox** statement:

```
If myCheck = vbNo Then
    Exit Sub
End If
```

> **Important** When you create a conditional expression using the result of the MsgBox function, you must not check for True or False. MsgBox has many types of buttons it can display, so it has many types of answers. If you use vbYesNo for the Buttons argument, MsgBox will always return either vbYes or vbNo. Neither of these enumerated values equals False, so comparing the result to False would be the same as always clicking Yes. When you test for a value that comes from an enumerated list, always be sure to use the appropriate enumeration constant.

The Exit Sub statement causes Visual Basic to stop the current macro immediately. To avoid making your macros hard to understand, you should use Exit Sub sparingly. One good use for Exit Sub is when you cancel the macro at the beginning, as in this case. The finished macro should look like this:

```
Sub CheckRun()
    Dim myCheck As VbMsgBoxResult

    myCheck = MsgBox("This takes a long time. Continue?", vbYesNo)
    If myCheck = vbNo Then
        Exit Sub
    End If

    MsgBox "Continue with slow macro..."
End Sub
```

9. Test the macro. Run it and click **Yes**, and then run it and click **No**. Make sure the rest of the macro runs only when you click **Yes**.

A message box is a powerful tool for asking simple questions. The MsgBox function is also a good example of how to use parentheses around argument lists: use parentheses if you use the return value of the function; otherwise, don't use them.

Creating Loops

Long before Henry Ford, and even before Marc Brunel, the economist Adam Smith reasoned that in a single day, a single worker could make only one straight pin, but ten people could subdivide the work and create 48,000 pins in the same day—an almost 5,000-fold increase in productivity. Similarly, you can get amazing increases in productivity by converting a macro that runs once into one that runs thousands of times in a loop.

Loop Through a Collection by Using a For Each Loop

Excel allows you to protect a worksheet so that users can change only cells that are explicitly unlocked. You must, however, protect each sheet individually. Suppose that you have a workbook containing budgets for ten different departments and that you want to protect all the worksheets.

The *Flow* text file includes a macro named *ProtectSheets*. Here's what it looks like:

```
Sub ProtectSheets()
    Dim mySheet As Worksheet
    Set mySheet = Worksheets(1)
    mySheet.Select
    mySheet.Protect "Password", True, True, True
End Sub
```

This macro assigns a reference to the first worksheet to the mySheet variable, selects that sheet, and then protects it. (Selecting the sheet really isn't necessary, but it makes it easier to see what the macro is doing.) Now see how you can convert this macro to protect all the worksheets in the workbook.

1. Copy the **ProtectSheets** macro from the text file, and paste it into a VBA module in the *Chapter07* workbook.

2. Click in the **ProtectSheets** macro, and press F8 repeatedly to step through the macro. Make sure you understand everything that the original macro does.

3. In the third line, replace **Set** with **For Each**, replace the equal sign with **In**, and re-move the parentheses and the number between them.

4. Indent the two statements that begin with **mySheet**, add a new line, and then type the statement **Next mySheet**.

   The finished macro should look like this:

```
Sub ProtectSheets()
    Dim mySheet As Worksheet
    For Each mySheet In Worksheets
        mySheet.Select
```

```
        mySheet.Protect "Password", True, True, True
    Next mySheet
End Sub
```

The For Each statement acts just like Set: It assigns an object reference to a variable. But instead of assigning a single object to the variable, it assigns each item from a collection to the variable. Then, for each (get it?) object in the collection, Visual Basic executes all the statements down to the Next statement. (Technically, you don't need to put the variable name after Next. If you do use it, Visual Basic requires that it match the variable name after For Each. Always use the loop variable after Next so that Visual Basic can help you avoid creating bugs in your macros.) Statements beginning with For Each and ending with Next are called For Each blocks or For Each loops.

5. Press F8 repeatedly to step through the macro, watching as it works on each worksheet in turn.

6. Switch to Excel, and try typing a value into a cell on any worksheet. Afterwards, close the error message box that opens.

7. Create a new macro named UnprotectSheets that unprotects all the worksheets.

Try to write the macro without looking at the finished code that follows. Hint: You'll need to use the Unprotect method of the worksheet object, with a single argument that gives the password.

> **Tip** A For Each loop is a handy way of browsing collections in the Immediate window. However, in the Immediate window, everything you type must be on a single line. You can put multiple statements on a single line by separating the statements with colons. For example, here's what you'd type in the Immediate window to see the names of all the worksheets in the active workbook: *For Each x In Worksheets: ?x.Name: Next x.* (In the Immediate window, it's all right to use short, meaningless names for variables.)

Here's what the UnprotectSheets macro should look like:

```
Sub UnprotectSheets()
    Dim mySheet As Worksheet
    For Each mySheet In Worksheets
        mySheet.Select ' This statement is optional.
        mySheet.Unprotect "Password"
    Next mySheet
End Sub
```

8. Save the workbook, press F5 to run the **UnprotectSheets** macro, and then test it by changing a value on a worksheet.

Looping through a collection is almost as easy as assigning a single object to a variable. The only differences are that you use For Each instead of Set, you specify a collection to loop through, and you add a Next statement to end the loop.

Loop with a Counter by Using a For Loop

Sometimes you want to perform actions repeatedly but can't use a For Each loop. For example, a For Each loop can work through only a single collection. If you want to compare two parallel collections—such as two ranges—you can't use a For Each loop. In that situation, Visual Basic has another, more generalized way to loop: a For loop.

The Compare worksheet in the *Chapter07* workbook contains two named ranges. The one on the left is named *Old*, and the one on the right is named *New*. You can think of these as being an original forecast and a revised forecast. The cells in the Old range contain values. The cells in the New range contain a formula that will calculate a random number each time you press F9 to recalculate the workbook. (The formula in those cells is =ROUND(RAND()*50+100,0), which tells Excel to calculate a random number between 0 and 1, multiply it by 50, add 100, and round to the nearest whole number. Because the numbers in the New range are randomly generated, the ones you see will differ from the ones in this graphic.)

	A	B	C	D	E	F	G	H
1								
2	Old				New			
3	143	116	110		146	110	106	
4	133	136	114		146	116	137	
5	123	113	120		123	143	119	
6	103	148	129		112	134	108	
7								

The *Flow* text file contains a macro named *CompareCells*, which looks like this:

```
Sub CompareCells()
    Dim i As Integer
    Calculate
    If Range("New").Cells(i) > Range("Old").Cells(i) Then
        Range("New").Cells(i).Interior.Color = rgbLightGreen
    Else
        Range("New").Cells(i).Interior.Color = rgbLightSteelBlue
    End If
End Sub
```

The macro first executes the Calculate method, which calculates new values for all the cells in the New range. Then the macro compares only the last cell in the New range with the last cell in the Old range. If the New value for that one cell is greater than the Old value, the cell turns light green; otherwise, it turns light steel blue. The macro assigns the Count of cells in the range to the variable *i*, which is a simple integer.

See Also If you're not comfortable with If blocks, review the first half of this chapter. For more information about cell color, see the section titled "Format the Interior of a Range" in Chapter 4, "Explore Range Objects."

Now see how you can convert this macro to use a loop to compare and color all the cells in the New range.

1. Copy the **CompareCells** macro from the text file, and paste it into a VBA module in the *Chapter07* workbook.

2. Click in the **CompareCells** macro, and press F8 repeatedly to step through the macro. Make sure you understand everything the original macro does.

	A	B	C	D	E	F	G	H
1								
2	Old				New			
3	143	116	110		117	141	129	
4	133	136	114		136	116	138	
5	123	113	120		103	117	109	
6	103	148	129		137	135	121	
7								

3. In the statement that assigns the **Count** to the variable, insert the word **For** in front of the variable, and then insert **1 To** after the equal sign.

4. Type **Next i** before the **End Sub** statement, and indent all the statements between **For** and **Next**.

The finished macro should look like this:

```
Sub CompareCells()
    Dim i As Integer
    Calculate
    For i = 1 To Range("New").Cells.Count
        If Range("New").Cells(i) > Range("Old").Cells(i) Then
            Range("New").Cells(i).Interior.Color = rgbLightGreen
        Else
            Range("New").Cells(i).Interior.Color = rgbLightSteelBlue
        End If
    Next i
End Sub
```

The keyword *For* works just like a simple assignment statement. It assigns a number to the variable. (The For statement assigns a number to an integer variable, while the For Each statement assigns a reference to an object variable.) The variable that holds the number is called a loop counter. You specify the start value for the loop counter (in this case, 1) and the stop value (in this case, the total number of cells in the range).

The For loop assigns the start value to the loop counter, executes all the statements down to the Next statement, adds 1 to the loop counter, and checks the loop counter against the stop value. If the loop counter is greater than the stop value, the For loop jumps to just past the Next statement. If the loop counter is less than or equal to the stop value, the For loop does it all again.

5. Press F8 repeatedly to watch the macro work. Step through at least two or three loops, and then press F5 to finish the macro.

▲	A	B	C	D	E	F	G	H
1								
2	Old				New			
3	143	116	110		121	121	142	
4	133	136	114		132	146	106	
5	123	113	120		149	145	128	
6	103	148	129		110	119	113	
7								

In many cases, using a For Each loop is more convenient than using a For loop. However, a For loop is a more general tool: you can always use a For loop to reproduce the behavior of a For Each loop. For example, here's how you could write the ProtectSheets macro without using For Each:

```
Sub ForProtectSheets()
    Dim mySheet As Worksheet
    Dim i As Integer
    For i = 1 to Worksheets.Count
        Set mySheet = Worksheets(i)
        mySheet.Select
        mySheet.Protect "Password", True, True, True
    Next i
End Sub
```

> **Troubleshooting** If you run a macro that contains an infinite loop, stop the macro by pressing Ctrl+Break.

The For loop is a little more dangerous than a For Each loop because you have to be sure to get the start and stop values correct. If you have a stop value that is smaller than the start value, the loop will run forever—a condition known as an infinite loop. With a For Each loop, it is impossible to create an infinite loop.

Loop Indefinitely by Using a Do Loop

A For Each loop works through a collection. A For loop cycles through numbers from a starting point to an ending point. In some situations, however, neither of these options works.

For example, suppose that you want to retrieve the names of all the Excel workbooks in the current folder. Visual Basic has a function that tells you the names of files in a folder (or directory). The function is named *Dir*, after the old MS-DOS operating system command of the same name. The first time you use Dir, you give it an argument that tells which kind of files you want to look at. To retrieve the name of the first Excel workbook in the current directory, you use the statement *myFile = Dir("*.xlsx")*. To get the next file that matches the same pattern, you use Dir again, but without an argument. You must run Dir repeatedly because it returns only one file name at a time. When Visual Basic can't find another matching file, the Dir function returns an empty string.

So how do you create a macro that retrieves the names of all the Excel files in the current folder? The list of files in the directory isn't a collection, so you can't use a For Each loop. You can't use a For loop either because you don't know how many files you'll get until you're finished. Fortunately, Visual Basic has one more way of controlling a loop: a Do loop.

The ListFiles macro in the *Flow* text file retrieves the first two Excel files from the current directory and puts their names into the first two cells of the first column of the active worksheet. Here's the original macro:

```
Sub ListFiles()
    Dim myRow As Integer
    Dim myFile As String

    myRow = 1
    myFile = Dir("*.xls")
    Cells(myRow, 1) = myFile

    myRow = myRow + 1
    myFile = Dir
    Cells(myRow, 1) = myFile
End Sub
```

Aside from the variable declaration statements, this macro consists of two groups of three statements each. In each group, the macro assigns a row number to myRow, retrieves a file name using the Dir function, and then puts the file name into the appropriate cell. The first time the macro uses Dir, it specifies the pattern to match. The next time, the macro uses Dir without an argument so that it will retrieve the next matching file.

Now see how you can convert this macro to loop until it has found all the files in the folder.

1. Copy the **ListFiles** macro from the text file, and paste it into a VBA module in the *Chapter07* workbook.

2. In the *Chapter07* workbook, activate the **Files** worksheet.

3. Make sure the current folder is the one containing the practice files for this book. (Click the **Microsoft Office Button**, click **Open**, change to the correct folder, and then click **Cancel**.)

4. In the Visual Basic editor, click in the **ListFiles** macro, and press F8 repeatedly to step through the macro. (The names of the files your macro retrieves might differ from those in the graphics.) Make sure you understand the original macro.

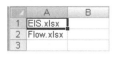

> **Tip** As you step through the macro, move the mouse pointer over a variable name to see the current value stored in that variable.

5. At the end of the first statement that contains a **Dir** function, insert a new line, and type `Do Until myFile = ""` (There is no space between the quotation marks.)

   This statement begins the loop. You begin the loop after the first Dir function because you use Dir with an argument only once.

6. At the end of the second statement that contains a **Dir** function, insert a new line, and type `Loop`.

   This statement ends the loop and sends Visual Basic back to the start of the loop to check if it's time to quit.

7. Delete the second **Cells(myRow, 1) = myFile** statement.

   You don't need this statement because the loop repeats the assignment statement as many times as needed.

8. Just before the **myRow = 1** statement, insert a line, and then enter the statement `Cells.Clear`.

   This ensures that the worksheet is empty in case you run the macro multiple times and some lists are shorter than others.

> **Tip** When you use a macro to write a list onto a worksheet, make sure there are no old lists left in the worksheet. You can use Cells.Clear to erase the worksheet, or use Worksheets.Add to create a new one.

9. Indent the three statements between the **Do** and **Loop** statements.

The revised macro should look like this:

```
Sub ListFiles()
    Dim myRow As Integer
    Dim myFile As String

    Cells.Clear
    myRow = 1
    myFile = Dir("*.xlsx")
    Do Until myFile = ""
        Cells(myRow, 1) = myFile

        myRow = myRow + 1
        myFile = Dir
    Loop
End Sub
```

The myFile = "" expression at the end of the Do Until statement is a conditional expression, precisely like one you'd use with an If statement. The conditional expression must be something that Visual Basic can interpret as either True or False. Visual Basic simply repeats the loop over and over until the conditional expression is True. Note that the condition may never be true, in which case the loop will never execute. For example, if there were no *.xlsx* files in the folder, the stop condition would be true the very first time it executes.

If you want to increment a number during the loop, you must enter a statement to do so. You must always be careful to cause something to happen during the loop that will allow the loop to end. In this case, you retrieve a new file name from the Dir function.

10. Press F8 repeatedly to watch the macro work. Step through at least two or three loops, and then press F5 to finish the macro.

	A	B
1	EIS.xlsx	
2	Flow.xlsx	
3	Graphics.xlsx	
4	Loan.xlsx	
5	Orders.xlsx	
6	Ranges.xlsx	
7	Budget.xlsx	
8		

> **Troubleshooting** If you run a macro that contains an infinite loop, stop the macro by pressing Ctrl+Break.

A Do loop is the most flexible of all the looping structures. Anything that you can do with a For loop or a For Each loop, you can do with a Do loop. If you had to be stranded on a desert island with only one loop structure, the Do loop would be the best one to have. For example, here is how you could write the ProtectSheets macro by using a Do loop.

```
Sub ProtectSheets()
    Dim mySheet As Worksheet
    Dim i As Integer
    i = 1
    Do Until i > Worksheets.Count
        Set mySheet = Worksheets(i)
        mySheet.Select
        mySheet.Protect "Password", True, True, True
        i = i + 1
    Loop
End Sub
```

The flexibility makes the Do loop a little more complicated than the others because you have to create and increment your own loop variable and provide your own condition for ending the loop. This makes a Do loop particularly vulnerable to becoming an infinite loop. For example, if you forgot to add the statement to retrieve a new file name, or if you had included the argument to the Dir function inside the loop (so that Dir would keep returning the first file name over and over), you'd have an infinite loop.

> **Tip** Do loops have several useful variations. You can loop until the conditional expression is True or while the expression is True. You can put the conditional expression at the top of the loop (in the Do statement) or at the bottom of the loop (in the Loop statement). To find out more about Do loop structures, select the word Do in the macro, and then press F1.

Managing Large Loops

A loop that executes only two or three times isn't much different from a program without a loop. It runs fast, and it's easy to step through to watch how each statement works. Once you start repeating a loop hundreds or thousands of times, however, you need some additional techniques to make sure the macro works the way you want it to.

Set a Breakpoint

The *Flow* text file includes a macro named *PrintOrders*. You can think of this macro as one that your predecessor wrote just before leaving the company. Or you can think of it as one that you almost finished three months ago. In either event, you have a macro that you don't completely understand and that doesn't work quite right.

The PrintOrders macro is supposed to print a copy of the entire *Orders* workbook, specifically one that is sorted by product Category. You give each Category manager the section of the report that shows orders only for that one category, so you need a new page every time the Category changes. Unfortunately, the macro doesn't do what it's supposed to. You need to find and fix the problem. Here's the macro as you first receive it:

```
Sub PrintOrders()
    Dim myRow As Long
    Dim myStop As Long
    Workbooks.Open FileName:="orders.xls"
    Columns("E:E").Cut
    Columns("A:A").Insert Shift:=xlToRight
    Range("A1").CurrentRegion.Sort Key1:="Category", _
        Order1:=xlAscending, Header:=xlYes
    myStop = Range("A1").CurrentRegion.Rows.Count
    For myRow = 3 To myStop
        If Cells(myRow, 1) <> Cells(myRow + 1, 1) Then
            Cells(myRow, 1).Select
            ActiveCell.PageBreak = xlPageBreakManual
        End If
    Next myRow
    Cells(myRow, 1).Select
    ActiveSheet.PageSetup.PrintTitleRows = "$1:$1"
    ActiveSheet.PrintPreview
    ActiveWorkbook.Close SaveChanges:=False
End Sub
```

The best approach is probably to start stepping through the macro.

1. Copy the **PrintOrders** macro from the text file, and paste it into a VBA module in the *Chapter07* workbook.

2. Make sure the current folder is the one containing the practice files for this book. (Click the **Office** Button, click **Open**, change to the correct folder, and then click **Cancel**.)

3. In the Visual Basic editor, click in the **PrintOrders** macro, and then press F8 three times to jump over the variable declarations and open the *Orders* workbook.

	A	B	C	D	E	F	G	H
1	Date	State	Channel	Price	Category	Units	Net	
2	January-05	Oregon	Wholesale	High	Art	670	$1,681.65	
3	January-05	Washington	Wholesale	High	Seattle	65	$178.75	
4	January-05	Washington	Wholesale	High	Art	50	$137.50	
5	January-05	Washington	Retail	High	Art	10	$55.00	

4. Press F8 three more times.

These statements move the Category field over to column A and then sort the list by Category.

	A	B	C	D	E	F	G	H
1	Category	Date	State	Channel	Price	Units	Net	
2	Art	January-05	Oregon	Wholesale	High	670	$1,681.65	
3	Art	January-05	Washington	Wholesale	High	50	$137.50	
4	Art	January-05	Washington	Retail	High	10	$55.00	
5	Art	January-05	Oregon	Wholesale	Mid	1,425	$2,738.24	
6	Art	January-05	Washington	Wholesale	Mid	75	$168.75	

5. Press F8 twice to assign a number to **myStop** and to start the loop. Hold the mouse pointer over **myStop** and then over **myRow** to see the values that were assigned.

The value of myStop is 3266, and the value of myRow is 3. Those values appear to be correct. The loop will execute from row 3 to row 3266.

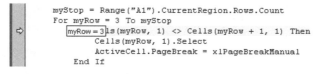

```
myStop = Range("A1").CurrentRegion.Rows.Count
For myRow = 3 To myStop
    myRow = 3 ls(myRow, 1) <> Cells(myRow + 1, 1) Then
        Cells(myRow, 1).Select
        ActiveCell.PageBreak = xlPageBreakManual
    End If
```

6. Press F8 several times.

Visual Basic keeps checking whether the cell in the current row matches the cell below it. How many rows are in the Art category? Pressing F8 repeatedly until the macro finds the last row in the category could take a long time. But if you just press F5 to run the rest of the macro, you can't watch what happens when the condition in the If statement is True. If only there were a way to skip over all the statements until the macro moves into the If block.

7. Click in the gray area to the left of the statement starting with **ActiveCell**.

A dark red circle appears in the margin, and the background of the statement changes to dark red. This is a breakpoint. When you set a breakpoint, the macro stops when it reaches the breakpoint statement.

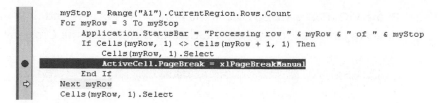

```
myStop = Range("A1").CurrentRegion.Rows.Count
For myRow = 3 To myStop
    Application.StatusBar = "Processing row " & myRow & " of " & myStop
    If Cells(myRow, 1) <> Cells(myRow + 1, 1) Then
        Cells(myRow, 1).Select
        ActiveCell.PageBreak = xlPageBreakManual
    End If
Next myRow
Cells(myRow, 1).Select
```

8. Press F5 to continue the macro.

   The macro stops at the breakpoint. When the macro reaches the breakpoint, the active cell is the first one that the If statement determined is different from the cell below it.

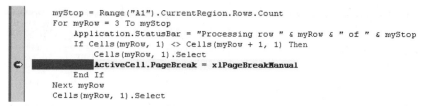

```
myStop = Range("A1").CurrentRegion.Rows.Count
For myRow = 3 To myStop
    Application.StatusBar = "Processing row " & myRow & " of " & myStop
    If Cells(myRow, 1) <> Cells(myRow + 1, 1) Then
        Cells(myRow, 1).Select
        ActiveCell.PageBreak = xlPageBreakManual
    End If
Next myRow
Cells(myRow, 1).Select
```

9. Press F8 to execute the statement that assigns a manual page break.

	A	B	C	D	E	F	G	H
517	Art	October-07	Nevada	Retail	Mid	75	$337.50	
518	Art	October-07	Oregon	Retail	Mid	50	$225.00	
519	Art	October-07	Oregon	Wholesale	Mid	50	$112.50	
520	Art	October-07	Utah	Retail	Mid	35	$157.50	
521	Art	October-07	Washington	Retail	Mid	22	$99.00	
522	Dinosaurs	January-05	Washington	Retail	Low	40	$140.00	

The page break appears above the row, not below the row. This is a problem. The macro shouldn't set the page break on the last cell of a Category; rather, it should set the break on the first cell of a Category. The If statement should check to see whether the cell is different than the one above it.

10. Change the plus sign (+) in the **If** statement to a minus sign (–).

    The revised statement should look like this:

    ```
    If Cells(myRow, 1) <> Cells(myRow - 1, 1) Then
    ```

11. Click the **Reset** button, press F5, and click **Yes** to reopen the *Orders* file. Then press F8 to watch the critical statement work—properly this time—as it assigns the page break after the Art category.

12. Click the red circle in the margin to turn off the breakpoint.

Setting a breakpoint is an invaluable tool for finding a problem in the middle of a long loop. In the following section, you'll learn an easy way to set a temporary breakpoint if you need to use it only once.

Set a Temporary Breakpoint

A breakpoint stops the macro each time the macro reaches the statement, and the breakpoint stays around until you remove it. What if you want to create a temporary breakpoint—one that you use only once? For example, suppose you're stepping through the middle of the PrintOrders macro. The code to assign a page break seems to be working properly. However, there are still some statements at the end of the macro that you'd like to step through.

1. If you're not already stepping through the macro, press F8 to start the macro.

2. Click anywhere in the **Cells(myRow, 1).Select** statement after the end of the loop to place the insertion point in that statement.

    You want a breakpoint on this statement, but one that you need to use only once.

3. On the **Debug** menu, click the **Run To Cursor** command.

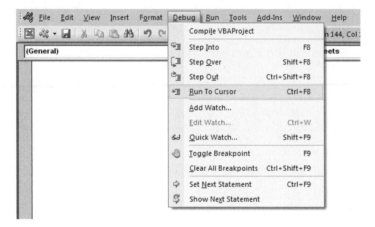

The macro runs through all the pages of the report and stops on the statement with the cursor.

4. Press F8 three times to scroll to the bottom of the list, set the print titles, and preview the report. Once the macro has stopped on a statement, you can continue stepping from there.

5. Review the report. Click **Next Page** repeatedly to get to page 10 to see the end of the Art category.

> **Troubleshooting** If you don't see the end of the Art category on page 10, simply click Next Page or Previous Page to locate the correct page. Your current printer driver might have placed the end of the category on a different page.

6. Close **Print Preview**, and press F8 twice more to finish the macro.

7. Save the *Chapter07* workbook.

Turning off a breakpoint is just as easy as turning one on: just click in the left margin of the Visual Basic editor window. But if turning a breakpoint on and off is still too much work, you can create a temporary one by running to the cursor.

Show Progress in a Loop

Even if the loop in a macro is working perfectly, you might get nervous about whether something has gone wrong if the macro takes a long time to execute. The best way to feel comfortable when a long loop is running (particularly if you're wondering whether you have time to get a cup of coffee) is to show the progress of the loop.

You can show progress with any kind of loop. But a For loop lends itself particularly well to showing progress because at any point in the loop, your macro can determine both the current value of the loop counter and also what its final value will be.

1. In the **PrintOrders** macro, immediately following the **For** statement, insert this statement:

```
Application.StatusBar = "Processing row " & myRow & " of " & myStop
```

The status bar at the bottom of the Excel window usually says "Ready." The StatusBar property of the Application object allows you to make the status bar say whatever you want. The best message is one that shows progress and also gives you an idea of how long the task will take.

The statement you added creates this message when it enters the loop the first time: "Processing row 3 of 3300." By using an ampersand (&) to join together message text with the numbers in the myRow and myStop variables, you can create a useful message. Just be careful to include an extra space before and after the numbers.

2. Press F5 to run the macro. Watch the status bar to see how the macro is progressing.

527	Dinosaurs	January-05	Washington	Retail
528	Dinosaurs	February-05	Washington	Retail
529	Dinosaurs	February-05	Washington	Wholesale

Orders

Processing row 1046 of 3266

3. Close the **Print Preview** screen to let the macro finish.

The status bar indicates that the macro is still running. The status bar doesn't automatically reset when your macro ends. To return control of the status bar to Excel, you must assign it a value of False.

4. After the Next statement, insert the statement:

```
Application.StatusBar = False
```

5. Run the macro again, close the **Print Preview** screen at the appropriate time, and then look at the status bar.

It's back to normal.

13			
14			
15			

Test / Compare / **Files**

Ready

6. Save the *Chapter07* workbook.

Visual Basic provides extremely powerful tools for repeating statements in a loop. Coupled with the decisions that you can make using If blocks, these tools let you create macros that are smart and very powerful.

CLOSE the *Chapter07.xlsm* workbook.

Key Points

- Use an If structure to make a decision. Add an Else clause if you need different actions for True and False conditions.

- When you use a MsgBox, use the Buttons argument to create explicit choices. When checking the result of a MsgBox, be sure to test against the proper constant.

- When you use an InputBox, be sure to think through all the possible types of input—valid, invalid, non-existent. Create an If structure to handle all the possible conditions.

- When you simply need to loop through a collection, a For Each is the easiest option.

- When you need a counter to help you as you work through a loop—for example, to keep two objects synchronized—use a For loop.

- When you need to loop for a while or until a condition is True, use a Do loop A Do loop is extremely flexible, but be careful that you don't create an infinite loop.

- Use permanent and temporary breakpoints when troubleshooting large macros or loops.

Chapter at a Glance

Function Arguments

Random

Midpoint	B3	=	1000
Range	C3	=	100
Round	D3	=	TRUE
		=	1016

No help available.

Round

Formula result = 958

Help on this function

Create a custom worksheet function **page 239**

Trap run-time errors, **page 255**

Microsoft Visual Basic

Run-time error '1004':

Cannot rename a sheet to the same name as another sheet, a referenced object library or a workbook referenced by Visual Basic.

Continue   End   Debug   Help

Repeat a command until an error is over, **page 254**

37				
38				

Report6 Report5 Report4 Report3 Repor

Ready

Create a customized error message, **page 258**

Microsoft Excel

Please notify Reed Jacobson of error 1004

'Bad File Name.xlsx' could not be found. Check the spelling of the file name, and verify that the file location is correct.

If you are trying to open the file from your list of most recently used files, make sure that the file has not been renamed, moved, or deleted.

OK

8 Extend Excel and Visual Basic

In this chapter, you will learn to:

✔ Create and use custom functions.

✔ Handle errors that occur while a macro is running.

A bacteria cell doesn't have a nucleus. A cell without a nucleus is called a *prokaryote*. Prokaryotes are very important. The first known fossils, dating from three and a half billion years ago, are all prokaryotes. They are also very small. In 1999, Heide Schulz discovered the prokaryote species *Thiomargarita namibiensis* whose individual organisms grow to be as large as 0.75 millimeter—about the size of the head of a fruit-fly. This is astonishingly large for a bacteria but doesn't seem very large compared to, say, a puppy.

A single-cell organism with a nucleus is called a eukaryote. Eukaryotes can become much larger than prokaryotes, because they have internal structure. Probably the largest single-celled organism is *Caulerpa taxifolia*. It is a type of seaweed—algae, really—that has been an uncontrollable weed in the Mediterranean Sea since 1984 and was discovered off the US coast near San Diego, California, in June 2000. One Caulerpa plant—consisting of a single cell—can grow to just under a meter in length. In the grand scheme of things, a single-celled Caulerpa is not very big, but it is orders of magnitude larger than a single-celled Thiomargarita. The difference is due to internal structure. The Caulerpa is a eukaryote with a nucleus, and the structure that comes with it. Structure enables functional size.

Recorded macros are like prokaryotes. The macro recorder puts everything you do into a single, unstructured procedure. And, like prokaryotes, single-procedure macros should be small. Large, sophisticated applications are more like eukaryotes. To get a large, sophisticated application to work properly, you must give it an internal structure—you must break it up into smaller procedures. And just as large, complex organisms need an immune system to deal with diseases, sophisticated applications need a mechanism for dealing with error conditions.

In this chapter, you'll learn how to create custom functions, use arguments in procedures, and handle errors—tools you'll need to create more powerful applications.

> **Important** Before you complete this chapter, you need to install the practice files from the book's companion CD to their default locations. See "Using the Book's CD" on page xv for more information.

> **USE** a new blank, macro-enabled workbook and the *Structure.txt* file. This practice file is located in the *Documents\MSP\ExcelVBA07SBS* folder. The *Structure* text file contains some initial macros that you will copy into your workbook and modify in the exercises in this chapter. The initial macros are stored in a simple text file so that you can be certain there is no malicious code before you put the code into a trusted location.
>
> **BE SURE TO** save the new macro-enabled workbook as *Chapter08.xlsm* in the trusted folder location that you created in Chapter 1.
>
> **OPEN** the *Chapter08.xlsm* workbook, and then rename Sheet1 to *TestFunction*.

Creating Custom Functions

Once you assign a value to a variable, you can use that value in any expression. For example, after you assign the number 25 to the variable myAge, the value of the conditional expression *myAge > 20* would be True because 25 is greater than 20. You use the variable as if it were the value that it contains.

A function is like a variable, except that a function is smarter. A function is a variable that figures out its own value whenever you use it. For example, Microsoft Visual Basic has a function named *Time*. When you use the conditional expression *Time > #8:00 PM#*, the Time function checks the time on your computer's clock to see whether it is later than 8:00 P.M.

Visual Basic has many built-in functions. Microsoft Office Excel 2007 also has many built-in functions. Those functions are useful, but they aren't customizable. Even if you found a Visual Basic function that's very close to what you need, you can't get inside of Visual Basic to change the way it works. You can, however, create a function of your own. Because your function can take advantage of any of the Excel or Visual Basic built-in functions, and because you can customize your function however you want, you get the same benefit you would get if you could make changes directly to the built-in functions.

Use a Custom Function from a Worksheet

Both Excel and Visual Basic have functions that return a random number between 0 and 1. The Excel function is named *RAND()*, and the Visual Basic function is named *Rnd*. You can use the Excel function in a worksheet cell, but you can use the Visual Basic function only in a macro.

You can't directly customize either the Visual Basic Rnd function or the Excel RAND() function, but you can create a custom random-number function—let's call it *Random*—that you can use from Excel. Why would you want to create your own random-number function when you could use Excel's built-in one? Because you want your Random function to behave just a little differently than Excel's. Once you create your own function, you can make it do whatever you want.

1. Enter the formula =Random() into cell **A3** on the **TestFunction** sheet.

    Excel displays the #NAME? error value. This is because the Random function doesn't exist yet.

2		
3	#NAME?	
4		
5		

2. Click the **Run Macro** button, type **Random** in the **Macro Name** box, and then click **Create**.

3. Double-click the word **Sub** at the beginning of the macro, and replace it with **Function**.

    The End Sub statement changes to End Function. You've now created a function. Next you need to tell Excel what to use as the value of the function.

    ```
    Function Random()

    End Function
    ```

4. Type the statement **Random = Rnd** as the body of the function.

    The revised function should look like this:

    ```
    Function Random()
        Random = Rnd
    End Function
    ```

    The way you tell a function what value to return is by assigning a value to the name of the function, as if the function name were a variable. This function simply takes the value of the Visual Basic Rnd function and assigns it to the Random function.

5. Switch back to Excel, select cell **A3**, and then click the **Insert Function** button next to the formula bar.

Excel displays the Function Arguments window, which explains that the Random function doesn't take any arguments.

Function Arguments

No help available.

This function takes no arguments.

Formula result = 0

Help on this function   OK   Cancel

6. Click **OK** to enter the random number into cell **A3**.

That's all there is to creating a simple worksheet function. In the Visual Basic editor, you replace the word *Sub* with the word *Function*, and then somewhere in the function, you assign a value to the function name. In Excel, you put the function name into a formula, followed by parentheses.

Add Arguments to a Custom Function

Suppose that in your worksheet, you want a formula that generates random whole numbers equal to 100 plus or minus 25. Or random whole numbers equal to 1000 plus or minus 100. The Excel RAND() function can't give you that kind of random number. Neither, for that matter, can yours, but because yours is a custom function, you can add capabilities to it by adding arguments.

When you add arguments to a function, you need to decide what would make good arguments. Good arguments 1) provide just the right amount of information, 2) are general enough to allow you to do a lot of things with the function, and 3) don't over-lap in a confusing way. One good set of arguments for your Random function would consist of the following three arguments: one to specify the midpoint, one to specify the plus or minus range, and one to specify whether or not to round the final number. You can add those arguments to your function.

1. In the Visual Basic editor, type **Midpoint, Range, Round** between the parentheses after the name of the function.

The statement that contains the function name and its arguments is called the *function declaration* statement. In the function declaration statement, you declare the name of the function and also the names of all the arguments. The revised function declaration statement should look like this:

```
Function Random(Midpoint, Range, Round)
```

These three words are arguments to the function. You can use them inside the function as variables that have been prefilled with values.

2. Change the statement that assigns a value to the function name to this:

```
Random = Rnd * (Range * 2) + (Midpoint - Range)
```

To understand the formula, assume that the desired range is 25 and the desired midpoint is 100. That means you want random numbers that equal 100 plus or minus 25, or, in other words, random numbers between 75 and 125. The total spread is 50, which is two times the range. The Visual Basic Rnd function returns a random number between 0 and 1. Multiplying Rnd by Range * 2 gives you a random number between 0 and 50. To get numbers between 75 and 125, you need to add 75. Subtracting Range from Midpoint gives you the 75 that you need.

3. Insert these three statements to round the number if requested:

```
If Round Then
    Random = CLng(Random)
End If
```

In Visual Basic, a Long is an integer that can include large numbers. The Visual Basic function CLng converts a number to a Long, rounding it along the way. You round the random number only if the value of the Round argument is True. (Because the value of the Round argument already equals True or False, you don't need to compare it to anything to get a conditional expression.) The complete function should look like this:

```
Function Random(Midpoint, Range, Round)
    Random = Rnd * (Range * 2) + (Midpoint - Range)
    If Round Then
        Random = CLng(Random)
    End If
End Function
```

> **Tip** To see other functions that convert between data types, in the Visual Basic editor, click CLng, press F1, and look for Type Conversion Functions.

4. In Excel, enter **100** into cell **B3**, **25** into cell **C3**, and **TRUE** into cell **D3**.

You'll use these values for the Midpoint, Range, and Round arguments of your function. The formula in cell C3 will turn into an error because it no longer matches the function declaration.

	A	B	C	D	E
1					
2					
3	#VALUE!	100	25	TRUE	
4					
5					

5. Select cell **A3**, and click the **Insert Function** button next to the formula bar.

The Function Arguments window appears, showing you the three new arguments of your function.

6. Click in the **Midpoint** box, and click cell **B3**. Click in the **Range** box, and click cell **C3**. Click in the **Round** box, and click cell **D3**. Then click **OK**.

Function Arguments		? X
Random		
Midpoint B3	📊	= 100
Range C3	📊	= 25
Round D3	📊	= TRUE
		= 113
No help available.		
	Midpoint	
Formula result = 103		
Help on this function	OK	Cancel

After adjusting the formula, cell A3 contains a random number between 75 and 125. You use arguments to pass values to a function.

7. Change cell **B3** to **1000** and cell **C3** to **100**.

The value of cell A3 changes to a random number between 900 and 1100. Whenever you change the value of a cell that the function refers to, the function calculates a new answer.

2				
3	1018	1000	100	TRUE
4				

Adding arguments is a way to make functions more flexible.

Make a Function Volatile

Most functions recalculate only when the value of a cell that feeds into the function changes. Other functions (such as Excel's RAND() function), are called *volatile functions* because they recalculate whenever any cell on the worksheet changes or whenever you press F9. You can make your function volatile so that it calculates a new random number whenever you press F9.

1. In Excel, press the F9 key repeatedly to see that the random number in cell **A3** doesn't change.

2. In the Visual Basic editor, insert this statement after the function declaration statement:

```
Application.Volatile True
```

3. Switch back to Excel, and press F9.

   The random number in cell A3 changes. Press F9 several times to verify that the function generates random numbers in the range specified by the arguments.

Most of the time, you don't want custom functions to be volatile. You want the function to recalculate only when a value that feeds into it changes. For those few cases in which you do want the formula to recalculate, just use the Application object's Volatile method with True as an argument.

Make Arguments Optional

The only problem with your new enhanced Random function is that it's now more complicated to use in those simple cases in which you don't need the new arguments. If you type =*Random()* in a cell without the arguments, Excel displays the #VALUE! error value. To avoid this error, you can tell Visual Basic that you want the arguments to be optional. Then you specify default values to use if an argument isn't supplied.

1. In the Visual Basic editor, type the word Optional in front of each of the three argument names. (If you want, you can insert a line continuation character to split the statement onto two lines.)

   The revised statement should look like this:

```
Function Random(Optional Midpoint, _
    Optional Range, Optional Round)
```

   You don't have to make all the arguments optional, but once you make one argument optional, all the arguments that follow it must be optional as well. In other words, you place optional arguments at the end of the argument list.

2. In the Visual Basic editor, type = 0.5 after the word *Midpoint*, = 0.5 after the word *Range*, and = False after the word *Round*. Break the statement into two lines after the first comma.

   The resulting statement should look like this:

```
Function Random(Optional Midpoint = 0.5, _
    Optional Range = 0.5, Optional Round = False)
```

   You can specify a default value for any optional argument. You assign the default value to the argument name in the same way you would assign a value to a variable—by using a simple equal sign.

3. In Excel, enter =Random() into cell **A4**.

   A random number between 0 and 1 appears.

4. Delete any formulas in the worksheet that include the Random function (cells **A3** and **A4**) so that you can step through other macros later in the chapter without stepping through the Random function.

Optional arguments allow you to add powerful features to a function while keeping it easy to use in cases in which you don't need the extra features. To make an argument optional, add the word *Optional* before the argument name. To add a default value for an optional argument, assign the value to the argument name the same way you would if it were a variable.

Use a Custom Function from a Macro

You can use a custom function from a macro just as easily as you can use it from a worksheet cell.

1. In the Visual Basic editor, type **Sub TestRandom** at the bottom of the module, and then press Enter to start creating a macro.

2. Type **MsgBox** and a space.

   Visual Basic displays the Quick Info box with the arguments for MsgBox.

3. Press Ctrl+Spacebar to show the list of global methods and properties, and then press the R key to scroll down to the words that begin with the letter *R*.

```
Sub TestRandom()
    MsgBox R
End  MsgB  ⬡ Random
            ⬡ Randomize
            ⬡ Range
            ⬡ Rate
            ⬡ Replace
            ⬡ Reset
            ⬡ RGB
```

   Your Random function is automatically included in the list. Your function has the icon for a method next to it. Excel methods are simply functions built into Excel. You create new global methods by writing new functions.

4. Press the Tab key to insert the function name into the statement, and then type an opening parenthesis to begin the argument list.

Visual Basic displays the Quick Info box with the arguments for your custom function. The Quick Info box even shows the default values for the optional arguments.

```
Sub TestRandom()
    MsgBox Random(
End Sub       Random([Midpoint = 0.5], [Range = 0.5], [Round = False])
```

5. Type 200, 5, True as the list of arguments, and then type a closing parenthesis.

6. Press F5 to run the macro, and click **OK** when your random number appears.

```
Microsoft Excel    [x]

200

      [   OK   ]
```

A function is a procedure like a Sub procedure, except that it returns a value that you can use either in a cell in Excel or from a macro.

> **Important** A function used in a worksheet cell can include only those actions that can be executed while Excel is recalculating a worksheet. (Remember that some cells might even recalculate more than once.) Actions such as opening files or displaying message boxes can be included in functions that are called from macros, but if you include them in a function that's called from a worksheet, the function simply returns the #VALUE! error value.

Handling Errors

Believe it or not, computer programs don't always work perfectly. Every now and then, you might actually write a macro that doesn't quite do what you want. These errors come in several types.

Syntax Errors

These are mistakes such as using an opening quotation mark and forgetting to type the closing quotation mark. When you type a statement in a procedure, the Visual Basic editor checks the statement for syntax errors as soon as you leave the statement.

Compiler Errors

Some mistakes can't be detected on a single-line basis. For example, you might start a For Each loop but forget to put a Next statement at the end. The first time you try to run a procedure, Visual Basic translates that procedure (along with all the other procedures in the module) into internal computer language. Translating to computer language is called *compiling*, and errors that Visual Basic detects while translating are called *compiler errors*. Syntax errors and compiler errors are usually easy to find and fix.

> **Tip** Visual Basic can check for spelling errors when you use variables. On the Visual Basic Tools menu, click the Options command, select the Require Variable Declaration check box, and then click OK. After you do this, Visual Basic adds the statement *Option Explicit* to any new module that you create. When Option Explicit appears at the top of a module, Visual Basic displays a compiler error any time you use a variable that you didn't explicitly declare.

Logic Errors

The computer can never detect some mistakes. For example, if you mean to change a workbook caption to My Workbook, but you accidentally spell the caption My Werkbook, the computer will never complain. Or if you compare the new values with the wrong copy of the old values, the computer won't find the error for you. You can toggle breakpoints, step through the procedures, and watch values, but you still have to find the problem on your own.

Run-Time Errors

Sometimes a statement in a procedure works under some conditions but fails under others. For example, you might have a statement that deletes a file on your hard disk. As long as the file exists and can be deleted, the statement works. However, if the file doesn't exist, Visual Basic doesn't know what else to do but quit with an error message. These errors can't be detected until you run the procedure, so they're called *run-time errors*. Some run-time errors indicate problems. Other run-time errors are situations that you can anticipate and program Visual Basic to deal with automatically. Visual Basic has tools that can help you deal with any kind of run-time error.

Ignore an Error

Suppose you want to create a macro that creates a temporary report worksheet. The macro should add a new worksheet named *Report* to the active workbook, replacing any existing worksheet named *Report*. The *Structure* text file contains the MakeReport macro, which creates and names the Report worksheet. Here's the original macro:

```
Sub MakeReport()
    Dim mySheet As Worksheet
    Set mySheet = Worksheets.Add
    mySheet.Name = "Report"
End Sub
```

The macro adds a worksheet, assigning a reference to the new worksheet to the mySheet variable. It then changes the Name property of the sheet.

1. Copy the **MakeReport** macro from the *Structure* text file, and paste it into a module in the *Chapter08* workbook.

2. Put the insertion point anywhere in the **MakeReport** macro, and then press F5 to run the macro.

   You should see a new worksheet named *Report* in the active workbook in Excel. The macro works fine. Or at least it seems to work fine. But what happens if you run the macro again?

3. Press F5 again to run the macro a second time.

   Visual Basic displays an error message informing you that you can't rename a sheet to the name of an existing sheet. The solution is simple: all you have to do is delete the old Report sheet before you rename the new one.

4. Click the **End** button to remove the error message, and then insert these two statements before the one that renames the worksheet:

```
Application.DisplayAlerts = False
Worksheets("Report").Delete
```

Setting DisplayAlerts to False turns off alert messages so that Excel doesn't ask whether you really want to delete the sheet.

5. Press F8 repeatedly to step through the macro.

> **Troubleshooting** If the macro steps through the Random function, stop the macro and clear any formulas in the workbook that use the Random function (most likely cells A3 and A4 of the TestFunction worksheet). If the macro already deleted the Report worksheet, continue with Step 7 below.

The macro creates a new worksheet, deletes the old Report worksheet, and then renames the new worksheet. Once again, the macro works fine. Or at least it seems to work fine. But what happens if there's no Report worksheet in the workbook?

6. Switch to Excel, delete the **Report** worksheet, switch back to the Visual Basic editor, and press F5 to run the macro.

Once again, you get an error message, this time informing you that the subscript is out of range. In other words, there's no item named *Report* in the Worksheets collection.

The interesting thing about this error is that you really don't care. You were just going to delete the worksheet anyway. If it already doesn't exist, so much the better.

7. Click the **End** button to clear the error message, and then insert this statement above the one that deletes the worksheet:

```
On Error Resume Next
```

This statement tells Visual Basic to ignore any run-time errors and simply continue with the next statement.

8. Press F5 to test the macro. Then test it again to see what happens when the Report worksheet exists.

Finally the macro seems to work properly. Some errors deserve to be ignored.

Ignore an Error Safely by Using a Subroutine

When you use an On Error Resume Next statement, Visual Basic ignores all run-time errors until you turn error checking back on or until Visual Basic gets to an End Sub or End Function statement. When you tell Visual Basic to ignore errors, you should be careful that you don't ignore errors you didn't mean to ignore.

1. In the **MakeReport** macro that you created in the previous section, remove the quotation marks from around the word *"Report"* in the statement that gives the worksheet a new name.

Removing these quotation marks creates a run-time error. The revised, erroneous statement should now look like this:

```
mySheet.Name = Report
```

> **Troubleshooting** If the statement *Option Explicit* appears at the top of the module, delete it.

2. Press F5 to test the macro.

The macro appears to run just fine, but you don't have a Report worksheet when it's finished. Visual Basic interpreted the word *Report* without the quotation marks as a new (empty) variable, and was unable to assign that empty name to the worksheet. Unfortunately, because you told Visual Basic to ignore errors, it didn't even warn you of the problem. (Of course, if you had inserted Option Explicit at the top of the module, Visual Basic would have complained about using an undefined variable.)

The best way to ignore errors for just one or two statements is to put the statements into a Sub procedure of their own. When Visual Basic gets to an *End Sub* or *End Function* statement, it cancels the effect of the *On Error Resume Next* statement.

3. Create a new macro named DeleteSheet.

4. Move the three statements that delete the worksheet into the **DeleteSheet** macro.

The new procedure should look like this:

```
Sub DeleteSheet()
    Application.DisplayAlerts = False
    On Error Resume Next
    Worksheets("Report").Delete
End Sub
```

The *On Error Resume Next* statement loses its effect at the *End Sub* statement, so you ignore a possible error only in the single Delete statement.

> **Important** In general, you can think of a *macro* as anything you can run from the Macros dialog box and use the more general term *procedure* for anything you have to run from code.

You never want to run the DeleteSheet procedure from the Macros dialog box. Rather, you should always call it from within another procedure—much like a custom function. To keep it out of the Macros dialog box, you can make it *private*.

5. Insert the word Private in front of Sub DeleteSheet(). Then move the insertion point outside of any macro and press F5 to verify that it no longer appears in the list.

6. In the **MakeReport** macro, type **DeleteSheet** where the three statements had been.

   The revised MakeReport macro (still containing the error) should look like this:

```
Sub MakeReport()
    Dim mySheet As Worksheet
    Set mySheet = Worksheets.Add
    DeleteSheet
    mySheet.Name = Report
End Sub
```

   The MakeReport macro no longer contains an *On Error Resume Next* statement, so Visual Basic should be able to alert you to the error. The DeleteSheet procedure is now a subroutine.

7. Press F5 to run the macro, and click the **End** button to close the error box.

8. Replace the quotation marks around the sheet name in the last line of the
    MakeReport macro, and test the macro when the Report worksheet exists as well
    as when it doesn't.

    This time, the macro really does work properly. It ignores the error you want to
    ignore while still warning you of other, inadvertent errors.

Add Arguments to Generalize a Subroutine

The DeleteSheet procedure that you created in the previous section quietly deletes the
Report worksheet if it happens to exist. Unfortunately, it deletes only the Report worksheet. What if you sometimes need to delete a sheet named *Report* and other times need
to delete a sheet named *Analysis*? This DeleteSheet procedure has too much potential
to limit it to deleting only one specific sheet. You can add an argument to generalize
the DeleteSheet procedure, in much the same way that you added an argument to the
Random function earlier in this chapter.

1. Type SheetName as an argument name between the parentheses after the
    DeleteSheet procedure name.

2. Replace "**Report**" with SheetName in the body of the **DeleteSheet** procedure.
    (SheetName shouldn't have quotation marks around it.)

3. In the **MakeReport** macro, type "Report" after **DeleteSheet**.

    Here's what the two revised procedures should look like:

    ```
    Sub MakeReport()
        Dim mySheet As Worksheet
        Set mySheet = Worksheets.Add
        DeleteSheet "Report"
        mySheet.Name = "Report"
    End Sub

    Private Sub DeleteSheet(SheetName)
        Application.DisplayAlerts = False
        On Error Resume Next
        Worksheets(SheetName).Delete
    End Sub
    ```

    The DeleteSheet procedure now knows absolutely nothing about the name of the
    sheet it will delete. It will simply delete whatever sheet it's given, without asking any
    questions and without complaining if it discovers its services aren't really needed.

4. Press F5 to test the **MakeReport** macro.

5. Create a new macro named MakeAnalysis. Make it an exact copy of the
    MakeReport macro, except have it create a sheet named *Analysis*.

The macro should look like this:

```
Sub MakeAnalysis()
    Dim mySheet As Worksheet
    Set mySheet = Worksheets.Add
    DeleteSheet "Analysis"
    mySheet.Name = "Analysis"
End Sub
```

6. Test the **MakeAnalysis** macro.

The DeleteSheet procedure now not only avoids the inconveniences associated with deleting a worksheet but is also a generalized tool—an enhancement to the built-in capabilities of Excel—that you can use from any macro you want.

> **Tip** When you add arguments to a Sub procedure, it no longer appears in the Run Macro dialog box, because there is no way to pass arguments to the procedure from the dialog box.

Check for an Error

When you use the *On Error Resume Next* statement in a macro, Visual Basic allows you to do more than merely ignore the error. Visual Basic contains a special debugging object named *Err*. The Err object has properties that you can check to see whether an error has occurred and, if so, what the error is.

Suppose that you want to create a Report worksheet but you don't want to delete any existing Report sheets. Instead, you want to add a suffix to the worksheet name, much as Excel does when you add a new worksheet. The *Structure* text file includes a macro named *MakeNextReport*. This macro creates a sheet named *Report1*. Here's the original MakeNextReport macro:

```
Sub MakeNextReport()
    Dim mySheet As Worksheet
    Dim myBase As String
    Dim mySuffix As Integer

    Set mySheet = Worksheets.Add
    myBase = "Report"
    mySuffix = 1

    On Error Resume Next
    mySheet.Name = myBase & mySuffix
End Sub
```

This macro creates a new worksheet and then tries to name it using Report as the base name and 1 as the suffix. The *On Error Resume Next* statement tells Visual Basic not to stop if Excel is unable to rename the sheet.

1. Copy the **MakeNextReport** macro from the *Structure* text file into a module in the *Chapter08* workbook. Then press F8 repeatedly to watch the macro work.

   The macro should rename the new worksheet properly.

2. Step through the macro a second time.

   The second time, the macro quietly fails, leaving the new sheet with the wrong name.

   It would be nice if this macro were smart enough to increment the suffix if the initial rename fails. The Err object—which watches errors even though the macro is ignoring them—has a Number property that is the key to knowing whether a statement failed.

3. Add the following statements immediately before the **End Sub** statement:

```
If Err.Number <> 0 Then
    mySuffix = mySuffix + 1
    mySheet.Name = myBase & mySuffix
End If
```

   The If statement checks to see whether the error number is something other than 0. A nonzero error number indicates that a statement failed. If a statement failed—that is, if the statement that attempted to rename the sheet failed—the macro increments the suffix and tries again.

4. Step through the macro.

   The code detects the failed rename and tries again, successfully renaming the sheet to Report2.

5. Press F5 to run the macro again.

   It silently fails because the error code executes only once.

Loop Until an Error Goes Away

It would be nice if this macro were smart enough to keep incrementing the suffix until it finds one that works. That sounds like a job for a loop structure, and since you can't know when the loop begins or how many times you'll have to repeat the loop, you should use a Do loop.

See Also For more information about Do loops, see the section titled "Loop Indefinitely by Using a Do Loop" in Chapter 7, "Control Visual Basic."

1. Replace the word **If** with **Do Until**, remove the word **Then** at the end of the statement, and change the not-equal sign (<>) to an equal sign (=). Then change **End If** to **Loop**.

    The last few lines of the macro should look like this:

    ```
    On Error Resume Next
    mySheet.Name = myBase & mySuffix
    Do Until Err.Number = 0
        mySuffix = mySuffix + 1
        mySheet.Name = myBase & mySuffix
    Loop
    ```

    The Do loop checks to see whether the rename occurred successfully. If it didn't, the loop increments the suffix, tries the rename again, and checks again until there is no error—at least, that's what you want it to do.

    > **Troubleshooting** Be sure to step through the macro, because the macro currently has an infinite loop. If you do run the macro, press Esc to stop the loop. You may need to press Esc more than once.

2. Press F8 repeatedly to step through the macro.

    The first time the macro tries to name the report sheet, it fails because Report1 already exists. As a result, the macro proceeds into the loop. At the end of the loop, the macro tries again to rename the sheet but fails again because Report2 already exists. So the macro reenters the loop a second time. At the end of the loop, the macro tries a third time to rename the sheet. This time it renames the sheet properly.

3. Keep stepping through the macro.

    Something is wrong. The macro goes into the loop again, renaming the sheet as Report4 and then as Report5. This renaming could go on forever.

The macro doesn't realize that the error is over. The value of Err.Number didn't automatically change back to 0 just because the macro successfully renamed the worksheet. You need to tell the macro that the error is no longer relevant.

4. Click the **Reset** button to stop the macro.

5. On the line immediately following the **Do** statement, type the statement Err.Clear.

Clear is the name of a method for the Err object. Clear resets the error number to 0 and makes Visual Basic forget that an error ever occurred.

> **Important** Some macro statements change the Err.Number value back to 0 when they complete successfully. Others don't. To be safe, you should clear the Err object immediately before the critical statement and then inspect the value of Err.Number right after that statement executes.

6. Press F5 to test the macro. Test it again. And again.

The macro is now able to create a new report sheet, incrementing as much as necessary—but no more!

Checking the value of Err.Number is meaningful only after you use an *On Error Resume Next* statement. Errors that occur above the *On Error Resume Next* statement cause Visual Basic to halt the macro with an error message box. Looking at the properties of the Err object is a good way to gain control over the way your macro handles errors.

Trap an Error

So far, you've seen three ways to handle a run-time error: 1) you can let Visual Basic display a standard error dialog box, 2) you can ignore the error altogether, or 3) you can check for a nonzero error number after each statement.

The first option—having Visual Basic display an error message—might not be a bad alternative if you're writing macros for yourself, but if you want to give a macro to someone else, you'll probably want more control over what the error message says. The second option—ignoring the error—is something you should do only in special circumstances. The third option—checking for a nonzero error value after every statement—can make your macros hard to read. Fortunately, there is a fourth option: Visual Basic can monitor the error value for you by trapping the error.

Suppose, for example, that you had a macro that opens, prints, and closes several work-books. It's possible that one of the workbooks might be missing when the macro runs. The *Structure* text file contains a CheckFiles macro that opens and closes several of the practice workbooks that came with this book. (In the interest of conserving trees, the macro doesn't actually print the workbooks.)

One of the workbook file names has been misspelled. Here's the original macro:

```
Sub CheckFiles()
    Workbooks.Open "Graphics"
    ActiveWorkbook.Close
    Workbooks.Open "Ranges"
    ActiveWorkbook.Close
    Workbooks.Open "Bad File Name"
    ActiveWorkbook.Close
    Workbooks.Open "Budget"
    ActiveWorkbook.Close
End Sub
```

Naturally, you can't tell which of the files won't be found until the macro actually runs.

1. In Excel, click the **Microsoft Office Button**, and click **Open**. Change to the folder containing the practice files for this book, and then click **Cancel**.

   This changes the current directory to the appropriate folder.

2. Copy the **CheckFiles** macro from the *Structure* text file into a module in the *Chapter08* workbook, and then press F5 to run the **CheckFiles** macro.

   You'll see the standard Visual Basic error message.

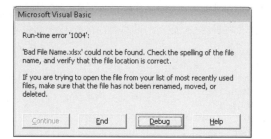

3. Click the **End** button to close the message box.

   You still need to add special code that Visual Basic will run whenever an error occurs.

4 Just before the **End Sub** statement at the end of the macro, type the statement **ErrorHandler:**.

   The statement *ErrorHandler:* is called a *label*. A label consists of a single word followed by a colon. (You can indent the label if you want, but you might prefer to keep it lined up with the Sub and End Sub statements because it behaves like an appendix to the macro.) A label must always end with a colon.

> **Tip** You can use any name you want for a label within the macro. You might want to always use the same name—such as ErrorHandler—as the error label in all your macros. That makes it easy to copy error-handling code from one macro to another.

5. Insert a line after the error-handler label, and type the statement **MsgBox Err.Number**.

   The statements below the label are the ones that the macro executes when it detects an error. These statements are called an *error handler*. The simplest error handler is a message box that displays the number of the error.

6. Immediately before the error-handler label, type the statement Exit Sub.

   You don't want the statements in the error handler to execute if the macro completes normally. If the macro gets to the Exit Sub statement, no error was detected.

> **Troubleshooting** Be sure to use the same label name in the On Error statement that you used for the error handler.

7. At the top of the macro, just under the **Sub** statement, type the statement On Error GoTo ErrorHandler.

   This statement tells Visual Basic that if it sees a run-time error, it should drop whatever it's doing and jump immediately to the label you specify. You don't put a colon after the label name here. You use a colon only when you create the actual label.

   The macro should look like this:

```
Sub CheckFiles()
    On Error GoTo ErrorHandler
    Workbooks.Open "Graphics"
    ActiveWorkbook.Close
    Workbooks.Open "Ranges"
    ActiveWorkbook.Close
    Workbooks.Open "Bad File Name"
    ActiveWorkbook.Close
    Workbooks.Open "Budget"
    ActiveWorkbook.Close
    Exit Sub
ErrorHandler:
    MsgBox Err.Number
End Sub
```

8. Press F5 to test the macro.

Visual Basic should display a simple message box showing only the message number.

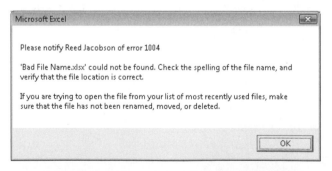

9. Click **OK** to close the message box.

You can make the message more elaborate. The Err object has a Description property that gives a longer text description of the error. That description is often a useful addition to an error message box. You can even add to the description with text of your own.

10. Delete the statement **MsgBox Err.Number**, and replace it with this statement:

```
MsgBox "Please notify Reed Jacobson of error " _
    & Err.Number & vbCrLf & vbCrLf _
    & Err.Description
```

You can string many pieces of text together to form an error message. Just put an ampersand between each piece. The word *vbCrLf* is a built-in Visual Basic constant that means "Carriage Return/Line Feed." Carriage Return/Line Feed is an archaic computer term for a new line and was often abbreviated as CRLF. You can put vbCrLf into a string anytime you want to force the message to go to a new line. (When you create your own macros, please substitute your name in the error message. Thanks.)

11. Press F5 to run the macro and see the more elaborate error message.

If you're creating an application for someone else to use and you don't want that person ever to see the Visual Basic default error dialog box, you should always include an error handler in every macro that the user launches directly. If you have some statements for which the error should be handled differently—either ignored or checked on a statement-by-statement basis—put those statements into a separate procedure and use an *On Error Resume Next* statement within that procedure. Visual Basic automatically restores the error handler when the procedure ends.

Errors are a frustrating but inevitable part of life when working with computers—that's especially the case when the human error factor compounds the likelihood of other types of errors. Of course, not all errors are equal. Some are serious, some are trivial, and some are even useful. It's fortunate that Visual Basic provides flexible tools for dealing with all kinds of errors.

CLOSE the *Chapter08.xlsm* workbook.

Key Points

- To create a new function that you can call from a worksheet, just change the word *Sub* to *Function*. You can also add arguments, the same as regular worksheet functions.

- Use the statement *Application.DisplayAlerts = False* to tell Excel not to display a warning message—for example, when deleting a worksheet.

- To simply ignore a possible error in one or two statements—for example, when deleting a file or worksheet—put the statements into a subroutine and add the statement *On Error Resume Next* at the top of the subroutine.

- Use the Err object—particularly the Number and Description properties—to find out information about an error that occurred in a macro statement.

- Use On Error GoTo along with the name of a label to force any errors to jump to a single error handler that begins with the specified label.

Chapter at a Glance

Enable the Developer tab in the Ribbon, **page 264**

Add a command button to a worksheet, **page 264**

Set properties for an ActiveX control, **page 265**

Insert | Design Mode | Properties | View Code | Run Dialog

Form Controls

ActiveX Controls

Command Button (ActiveX Control)

Insert a command button control.

Navigate a VBA project by using the Project Explorer, **page 272**

Properties

btnZoomIn CommandButton

Alphabetic	Categorized
(Name)	btnZoomIn
Accelerator	
AutoLoad	False
AutoSize	False
BackColor	☐ &H8000000F&
BackStyle	1 - fmBackStyleOpaque
Caption	Zoom In
Enabled	True
Font	Arial
ForeColor	■ &H80000012&
Height	25.5
Left	0
Locked	True
MouseIcon	(None)
MousePointer	0 - fmMousePointerDefault
Picture	(None)

Microsoft Visual Basic - Chapter09.xlsm - [MyNewSheet (Code)]

File Edit View Insert Format Debug Run Tools Add-Ins W

Project - VBAProject

- VBAProject (Chapter09.xlsm
  - Microsoft Excel Objects
    - MyNewSheet (Sheet1 (2)
    - Sheet1 (Sheet1)
    - Sheet2 (Sheet2)
    - Sheet3 (Sheet3)
    - ThisWorkbook
  - Modules
    - Module1

btnZoomIn

```
Private Sub btnZoomIn_Clic
    ZoomIn
End Sub

Private Sub btnZoomOut_Click()
    ZoomOut
End Sub

Private Sub btnZoomOut_MouseMove(ByVal Button As Inte
    If Shift = 1 Then
        ZoomIn
    ElseIf Shift = 2 Then
        ZoomOut
    End If
End Sub
```

Create macros that run when the user moves the mouse, **page 270**

Create macros that run when the user changes the selection, **page 274**

Properties - MyNewSheet

MyNewSheet Worksheet

Alphabetic	Categorized
(Name)	MyNewSheet
DisplayPageBreaks	False
DisplayRightToLeft	False
EnableAutoFilter	False
EnableCalculation	True
EnableFormatCond	True
EnableOutlining	False

Set properties for VBA project objects, **page 274**

	A	B	C	D	E	F	G	H
1	Zoom In							
2								
3	Zoom Out							
4								
5								
6								
7								
8								
9								
10								
11								

9 Launch Macros with Events

In this chapter, you will learn to:

✔ Create custom command buttons.

✔ Add additional event handlers to a command button.

✔ Create worksheet and workbook event handlers.

My grandmother used to embroider names on outfits for us with her sewing machine. She had a powerful old sewing machine, with lots of pulleys and levers and loops. When she changed the thread, she had to poke the new thread up, over, and through countless turns, spools, and guides, before even getting to the needle. I still don't know how she managed to embroider the names. She'd move levers and twist the fabric, and the names somehow appeared. She was very good, and the results were beautiful. She was a skilled professional.

Now even I can embroider names onto clothes. I flip the thread around a couple of guides and the sewing machine is threaded. I type in the name, select the lettering style, and push another button to embroider the name. The machine makes it easy to sew in all directions—I don't even have to turn the fabric. Anyone can use a sewing machine these days.

Macros can simplify your life. But you don't want the benefit of macros to be limited to skilled professionals such as yourself. If you add the buttons and controls and event handlers you'll learn about in this chapter and the chapters that follow, you can create powerful macros that anyone can use these days.

Important Before you complete this chapter, you need to install the practice files from the book's companion CD to their default locations. See "Using the Book's CD" on page xv for more information.

USE the *Events.txt* file. This practice file is located in the *Documents\MSP\ExcelVBA07SBS* folder. This file contains some initial macros that you will copy into your workbook and modify during this chapter. The initial macros are stored in a simple text file so that you can be certain there is no malicious code before you put the code into a trusted location.

BE SURE TO save a blank workbook as a macro-enabled workbook named *Chapter09.xlsm* in the trusted location you created in Chapter 1.

OPEN the *Events* text file.

Creating Custom Command Buttons

You might feel perfectly comfortable running a macro by pressing a shortcut key combination or even pressing F5 in the Microsoft Visual Basic editor. But if you're going to give a macro to somebody else, you want to make it as easy to run as possible. In Chapter 1, "Make a Macro Do Simple Tasks," you learned two ways of making macros easy to run: by assigning a shortcut key to a macro and by assigning a macro to a button on the Quick Access Toolbar. However, most people won't know the shortcut key, and sometimes you want something more noticeable than a button on the Quick Access Toolbar.

In this section, you'll learn how to launch a macro from a command button on a worksheet. This creates an easy and obvious way run a macro with just a simple click. But a command button can also respond to other actions. For example, you can make a macro run by simply moving the mouse over the button. Because a command button can respond to a complex set of events, it requires a whole new way of running a macro. This new approach uses what are called *event handler procedures*. Event handler procedures are special macros that are linked to an object such as a command button. Before you create command buttons, first set up some simple sample macros that the buttons can execute.

Try the ZoomIn and ZoomOut Macros

Each worksheet window in Excel has a Zoom level. You can change the level interactively.

1. Drag the **Zoom** control at the lower-right corner of the Excel window left and right to see the Zoom effect. When you're finished, leave the zoom at 100%.

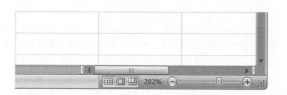

The *Events* text file contains two simple macros, ZoomIn and ZoomOut, that do the same thing as the Zoom control. They are macros that you'll run by using various events. Here are the macros:

```
Sub ZoomIn()
    Dim myZoom As Integer
    myZoom = ActiveWindow.Zoom + 10
    If myZoom <= 400 Then
        ActiveWindow.Zoom = myZoom
    End If
End Sub

Sub ZoomOut()
    Dim myZoom As Integer
    myZoom = ActiveWindow.Zoom - 10
    If myZoom >= 10 Then
        ActiveWindow.Zoom = myZoom
    End If
End Sub
```

Each macro retrieves the current value for the Zoom property of the active window. If it can change the value and stay within the acceptable limits (between 10 and 400, corresponding to the zoom percent limits in Excel), it changes the property; otherwise it does nothing.

2. Copy the two macros from the *Events* text file, and paste them into a new module in the macro-enabled *Chapter09* workbook.

3. On the **Visual Basic** toolbar, click in the **ZoomIn** macro, and press F5 a few times to see how the worksheet zooms in. Step through the macro to become comfortable with how it works.

4. Click in the **ZoomOut** macro. Press F5 as necessary to return the window to the normal zoom level.

These are "typical" macros. In this chapter, you'll learn new ways to run them. The first technique you'll learn is to run them by using command buttons.

Enable the Developer Tab in the Ribbon

As you know, the Ribbon has a special tab just for Developers. You can write, run, and edit macros just fine without using the Developer tab, but you need the Developer tab to add custom controls such as command buttons to a worksheet. If you haven't already done so, here's how to display the Developer tab.

Microsoft Office
Button

1. Click the **Microsoft Office Button**, and click **Excel Options**.

2. On the **Popular** page, select the **Show Developer tab in the Ribbon** check box.

3. Click **OK** to close the **Excel Options** dialog box, and then click the **Developer** tab.

The Code group of the tab contains commands for creating macros; all of these commands are also readily available in other places. The XML group is not related to macros at all. The Controls group has what you need for adding a command button to a worksheet.

Create a Custom Command Button

A command button is useful for running macros that relate to a specific worksheet. Command buttons are usually large and easy to click, with a label describing what the button does.

The Insert list on the Developer tab contains a number of controls that you can use on a worksheet or form. These controls are called *ActiveX controls*. These ActiveX controls are a special kind of drawing object that can carry out an action when you click them. The ActiveX control we'll work with in this chapter is the Command Button control.

See Also In Chapter 11, "Create a Custom Form," you'll use other ActiveX controls on a worksheet. In Chapter 10, "Use Dialog Box Controls on a Worksheet," you'll use ActiveX controls in a custom dialog box.

1. In the **Controls** group of the **Developer** tab, click the **Insert** arrow, and then click **Command Button** in the **ActiveX Controls** group.

2. Drag a rectangle on the worksheet from the upper-left corner of cell **A1** to the lower-right corner of cell **B2**.

   A command button appears on the worksheet. The white handles on the edges indicate that it is currently selected.

   Tip You can easily "snap" any drawing object to align with the corners of a cell by pressing the Alt key as you drag a rectangle for the object. You can move the edges of an existing drawing object to cell gridlines by holding down the Alt key as you move or resize the object.

   While the command button is selected, you can change its properties. In the same way that you can use Visual Basic to change the properties of an object in a macro, you can use the Properties window to change the properties of an object interactively.

3. In the **Controls** group of the Ribbon, click the **Properties** button.

   The Properties window appears. The box at the top shows you which object's properties are being displayed. In this case, it's CommandButton1, which is a CommandButton object.

   The Properties window shows various properties of the command button. One important property of the command button is its name, which appears as *(Name)* in the Properties window. (The parentheses make the Name property sort to the top of the list.) The Name property affects how you use the button in your macros. The name has to be something you could use for a macro name, which means you can't include spaces or other special characters.

4. Replace the default value of the **Name** property with **btnZoomIn**.

When naming controls, many people use three-letter prefixes to help identify what kind of control it is; in this case, *btn* stands for *button*.

Changing the name of the button doesn't change the label displayed on it. That's the function of the Caption property.

5. Replace the default value of the **Caption** property with **Zoom In**.

It is fine to include spaces in a caption. As soon as you change the Caption property, the caption on the button changes.

There's another property that you should set when you create a custom command button. It controls how the command button interacts with the active cell in Excel. Suppose cell B4 is the active cell when you click the command button. You'd normally expect cell B4 to be the active cell even after clicking the button (unless the button runs a macro that changes the active cell). But the default behavior of a command button is to remove the dark border around the active cell, making it impossible to see which cell is active.

6. Double-click the **TakeFocusOnClick** property to change its value to False.

TakeFocusOnClick is a complicated name for a simple property. Setting it to False simply means, "Leave the active cell alone when you click this button."

You've now created and customized the command button. All that's left is to link it to a macro and make it run.

Link a Command Button to a Macro

You don't assign a macro to a command button. Instead, you create a macro with a special name, in a special place, and the macro automatically links to the button. Fortunately, the Control group of the Developer tab has a button that will do all the work of naming the macro for you.

View Code

1. With the command button still selected, click the **View Code** button.

   The Visual Basic editor window appears with a new macro. The word *Private* before the macro name means that this macro won't appear in the Run Macro dialog box. The macro name is *btnZoomIn_Click*. The name is important. The part of the name that precedes the underscore matches the name of the command button. The part of the name that follows the underscore matches the name of the event that this macro will handle. In this example, the macro runs whenever you click the button. A macro linked to an event like this is called an *event handler*.

   > **Important** The word *procedure* is a technical synonym for a macro. Excel uses the word *macro* because *macro recorder* is less intimidating than *procedure recorder*. In general, this book uses *macro* to refer to the procedures that you can run from the Macro dialog box and *procedure* to refer to functions and event handlers.

   You could copy the code from the ZoomIn macro into the btnZoomIn_Click procedure, but it's easier simply to run that macro (since it already exists) from this one.

2. Type ZoomIn as the body of the procedure.

   The final procedure should look like this:

   ```
   Private Sub btnZoomIn_Click()
       ZoomIn
   End Sub
   ```

   You're now ready to try clicking the button.

3. Switch back to Excel, click in any cell in the worksheet to deselect the button, and then click the button.

   The procedure doesn't run. You simply reselected the button. You need some way of letting Excel know whether clicking an ActiveX control should run the event handler or simply select the control. You do that by controlling *design mode*. When Excel is in design mode, clicking a control selects it. When Excel isn't in design mode, it's in *run mode*, and clicking a control runs the event handler procedure.

Whenever you put an ActiveX control on a worksheet, Excel automatically switches to design mode. When Excel is in design mode, the Design Mode button on the Developer tab is highlighted.

4. Click the **Design Mode** button to turn off design mode.

   The selection handles disappear from the command button.

5. To try the **Zoom In** button, click it.

6. Click the **Design Mode** button to turn design mode back on, and click the command button.

The selection handles appear on the command button, but the code does not run.

ActiveX Controls and Forms Controls

The Insert button on the Developer tab includes two different sets of controls: ActiveX controls and Forms controls. As you can tell by looking at the buttons, the sets are almost identical. So what is the difference? Forms controls are simpler. They have a very limited number of properties and don't have event handlers. You can think of Forms controls as belonging to Excel directly, and ActiveX controls as belonging to Visual Basic. Forms controls are not affected by the Design Mode button. To select an existing Forms control, you hold down the Ctrl key as you click the control.

In this book, you learn how to use ActiveX controls for two reasons. First, to create a custom dialog box, you use ActiveX controls. Second, because Forms controls are simpler, if you learn how to create an ActiveX control, you can easily transfer the knowledge to a Forms control. If all you want from a control is the ability to run a simple macro, a Forms control may be better. If you want more "control" over the control, an ActiveX control may be better. If you need to create an application that will work with different character sets—for example, Arabic or Chinese—there is a significant difference between the two types of control. The Forms controls are actually part of Excel, and because Excel supports Unicode, Forms controls can display captions in any language supported by your operating system and fonts. But the ActiveX controls are part of Visual Basic for Applications, and because VBA supports code pages for localization, ActiveX controls can support only the language of the current code page. If the terms *code page* and *Unicode* don't mean anything to you, then you should be able to use either ActiveX controls or Forms controls.

Create an Event Handler on Your Own

Although you can create a handler for the click event for a control by just clicking the View Code button, you might find it enlightening to see how you can also create an event handler directly in the Visual Basic editor.

1. To create a Zoom Out command button over cells **A3** and **A4**, drag a rectangle on the worksheet from the upper-left corner of cell **A3** to the lower-right corner of cell **B4**. In the **Properties** window, assign the name **btnZoomOut** and the caption **Zoom Out**, and set the **TakeFocusOnClick** property to **False**. Don't click the **View Code** button.

   See Also For detailed instructions, see steps 2 through 6 of the section titled "Create a Custom Command Button."

2. On the **Developer** tab of the Ribbon, click the **Design Mode** button to turn off design mode.

   You can create the event handler in Visual Basic even if design mode is turned off.

3. Switch to the Visual Basic editor, click anywhere in the **btnZoomIn_Click** procedure, and look at the bar just above the code.

Above the code portion of the window are two boxes. The box on the left contains the first half of the procedure name (btnZoomIn), and the box on the right contains the second half of the procedure name (Click). These two boxes are named Object and Procedure, respectively.

4. Click the **Object** arrow.

   The list shows all the objects related to the current worksheet that can have event handlers. In this case, they are btnZoomIn, btnZoomOut, and Worksheet.

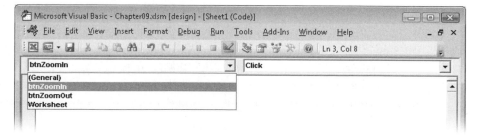

5. Select **btnZoomOut** from the list.

   A new procedure appears. *Click* is the default event for a button, so the new procedure is named *btnZoomOut_Click*, which is precisely what you need.

6. Type ZoomOut as the body of the procedure.

7. Switch to Excel, and try both buttons.

   The lists at the top of the code window can help you build event handlers by combining an object name with an event name.

> **Tip** You can also create an event handler simply by typing the correct name for the macro. As long as you spell the object name and the event name properly, the event handler will work. The object and procedure lists just help you avoid errors.

Make a Button Respond to Mouse Movements

The command button can recognize several different events. Three of the most useful events are a click (the Click event), a double-click (the DblClick event), and a mouse movement (the MouseMove event). The MouseMove event is especially fun to write an event handler for because it has arguments you can use to control the way the procedure works.

1. In the Visual Basic editor, select **btnZoomOut** from the **Object** list, and then select **MouseMove** from the **Procedure** list.

   The declaration for the new procedure is relatively long. This is what it looks like when divided into shorter lines:

```
Private Sub btnZoomOut_MouseMove( _
    ByVal Button As Integer, _
    ByVal Shift As Integer, _
    ByVal X As Single, _
    ByVal Y As Single)
```

   This event handler procedure has four arguments: *Button, Shift, X,* and *Y.* (The word *byVal* means that Excel will ignore any changes the procedure makes to an argument.) The arguments communicate information that you can take advantage of as you write the macro. The *Button* argument indicates whether a mouse button is down as the mouse moves. The *Shift* argument indicates whether the Shift, Ctrl, or Alt key is pressed. The *X* and *Y* arguments indicate the horizontal and vertical position of the mouse.

2. Insert ZoomOut as the body of the new procedure, switch to Excel, and move the mouse over the **Zoom Out** button. (You don't even have to click. Just moving the mouse over the button causes the procedure to run. Events can happen quickly.)

   You can use the arguments that the MouseMove event provides to control the procedure. The most useful argument is *Shift*. Specifically, Shift equals 1 if the Shift key is down, 2 if the Ctrl key is down, and 4 if the Alt key is down. If multiple keys are down, the argument equals the sum. Thus if the argument value is 3, both the Shift and the Ctrl keys are down. By creating an If block based on the Shift value, you can change the procedure so that it zooms *in* when the Shift key is down, and *out* when the Ctrl key is down—and does nothing otherwise.

3. Replace the body of the **btnZoomOut_MouseMove** procedure with these statements:

```
If Shift = 1 Then
    ZoomIn
ElseIf Shift = 2 Then
    ZoomOut
End If
```

> **Tip** The ElseIf keyword allows you to combine Else and If statements into a single statement.

4. Switch to Excel, and try the event handler. Try moving the mouse by itself. Then try pressing and holding the Shift key as you move the mouse. Then try pressing and holding the Ctrl key as you move the mouse.

As you move the mouse over the button, you can practically see the procedure running over and over. Each time the button detects the mouse moving, it triggers another event and the event handler procedure runs again. Event handler procedures can be a powerful way to make things happen.

Explore the Visual Basic Project

You might wonder where all these event handlers are stored and how they relate to the macros that you create with the macro recorder. When you use the macro recorder to create a macro, the macro is stored in a module. You can have multiple macros in a single module, and you can have multiple modules in a workbook. (Each time you close and reopen a workbook, the macro recorder creates a new module for any new macros you record.) Event handler procedures for a command button are attached to the worksheet that contains that button. Visual Basic refers to all the code in a single workbook—whether the code is in a module or attached to a worksheet—as a *project*. The Visual Basic editor has a special window that allows you to explore the project. In the Excel file, the Visual Basic project is stored separately from everything else in the workbook. This makes it easy for Excel to refuse to open a workbook that contains macros unless the file is explicitly saved as a macro-enabled workbook.

1. In the Visual Basic editor, click the **Project Explorer** button.

   Project Explorer

   The Project window appears. This is a dockable window, so you can move it to the edge of the Visual Basic editor or make it float. In the window, you see that the name of the project is *VBAProject*. The name of the workbook (*Chapter09.xlsm*) appears in parentheses. Procedures can be stored either in ordinary modules (grouped under the Modules heading in the Project window) or attached to workbooks and worksheets (grouped under Microsoft Excel Objects in the Project window).

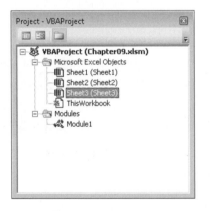

   Associated with each worksheet is a page that contains any code for that worksheet or for objects on that worksheet. When you create a new worksheet, a new code page appears in the Project window. When you delete a worksheet, the worksheet's code page disappears.

2. Double-click the entry labeled **Module1**.

The main Visual Basic editor window displays the macros stored in Module1.

3. Double-click the entry labeled **Sheet1**.

The main Visual Basic editor window displays the event handlers for the objects on Sheet1.

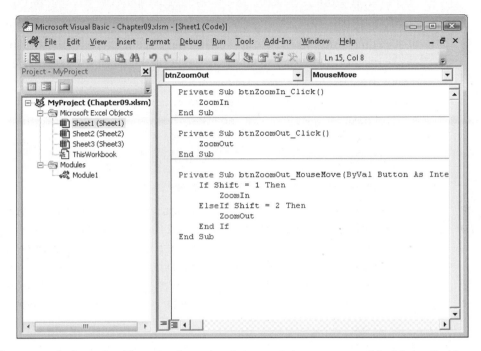

4. In Excel, drag the **Sheet1** tab to the right, and then press and hold the Ctrl key as you release the mouse button.

Excel creates a copy of the sheet. The copy's name is *Sheet1 (2)*, and it has its own copy of the command buttons.

5. Switch to the Visual Basic editor, and look at the **Project** window.

There's a new sheet in the list under Microsoft Excel Objects.

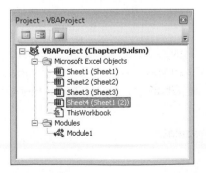

The name in parentheses, *Sheet1 (2)*, matches the name on the worksheet tab. The name in front of the parentheses, *Sheet4*, is a unique name that Visual Basic generates. (Now that you have a sheet with Sheet4 as the internal name, if you use Insert Worksheet to create a new Sheet4, Visual Basic will give it Sheet5 as its internal name!) You can use the Properties window to change the internal name of the sheet.

6. Click the **Properties** button, and in the **Properties** window, change the value of the **(Name)** property to MyNewSheet.

Properties

7. Double-click the **MyNewSheet** worksheet item in the **Project** window.

The main Visual Basic editor window now shows the event handler procedures for the copies of the command buttons. These procedures look just like the procedures that are linked to the command buttons on Sheet1, but they're separate copies. Even if you change the btnZoomIn_Click procedure on MyNewSheet, the btnZoomIn_Click procedure on Sheet1 remains unchanged.

8. In Excel, delete the **Sheet1 (2)** worksheet. Then switch back to the Visual Basic editor, and look at the **Project** window.

As you probably anticipated, the entry for MyNewSheet has disappeared, along with the procedures that were associated with it.

> **Important** When you delete a worksheet that has event handler procedures associated with it, all the procedures are destroyed with the worksheet. Save your work frequently when you write event handlers so that you can recover your work if you accidentally delete a worksheet.

Handling Worksheet and Workbook Events

ActiveX controls aren't the only objects in Excel that can have events. Worksheets and workbooks have events, too. Each of these objects has different events that it can respond to.

Run a Procedure When the Selection Changes

One event you can respond to from a workbook is when the user changes the selection. You can create an event handler that runs every time the selection changes.

1. In the Visual Basic editor, activate the **Sheet1** code window. (In the **Project** window, double-click **Sheet1**.)

2. From the **Objects** list, at the top left of the code window, select **Worksheet**.

A new procedure appears with the name *Worksheet_SelectionChange*. This event happens whenever you change the selection on the worksheet. It doesn't matter whether you click in a cell or use the arrow keys to move around; the event happens either way.

3. Just to see what events are available for a worksheet, click the **Procedure** arrow, at the upper right of the code window. The list shows the nine events that a worksheet can respond to. *SelectionChange* is the default event for a worksheet, just as *Click* is the default event for a command button.

4. Press Esc to close the list of events, and enter these statements as the body of the **Worksheet_SelectionChange** procedure:

```
If ActiveCell.Interior.Color = rgbLightBlue Then
    Selection.Interior.Color = rgbLightGreen
Else
    Selection.Interior.Color = rgbLightBlue
End If
```

The procedure now changes all the newly selected cell to light blue unless the new active cell already happens to already be light blue.

5. Activate **Sheet1** in Excel, and click in several different cells. Press arrow keys to move between cells. Drag a selection rectangle through several cells. The cell colors change each time you change which cells are selected.

⬓	A	B	C	D	E	F	G	H
1								
2	Zoom In							
3								
4	Zoom Out							
5								
6								
7								
8								
9								
10								
11								

6. Now activate **Sheet2** and select a cell.

Nothing happens. The Worksheet_SelectionChange event handler is active only for the associated worksheet.

Handle an Event on Any Worksheet

When you create an event handler for the Sheet1 SelectionChange event, that handler applies only to that worksheet. If you activate Sheet2 and change the selection, nothing happens. Worksheet event handlers respond to events only on their own worksheet. To handle an event on any worksheet, you must use a workbook-level event handler.

1. In the Visual Basic editor, activate the **Project** window and double-click the **ThisWorkbook** item.

2. From the **Object** list, select **Workbook**.

   A new procedure appears with the name *Workbook_Open*. *Open* is the default event for a workbook. This is the event you'd use if you wanted to run a procedure every time you open the workbook.

3. Click the **Procedures** list to see the events available for a workbook. Scroll down to see the ones that start with the letter *S*.

   ```
   Open                        ▼
   RowsetComplete              ▲
   SheetActivate
   SheetBeforeDoubleClick
   SheetBeforeRightClick
   SheetCalculate
   SheetChange
   SheetDeactivate
   SheetFollowHyperlink
   SheetPivotTableUpdate
   SheetSelectionChange
   Sync
   WindowActivate              ▼
   ```

   A workbook can respond to any of 29 different events. It just so happens that *nine* of the events begin with *Sheet*. And these *nine* workbook Sheet events just happen to correspond to the *nine* events for a worksheet, except that they apply to any worksheet in the workbook, even worksheets that don't exist yet.

4. Select the **SheetSelectionChange** event.

   This creates a new Workbook_SheetSelectionChange procedure.

5. Delete the **Workbook_Open** procedure. You won't need this one.

6. Type **Selection.Interior.Color = rgbLightSalmon** as the body of the new procedure.

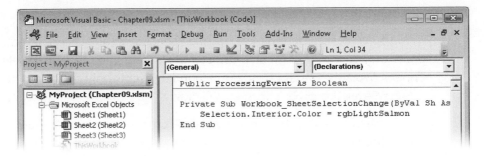

7. Switch to Excel, activate **Sheet2**, and click in various cells. The cells change to light salmon.

8. Activate **Sheet1**, and click in various cells.

   The cells change to light salmon on this sheet as well. What happened to the SelectionChange event handler procedure for Sheet1? It might seem that the event handler for the workbook replaces the one for an individual sheet, but that's not quite true. In fact, they both ran; the workbook one just ran last. The property for the interior color of the cell changed to light blue (or light green) and then quickly changed to light salmon. You didn't see the intermediate color because Windows doesn't refresh the screen until the macro finishes. So all you ever see is the final color. (If you don't believe me, put breakpoints in both the workbook procedure and the worksheet procedure and then click a cell on Sheet1.)

In summary, you can create event handler procedures for any of nine different events that take place on a worksheet. You can put those event handler procedures either at the worksheet level or at the workbook level. If the procedure is at the workbook level, it handles events for all worksheets, regardless of whether a worksheet has an event handler of its own.

Suppress a Workbook Event

It might seem strange that a worksheet event handler wouldn't override a workbook event handler for the same event. In fact, having the worksheet event occur first gives you a great deal of control over how to take advantage of events.

If you want both event handlers to run, you don't have to do anything. For example, the workbook handler might set the border of the selection while the worksheet handler sets the interior color. But if you do want the worksheet event handler to suppress the workbook event handler, you can set it up to do that. You just make the worksheet event handler tell the workbook event handler to do nothing. The way you do that is by creating a very simple custom property at the workbook level.

1. Double-click **ThisWorkbook** in the **Project** window. At the top of the code window, enter this statement above the event handler procedure:

```
Public ProcessingEvent As Boolean
```

This declares *ProcessingEvent* as a *public* variable in ThisWorkbook. When you declare a variable above all the procedures in a module, the variable becomes visible to all the procedures in that one module and is called a *module-level* variable. If you use the word *Public* to declare a module-level variable, that variable is then visible to any procedure in the entire workbook. A public variable is essentially a simple property. Declaring the variable as Boolean means that it can be only True or False. If you don't assign something to it, it will be False.

2. Change the body of the **Workbook_SheetSelectionChange** event handler to this:

```
If ProcessingEvent = True Then
    ProcessingEvent = False
Else
    Selection.Interior.Color = rgbLightSalmon
End If
```

The event handler will now change the color of the selection only if the *ProcessingEvent* variable is not True. If *ProcessingEvent* is True, the event handler changes the variable back to False. (If you didn't change *ProcessingEvent* back to False, suppressing the event handler once would disable this event handler until you close the workbook.)

3. Double-click **Sheet1** in the **Project** window. In the **Worksheet_SelectionChange** event handler, type ThisWorkbook.ProcessingEvent = True just before the **End Sub** statement.

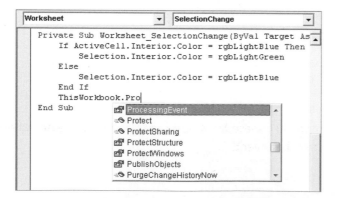

Notice that the new ProcessingEvent property is in the list of members. It even has a standard Property icon next to it. With this statement, the worksheet event handler tells the workbook event handler that it's in the middle of processing the event itself. The code in the workbook event handler uses that information to decide whether to do anything or not.

4. Activate **Sheet1** in Excel, and change the selection.

> **Troubleshooting** If you set breakpoints in any of the procedures, you may want to remove them before you continue.

The selection should change to light green or light blue. The worksheet event handler is suppressing the workbook event handler.

5. Activate **Sheet3**, and change the selection.

The selection should change to light salmon. The workbook event handler still functions properly as long as it's not suppressed by the worksheet.

Creating a public variable inside ThisWorkbook creates a very simple custom property that allows you to suppress the workbook event handler. You now have total control over which event handlers function at which time. You can have an event handler run only at the worksheet level, only at the workbook level, or at both levels. You are the master.

Cancel an Event

Some events are made to be canceled. For example, Excel displays a shortcut menu and formatting toolbar as popups when you right-click a worksheet.

What if you want to prevent these from appearing? You can create an event handler procedure that cancels that event.

Events that can be canceled all have the word *Before* in front of the event name. A worksheet has a BeforeDoubleClick event and a BeforeRightClick event. A workbook has corresponding SheetBeforeDoubleClick and SheetBeforeRightClick events, and also BeforeClose, BeforeSave, and BeforePrint events. Each event procedure that can be canceled has a *Cancel* argument. Cancelling an event suppresses the normal event handler that Excel would execute for that event. To cancel an event, assign True to the Cancel argument in your event handler procedure.

1. In the **Sheet1** code window, select **Worksheet** from the **Object** list, and **BeforeRightClick** from the **Procedures** list.

2. In the event handler procedure that appears, enter the statement Cancel = True as the body.

3. Activate Excel, and select **Sheet1**. Try right-clicking a cell.

   The color changes because of the SelectionChange procedure, but the normal pop-up windows don't appear. Your custom event handler executed before the built-in handler and prevented that built-in handler from executing.

4. Select **Sheet2**, and try right-clicking a cell.

   The color changes, but the pop-up windows also appear.

5. Press Esc to close the pop-up windows. Then save and close the *Chapter09* workbook.

Toolbars and menus can be linked to macros. Command buttons, worksheets, and workbooks can be linked to event handlers. All these tools allow you to create applications that are easy for anyone to use.

> **CLOSE** the *Chapter09.xlsm* workbook.

The Ribbon and Visual Basic for Applications

In previous editions of Excel, it was possible to use VBA macros to make changes to menus and toolbars. In Excel 2007, menus and toolbars are replaced by the Ribbon. It is possible to programmatically control the Ribbon, but you can't do it from VBA. Instead, you must create a full managed code add-in using a language such as C# or Visual Basic .NET. For backwards compatibility, any menus and toolbars created in a VBA macro are put on the Add-Ins tab of the Ribbon. You probably don't want to create new macros that put controls onto the Add-Ins tab.

The new Ribbon allows for more user interface options than menus and toolbars— a developer can add many different types of controls to a Ribbon tab. But it is also more complex, which is why you can't customize the Ribbon from VBA. Specifically, when you create a Ribbon control, you must create custom events for the control. In VBA, you can create a procedure for any of a pre-defined list of events, but you can't define a new event.

Key Points

- Add a custom command button to a worksheet to provide an easy way to launch a macro. Give the button a meaningful name before you create an event handler for it.

- Assign a MouseMove event handler to a control to get extremely frequent events that don't even require a click. Use the Shift argument of the MouseMove event to fine-tune the behavior of the event handler.

- If you want a worksheet event handler to run for any worksheet in the workbook— including new worksheets—create the event handler at the workbook level.

- Any event handler that begins with the word *Before* can be cancelled. Just add the statement *Cancel=True* to the body of the event handler to block what Excel would otherwise automatically do with that event.

Chapter at a Glance

Add a spin button to a worksheet, **page 288**

Add a list box to a worksheet, **page 292**

Add a scroll bar to a worksheet, **page 291**

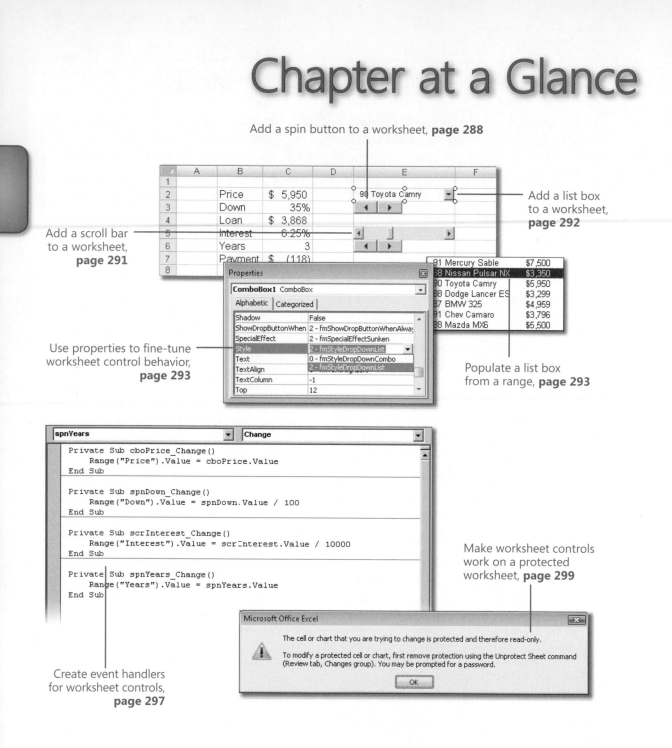

Use properties to fine-tune worksheet control behavior, **page 293**

Populate a list box from a range, **page 293**

Make worksheet controls work on a protected worksheet, **page 299**

Create event handlers for worksheet controls, **page 297**

10 Use Dialog Box Controls on a Worksheet

In this chapter, you will learn to:

✔ Add ActiveX controls to a worksheet.

✔ Link the value of a control to a worksheet cell.

✔ Link a list box to a worksheet range.

✔ Create a list box with multiple columns.

✔ Protect a worksheet that uses ActiveX controls.

Microsoft Office Excel 2007 is a great program. Many people purchase it to use at work. At least, people *say* they're going to use it at work. Of course, we all know the real reason most of us buy it is to calculate car payments. (The rest of us buy it to figure out mortgage payments.) It's *after* buying it that we discover that it's also good for one or two other projects as well.

Anyway, suppose you have a friend who just bought Excel but doesn't know how to use it very well yet. You want to help out by building a model your friend can use for calculating car loan payments. You want your friend to be able to try several possible prices, interest rates, and repayment periods, but you want to minimize the chance for mistakes. Excel has some powerful tools to help you do just that.

Important Before you complete this chapter, you need to install the practice files from the book's companion CD to their default locations. See "Using the Book's CD" on page xv for more information.

USE the *Loan.xlsx* workbook. This practice file is located in the *Documents\MSP\ ExcelVBA10SBS* folder.

BE SURE TO save a macro-enabled copy of *Loan.xlsx* as *Chapter10.xlsm* in the trusted folder you created in Chapter 1.

OPEN the *Chapter10.xlsm* workbook.

Important ActiveX controls do not require a macro-enabled workbook unless you add event handlers to the controls. You will add event handlers in the section titled "Protecting the Worksheet" at the end of this chapter. For information about ActiveX controls and event handlers, see Chapter 9, " Launch Macros with Events."

Using a Loan Payment Calculator

When you interact with Excel, you do so through Excel's graphical user interface. A graphical user interface includes buttons, task panes, dialog boxes, list boxes, scroll bars, and other graphical images. A graphical user interface makes a program easier to learn and also helps reduce errors by restricting choices to valid options.

Historically, creating a graphical user interface was the domain of professional computer scientists. More recently, users of advanced applications have been able to add graphical controls to custom dialog boxes. Now, with Excel, you can take advantage of dialog box–style controls directly on the worksheet, without doing any programming at all.

In this chapter, you'll create a worksheet model to calculate a car loan payment. You'll add ActiveX controls to the worksheet to make it easy to use, even for a friend who is unfamiliar with spreadsheets. In the process, you'll become familiar with how ActiveX controls work, which will be useful when you create custom forms.

Create a Loan Payment Model

Cells B2 through B7 of the Loan sheet of the *Chapter10* workbook contain the labels *Price*, *Down*, *Loan*, *Interest*, *Years*, and *Payment*. These labels will help you create a model that uses an Excel worksheet function to calculate the monthly payments for a car loan.

	A	B	C	D
1				
2		Price		
3		Down		
4		Loan		
5		Interest		
6		Years		
7		Payment		
8				

The following steps create a fully functional loan payment calculator.

> **Tip** If you are in a location that does not use the dollar sign as a currency symbol, your workbook will show your local currency symbol.

1. Type **5000** in cell **C2** (to the right of Price), type **20** in cell **C3** (to the right of Down), type **8** in cell **C5** (to the right of Interest), and type **3** in cell **C6** (to the right of Years).

	A	B	C	D
1				
2		Price	$ 5,000	
3		Down	20%	
4		Loan		
5		Interest	8.00%	
6		Years	3	
7		Payment		
8				

2. Select the range **B2:C7**, and then on the **Formulas** tab of the Ribbon, in the **Defined Names** section, click the **Create from Selection** button, make sure that only **Left column** is selected, and then click **OK**.

Create from Selection

This uses the label in column B to name the corresponding cell in column C, which will make formulas easier to understand.

	A	B	C	D
1				
2		Price	$ 5,000	
3		Down	20%	
4		Loan		
5		Interest	8.00%	
6		Years	3	
7		Payment		
8				

Create Names from Selection

Create names from values in the:

- ☐ Top row
- ☑ Left column
- ☐ Bottom row
- ☐ Right column

OK   Cancel

3. In cell **C4** (to the right of Loan), type =Price*(1-Down) and press Enter.

The value $4,000 appears in the cell.

	Loan		▾	f_x	=Price*(1-Down)	
	A	B	C	D	E
1					
2		Price	$ 5,000		
3		Down	20%		
4		Loan	$ 4,000		
5		Interest	8.00%		
6		Years	3		
7		Payment			
8					

4. In cell **C7** (to the right of Payment), type =PMT(Interest/12,Years*12,Loan) and press Enter.

The payment amount, $125, appears in the cell.

	Payment		▾	f_x	=PMT(Interest/12,Years*12,Loan)	
	A	B	C	D	E
1					
2		Price	$ 5,000		
3		Down	20%		
4		Loan	$ 4,000		
5		Interest	8.00%		
6		Years	3		
7		Payment	$ (125)		
8					

The result is the monthly payment amount for the hypothetical car. The parentheses around the number in the worksheet indicate a negative number. Unfortunately, you don't receive this amount; you pay it. (If you want to change the monthly payment to a positive number, put a minus sign in front of Loan in the formula.)

Use the Loan Payment Model

Now that you have all the formulas set up for the loan payment model, you can replace values in the input cells and see the effect on the price. For example, you can see what the monthly payment would be for a more expensive car.

1. Enter 12000 in cell **C2**, and press Enter.

The loan amount should change to $9,600, and the payment should change to $301.

	A	B	C	D
1				
2		Price	$12,000	
3		Down	20%	
4		Loan	$ 9,600	
5		Interest	8.00%	
6		Years	3	
7		Payment	$ (301)	
8				

This simple model calculates monthly loan payments for a given set of input variables. You change the input variables to anything you like, and the payment changes accordingly. You can even enter outlandish values.

2. Enter $1,500,000 as the price of the car.

This is a very expensive car. The payment formula bravely calculates the monthly payment, but you can't read it because it's too big. (In case you're interested, the monthly payment for this expensive car is $37,604.)

Price	▾	f_x	1500000	
	A	B	C	D
1				
2		Price	######	
3		Down	20%	
4		Loan	######	
5		Interest	8.00%	
6		Years	3	
7		Payment	######	
8				

Undo

3. Click the **Undo** button on the Quick Access Toolbar to change the price back to $12,000.

One problem with this model is that it's *too* flexible. You can enter a ridiculously large price or a ridiculously high interest rate, such as 500%. You can even enter something totally useless as the number of years, such as *Dog*. The wide spectrum of choices available—only a few of which are meaningful—might be confusing to your friend. You can add controls to the worksheet that will avoid the potential for this kind of confusion.

Creating an Error-Resistant Loan Payment Calculator

Excel has tools that enable you to make a loan payment calculator error-resistant. By restricting options to valid items, you can make your model less likely to produce erroneous results, as well as much easier to use. The Insert list on the Developer tab of the Ribbon contains various ActiveX controls that you can put on a worksheet.

See Also For more information about ActiveX controls or for instructions for enabling the Developer tab of the Ribbon, see the section titled "Creating Custom Command Buttons" in Chapter 9, "Launch Macros with Events."

Restrict the Years to a Valid Range

Start by making it difficult to enter an invalid number of years. Typically, for car loans you can borrow for up to five years in units of a year. Just to be safe, allow values from 1 to 6 for the number of years. A *spin button* is an effective way to specify such integer values.

Spin Button (ActiveX Control)

1. On the **Developer** tab of the Ribbon, click the **Insert** arrow, and then click the **Spin Button (ActiveX Control)** button.

2. Press and hold the Alt key, and then click near the upper-left corner of cell **E6**.

   Pressing the Alt key while you click makes the control snap to the cell grid line.

3. Release the Alt key, and then drag the lower-right corner of the new spin button to the bottom center of cell **E6**.

   The spin button rotates sideways so that it fits on the row.

	A	B	C	D	E
1					
2		Price	$12,000		
3		Down	20%		
4		Loan	$ 9,600		
5		Interest	8.00%		
6		Years	3		◄ ►
7		Payment	$ (301)		
8					

4. On the **Developer** tab of the Ribbon, click the **Properties** button to display the **Properties** window.

   An ActiveX control has many properties. For most of the properties, you can simply accept the default values. Change only the properties for which you need a custom value.

5. Type **6** as the value of the **Max** property, and type **1** as the value of the **Min** property.

Properties	
SpinButton1 SpinButton	

Alphabetic | Categorized

Max	6
Min	1
MouseIcon	(None)
MousePointer	0 - fmMousePointerDefault
Orientation	-1 - fmOrientationAuto
Placement	2
PrintObject	True
Shadow	False

You want the spin button to control the value in cell C6, which is named *Years*. The LinkedCell property determines which cell the control will change.

6. For the **LinkedCell** property, type **Years** and press Enter.

Properties		
SpinButton1 SpinButton		▾

Alphabetic | Categorized |

Left	206.25	▲
LinkedCell	Years	
Locked	True	
Max	6	≡
Min	1	
MouseIcon	(None)	
MousePointer	0 - fmMousePointerDefault	
Orientation	-1 - fmOrientationAuto	▼

7. Click the **Design Mode** button to turn off design mode, and then click the spin button on the worksheet.

The number in cell C6 changes as you click the spin button, and the payment amount changes accordingly. Now your friend will find it easy to select only valid loan durations.

Restrict the Down Payment to Valid Values

Unfortunately, your friend can still enter an invalid value for the down payment percentage (–*50%*, for example, or *Dog*). You need to help out.

You specify the down payment as a percentage. A reasonable range of values for the down payment would be anywhere from 0 percent to 100 percent, counting in 5 percent increments. The minimum change for a spin button is an integer, but even though the down payment is a fraction, not an integer, you can still use a spin button as long as you utilize an extra cell to hold the intermediate value.

1. Click the **Design Mode** button to turn on design mode.

2. Press and hold both the Alt key and the Ctrl key, and drag the spin button from cell **E6** to cell **E3**.

> **Troubleshooting** Be sure to release the mouse button before releasing the Ctrl and Alt keys.

When you release the mouse button, a copy snaps to the upper-left corner of cell E3. Copying the control makes both controls exactly the same size.

◢	A	B	C	D	E
1					
2		Price	$ 12,000		
3		Down	20%		◀ ▶
4		Loan	$ 9,600		
5		Interest	8.00%		
6		Years	3		◀ ▶
7		Payment	$ (301)		
8					

3. In the **Properties** window, type **100** as the value of the **Max** property, **0** (zero) as the value of the **Min** property, and **H3** as the value of the **LinkedCell** property.

> **Troubleshooting** If you try to enter H3 as the LinkedCell property before you set the Min value to 0, you will get an error message. That's because the current Min value is 1 and H3 is empty, which is the same as 0.

Cell H3 holds an intermediate—integer—value because the spin button can increment only in integers. Later, you will divide the value in cell H3 by 100 to convert the integer created by the spin button into a percentage suitable for use as a down payment.

4. As the value of the **SmallChange** property, type 5 and press Enter.

This property controls how much the number will change each time you click the arrows on the spin button.

Properties	⊠
SpinButton2 SpinButton	▾

Alphabetic	Categorized	
Left	206.25	
LinkedCell	H3	
Locked	True	
Max	100	
Min	0	
MouseIcon	(None)	
MousePointer	0 - fmMousePointerDefault	
Orientation	-1 - fmOrientationAuto	
Placement	2	
PrintObject	True	
Shadow	False	
SmallChange	5	
Top	27.75	

5. Click the **Design Mode** button to exit design mode, and then click the spin button.

The value in cell H3 changes to a multiple of 5 between 0 and 100. Now you need a corresponding value in cell C3 of between 0 percent and 100 percent.

6. Select cell **C3**, type =H3/100 and press Enter.

An appropriate percentage value appears in the cell.

	A	B	C	D	E	F	G	H	I
	Down		f_x =H3/100						
1									
2		Price	$ 12,000						
3		Down	35%		◄ ►			35	
4		Loan	$ 7,800						

7. Click the spin button to see both the integer in cell **H3** and the derived value in cell **C3** change in tandem. Because the loan and payment cells contain formulas that depend on the down payment, they also change. One simple click, so many effects.

Restrict the Interest Rate to Valid Values

The interest rate is another input value your friend might enter incorrectly. The interest rate is similar to the down payment rate; both are percentages. You probably want to allow interest rates to vary by as little as 0.25 percent, and within a range from 0 percent through about 20 percent. Because you're allowing so many possible values, you'll have many more increments than with the down payment rate, so you'll use a scroll bar control instead of a spin button. Like a spin button, the scroll bar returns only integers, so you'll link the control to an intermediate cell.

Scroll Bar
(ActiveX Control)

1. On the **Developer** tab of the Ribbon, click the **Insert** arrow, and then click the **Scroll Bar (ActiveX Control)** button.

2. Press and hold the Alt key as you click the upper-left corner of cell **E5**, and then continue to hold down the Alt key as you drag the lower-right corner of the new scroll bar to the lower-right corner of cell **E5**. Release the mouse before you release the Alt key.

	A	B	C	D	E	F
1						
2		Price	$ 12,000			
3		Down	35%		◄ ►	
4		Loan	$ 7,800			
5		Interest	8.00%		◄ ►	
6		Years	3		◄ ►	
7		Payment	$ (244)			
8						

3. In the **Properties** window, type **2000** as the value of the **Max** property, **25** as the value of the **SmallChange** property, **100** as the value of the **LargeChange** property, and **H5** as the value of the **LinkedCell** property. Then press Enter.

4. Click the **Design Mode** button to turn off design mode, and then try the scroll bar control by clicking its arrows as well as the area between them.

   If you click one of the arrows on either end, the number in cell H5 changes by 25 (the SmallChange value). If you click between the box and the end, the number changes by 100 (the LargeChange value). You can also drag the scroll bar handle to get any value between 0 and 2000.

5. Select cell **C5**, type =H5/10000 and press Enter.

	Interest		f_x	=H5/10000				
	A	B	C	D	E	F	G	H	I
1								
2		Price	$12,000					
3		Down	35%	◄ ►				35
4		Loan	$ 7,800					
5		Interest	6.25%	◄ ►				625
6		Years	3	◄ ►				
7		Payment	$ (238)					
8								

You divide by 100 to turn the number from H5 into a percentage and by another 100 (100 * 100 = 10000 total) to allow for hundredths of a percent.

Now your friend can easily modify the number of years for the loan (using one spin button), the down payment percentage (using the other spin button), or the interest rate (using the scroll bar control).

Retrieving a Value from a List

You could specify the price of the car by creating another scroll bar, but the price of a car is actually determined by which car you want to buy. You know that your friend has been looking through the classified ads and has come up with a list of used cars to consider. You can make the worksheet easy to use by allowing your friend to select the description of the car and have the price appear automatically in the Price cell.

Prepare a List of Cars

The *Chapter10* workbook contains a list of the cars your friend is interested in, along with their prices. The list starts in cell K2. You can create a list box that displays this list of cars.

	J	K	L	M
1				
2		91 Mercury Sable	$7,500	
3		88 Nissan Pulsar NX	$3,350	
4		90 Toyota Camry	$5,950	
5		88 Dodge Lancer ES	$3,299	
6		87 BMW 325	$4,959	
7		91 Chev Camaro	$3,796	
8		88 Mazda MX6	$5,500	
9				

To make the formulas easier, you'll start by naming the range that contains the list.

1. Select the range **K2:L8**. Then right-click the range, and click **Name a Range** on the shortcut menu. In the **New Name** dialog box, type **CarList** as the name of the list, and click **OK**.

New Name dialog box:

Name:	CarList
Scope:	Workbook
Comment:	
Refers to:	=Loan!$K$2:$L$8

OK   Cancel

The defined name contains both the list of car names and the corresponding list of prices.

Combo Box
(ActiveX Control)

2. On the **Developer** tab of the Ribbon, click the **Insert** arrow, and click **Combo Box (ActiveX Control)**. Then press and hold the Alt key, and drag a rectangle from the upper-left corner to the lower-right corner of cell **E2**.

	A	B	C	D	E	F
1						
2		Price	$ 12,000			
3		Down	35%			
4		Loan	$ 7,800			
5		Interest	6.25%			
6		Years	3			
7		Payment	$ (238)			
8						

A combo box can have either of two styles. It can be a list box, allowing you to select only items from the list, or it can be a list box combined with an edit box, allowing you to enter new values as well as select from the list. Because you want to confine your friend to the existing list of cars and prices, you want the combo box to be a simple list box.

3. In the **Properties** window, for the value of the **Style** property, select **2 – fmStyleDropDownList.**

Properties	☒
ComboBox1 ComboBox	▾

Alphabetic	Categorized

Shadow	False
ShowDropButtonWhen	2 - fmShowDropButtonWhenAlway
SpecialEffect	2 - fmSpecialEffectSunken
Style	2 - fmStyleDropDownList ▾
Text	0 - fmStyleDropDownCombo
TextAlign	2 - fmStyleDropDownList
TextColumn	-1
Top	12

The list box has a sunken appearance. On a worksheet, it would look better if there simply appeared to be an arrow in the cell. You can get that effect by changing a couple of properties on the control.

4. In the **Properties** window, change the value of the **SpecialEffect** property to **0 – fmSpecialEffectFlat** and the value of the **BackStyle** property to **0 – fmBackStyleTransparent**. Click anywhere on the worksheet so that you can see the effect of your changes to the button's properties.

	A	B	C	D	E	F
1						
2		Price	$12,000		▾	
3		Down	35%		◄ ►	
4		Loan	$ 7,800			
5		Interest	6.25%		◄ ▌ ►	
6		Years	3		◄ ►	
7		Payment	$ (238)			
8						

5. Select the **ComboBox** control. Change the value of the **LinkedCell** property to Price and press Enter.

The price from cell C2 appears as the value of the combo box. Now you can change the combo box to retrieve the list of cars.

6. Change the value of the **ListFillRange** property to CarList and press Enter.

Nothing seems to happen because the value in cell C2 doesn't match any of the values from the list. But the combo box now knows to get its list of values from the CarList range. You can watch the value of cell C2 change when you select a new car from the combo box.

7. Click the **Design Mode** button to turn it off. Then click the arrow on the combo box, and select **90 Toyota Camry** from the list.

   The name of the car appears in the combo box, but it also appears in cell C2, and the formulas don't work well when a car name is entered as the price.

	A	B	C	D	E	F
1						
2		Price	90 Toyota Camry		90 Toyota Camry	
3		Down	35%			
4		Loan	#VALUE!			
5		Interest	6.25%			
6		Years	3			
7		Payment	#VALUE!			
8						

Retrieve the Price from the List

You can now select a car name from the combo box, but you want the combo box to put the price of the car—not the name of the car—into cell C2. Because the CarList range you are using to populate the list contains a column with the car prices, you can tell the combo box to get the value from that column.

1. Click the **Design Mode** button, and then click the combo box.

2. In the **Properties** window, change the **ColumnCount** property to 2 and press Enter.

   The ColumnCount property informs the combo box that there are two columns of values in the ListFillRange.

3. Change the **BoundColumn** property to 2 and press Enter.

   The BoundColumn property tells the combo box which column's value to put into the linked cell. And sure enough, the price of the Toyota, $5,950, appears in the cell.

	A	B	C	D	E	F
1						
2		Price	$ 5,950		90 Toyota Camry	
3		Down	35%			
4		Loan	$ 3,868			
5		Interest	6.25%			
6		Years	3			
7		Payment	$ (118)			
8						

Properties

ComboBox1 ComboBox

Alphabetic | Categorized

BorderStyle	0 - fmBorderStyleNone
BoundColumn	2
ColumnCount	2
ColumnHeads	False
ColumnWidths	
DragBehavior	0 - fmDragBehaviorDisabled
DropButtonStyle	1 - fmDropButtonStyleArrow

4. Turn off design mode, and click the arrow on the combo box.

	A	B	C	D	E	F
1						
2		Price	$ 5,950		90 Toyota Camry	
3		Down	35%		91 Mercury Sa $7,500	
4		Loan	$ 3,868		88 Nissan Puls $3,350	
5		Interest	6.25%		90 Toyota Carr $5,950	
6		Years	3		88 Dodge Lanc $3,299	
7		Payment	$ (118)		87 BMW 325 $4,959	
8					91 Chev Camai $3,796	
9					88 Mazda MX6 $5,500	
10						

5. Select **87 BMW 325** from the list of cars.

   The price changes to $4,959, and the other formulas recalculate as well.

Now your friend won't accidentally calculate the payment for a $1,500,000 car. Your friend can just select various cars from the list, and Excel will automatically insert the correct price in the Price cell.

Set the Column Widths

The combo box works fine, but while the list is displayed, it has a horizontal scroll bar across the bottom, and car names are cut off. The combo box makes the price column as wide as the car name column. By default, a combo box uses the same width for each column. If, as in this example, you want the columns to have different widths, you can manually control the column widths.

1. Drag the heading for column **E** to the right to set the width to **30**.

2. Turn on design mode, and select the combo box.

3. In the **Properties** window, change the value of **ColumnWidths** to 1.5 in; .5 in, and press Enter.

This specifies 1.5 inches for the first column and 0.5 inch for the second column. The displayed value of the property changes to *108 pt; 36 pt*, the equivalent value in points. (A point is equal to 1/72 inch.) You can type the value of the property in inches (in), centimeters (cm), or points (pt), but the Properties window always displays the value in points.

4. Turn off design mode, and click the combo box arrow.

	A	B	C	D	E	F
1						
2		Price	$ 4,959		87 BMW 325	
3		Down	35%		91 Mercury Sable $7,500	
4		Loan	$ 3,223		88 Nissan Pulsar NX $3,350	
5		Interest	6.25%		90 Toyota Camry $5,950	
6		Years	3		88 Dodge Lancer ES $3,299	
7		Payment	$ (98)		87 BMW 325 $4,959	
8					91 Chev Camaro $3,796	
9					88 Mazda MX6 $5,500	

The combo box, with its new customized column widths, looks great!

Protecting the Worksheet

The model works, it doesn't require any typing into cells, and you were able to create it without using any macros! However, the model still isn't bulletproof. There's nothing in the model to prevent your friend from accidentally typing *Dog* as the price of the car in cell C2, thereby creating errors in all the formulas.

You can protect the worksheet to prevent your friend from typing invalid values into the model. Unfortunately, that will also prevent the ActiveX controls from changing the values of the linked cells. You can, however, set the worksheet protection in such a way that Microsoft Visual Basic for Applications procedures can still change the cells. All you need are some simple event handler procedures to protect the model effectively.

Create an Event Handler for the Combo Box

Right now, each of the four ActiveX controls links directly to a cell. Once you protect the worksheet, the direct links won't work, so you need to create event handler procedures to put the new values into the cells.

> **Tip** Note that up until this point, you could keep saving the workbook as a regular workbook. You can use ActiveX controls in a standard workbook as long as they don't have any code associated with them. As soon as you add code, you must save the workbook as a macro-enabled workbook. If you already saved the workbook as macro-enabled, you don't have to do anything different at this time.

1. Turn on design mode, and select the combo box.

2. In the **Properties** window, change the **Name** property to **cboPrice**. (The prefix *cbo* stands for "combo box.") Clear the **LinkedCell** property box, and then right-click the control and click **View Code**.

   A new event handler procedure named *cboPrice_Change* appears. *Change* is the default event for a combo box.

3. As the body of the macro, insert this statement:

   ```
   Range("Price").Value = cboPrice.Value
   ```

   This event handler procedure changes cell C2 to match the new value of the combo box whenever that value changes.

4. Activate Excel, turn off design mode, and try out the combo box.

   The value in cell C2 should change to the correct price each time you select a new car, as it did when the LinkedCell property connected the control directly to the cell.

5. Repeat Steps 1 through 4 for the spin button that sets the down payment percentage. Give it the name **spnDown**, clear the **LinkedCell** property box, and in its event procedure enter the following statement:

   ```
   Range("Down").Value = spnDown.Value / 100
   ```

6. Repeat Steps 1 through 4 for the scroll bar that sets the interest rate. Give it the name **scrInterest**, clear the **LinkedCell** property box, and in its event procedure enter the statement:

   ```
   Range("Interest").Value = scrInterest.Value / 10000
   ```

7. Repeat Steps 1 through 4 for the spin button that sets the number of years. Give it the name **spnYears**, clear the **LinkedCell** property box, and in its event procedure enter the statement:

   ```
   Range("Years").Value = spnYears.Value
   ```

```
spnYears                          ▼   Change                              ▼
    Private Sub cboPrice_Change()                                         ▲
        Range("Price").Value = cboPrice.Value
    End Sub

    Private Sub spnDown_Change()
        Range("Down").Value = spnDown.Value / 100
    End Sub

    Private Sub scrInterest_Change()
        Range("Interest").Value = scrInterest.Value / 10000
    End Sub

    Private Sub spnYears_Change()
        Range("Years").Value = spnYears.Value
    End Sub
```

8. On the worksheet, clear cells **H3** and **H5**, since you no longer need the values in them.

You now have an event handler procedure for each control, and none of the controls is linked to a cell. You're finally ready to protect the worksheet.

Protect the Worksheet

You typically protect a worksheet by clicking the Protection command on the Tools menu and then clicking the Protect Sheet command. When you protect a worksheet this way, you can't subsequently change the value of any locked cells, even with a macro or event handler procedure.

However, if you use a macro to protect the worksheet, the Protect method has a special argument that tells Excel to allow a macro or an event handler to change the protected cells. This special kind of protection doesn't persist when you close and reopen the workbook, so you must protect the worksheet each time you open the workbook. You can set the protection in the workbook's Open event handler.

Project Explorer

1. In the Visual Basic editor, click the **Project Explorer** button, and then double-click the **ThisWorkbook** object.

2. From the **Object** list (above the code window), select **Workbook**.

3. Insert this statement as the body of the Workbook_Open procedure:

```
Worksheets("Loan").Protect UserInterfaceOnly:=True
```

The UserInterfaceOnly argument to the Protect method is what allows a macro to make changes even if a user or control can't.

4. Save and close the *Chapter10* workbook. Then reopen it, allowing Excel to enable macros.

5. Try typing numbers into the model.

Excel politely explains that the worksheet is protected.

6. Try changing the model by using the ActiveX controls to verify that everything works correctly.

The loan payment calculator model is now robust and ready to give to your friend. Your friend can experiment with various scenarios without having to worry about typing invalid entries into the model. In fact, your friend can't type anything into the model because the worksheet is protected. Besides, there's actually no need to type. Your friend can control everything on the worksheet just by clicking controls with the mouse. One of the greatest benefits of a graphical user interface is the ability to restrict choices to valid values, thereby reducing or eliminating user error while also making a model easier to use.

CLOSE the *Chapter10.xlsm* workbook.

Key Points

- Use a spin control to choose between a small range of numbers, and a scroll bar to choose between a large range of numbers.

- Use a combo box control to select an item from a list. If the list has multiple available columns, use the BoundColumn property to determine which one the combo box returns.

- Use the UserInterfaceOnly argument for the Protect method to protect a worksheet while giving your macros special privileges.

- Use event handler procedures to allow ActiveX controls to change protected cells.

Chapter at a Glance

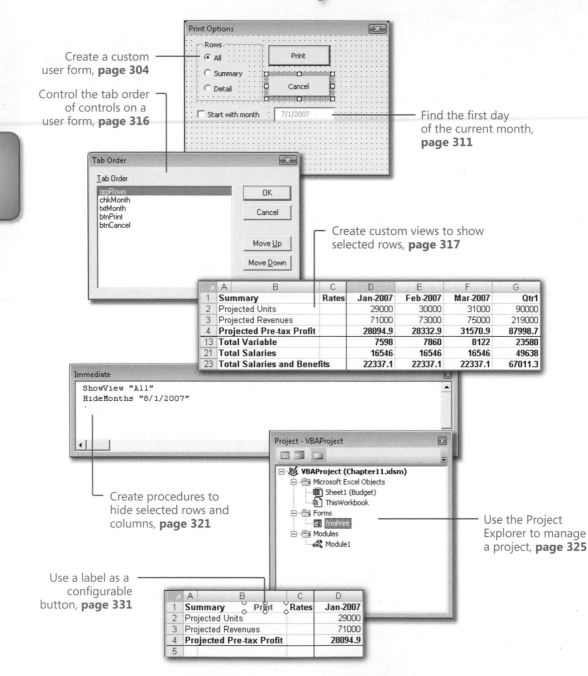

Create a custom user form, **page 304**

Control the tab order of controls on a user form, **page 316**

Find the first day of the current month, **page 311**

Create custom views to show selected rows, **page 317**

Create procedures to hide selected rows and columns, **page 321**

Use the Project Explorer to manage a project, **page 325**

Use a label as a configurable button, **page 331**

11 Create a Custom Form

In this chapter, you will learn to:

✔ Create a custom form.

✔ Initialize a form.

✔ Check for invalid input values in a text box.

✔ Run macros from a form.

Get a 3-foot-by-4-foot piece of plywood and some cans of blue, yellow, and orange paint. Drip, dribble, splash, and spread the paint on the plywood. You now have—a mess. But put a $500 frame around the painted plywood, and you now have—a work of art! Even serious art doesn't look earnest without a good frame.

And even the finest diamond brooch doesn't look like a precious gift if given in a paper bag.

Similarly, you can write macros that are practical, convenient, and useful, but until you put a frame around them—until you tighten them up, make them easy to use, and package them—you don't have a truly valuable application. One excellent way to make a functional macro easy to use and valuable is by creating a custom dialog box, or *user form*.

In this chapter, you'll learn how to create the user interface of a user form, create the functionality for the form, and implement the form by linking the two together into an integrated tool.

 Important Before you complete this chapter, you need to install the practice files from the book's companion CD to their default locations. See "Using the Book's CD" on page xv for more information.

> **USE** the *Budget.xlsx* workbook. This practice file is located in the *Documents\MSP\ ExcelVBA07SBS* folder.
>
> **BE SURE TO** save a macro-enabled copy of the *Budget.xlsx* workbook as *Chapter11.xlsm* in the trusted folder location you created in Chapter 1.
>
> **OPEN** the *Chapter11.xlsm* workbook.

Creating a Form's User Interface

The Budget worksheet in the *Chapter11* workbook shows detailed budget information for the year 2007. It includes both detail and summary rows.

	A	B	C	D	E	F
1	**Summary**		Rates	Jan-2007	Feb-2007	Mar-2007
2	Projected Units			29000	30000	31000
3	Projected Revenues			71000	73000	75000
4	**Projected Pre-tax Profit**			**28094.9**	**28332.9**	**31570.9**
5						
6	Variable					
7	Potting Soil		0.095	2755	2850	2945
8	Pots		0.012	348	360	372
9	Seeds		0.002	58	60	62
10	Fertilizer		0.002	58	60	62

Suppose that you need to print different versions of the budget. The managers want a version that shows only the summary rows. The data entry person wants a version that shows only the detail rows, without the totals. The budget analyst wants both the detail and the summary rows, but doesn't want to see months that are completed.

To make it easy to print the various versions of the report, you can create a user form. Here's the overall strategy for creating the form:

- Design the form. The layout of the form is the first thing that the user sees, and it should suggest how to use the form. How the form looks and acts is called the *user interface*. The easiest way to design a form in Microsoft Visual Basic for Applications (VBA) is to just jump in and create it.

- Create the macros that make the form work. These are the procedures that interact with Microsoft Office Excel objects. The tasks that the form executes are called its *functionality*. Adding functionality might involve making changes to the worksheet to enable the macros to work.

- Make the form run the macros, and provide a way to show the form. Integrating the user interface with the functionality of the form is the final step, which is called *implementation*.

> **Tip** If you want to create a more sophisticated user interface for an Excel application, you can use Microsoft Visual Studio 2005, together with the Visual Studio Tools for Office (VSTO), to create a managed code (Microsoft .NET) application that can control the Excel object model.

Create the Form

The process of designing the form's user interface can help you figure out what functionality you need to develop.

1. With the *Chapter11* workbook open, right-click the **Budget** worksheet tab, and click **View Code** to open the Visual Basic editor.

2. On the **Insert** menu, click **UserForm** to create a new, empty user form.

   The form is stored in your project just as a module is. You can run the form from VBA in the same way that you run a macro.

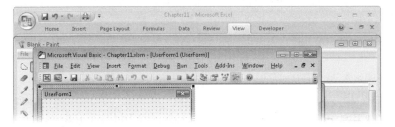

Run Sub/
UserForm

3. Click the **Run Sub/UserForm** button to display the form, and then click the **Close** button to close it.

   By default, the caption of the form is *UserForm1*. If you create a second form, it will have the caption *UserForm2*, and so on—similar to the way Excel creates new default worksheet names. The caption is a property; you can change the caption in the Properties window.

Properties
Window

4. Click the **Properties Window** button, and change the value of the **Caption** property to Print Options.

The caption changes in the form as you change the value in the Properties window.

5. Change the value of the **(Name)** property to frmPrint.

The Name property has parentheses around it to make it appear at the top of the list. The prefix *frm* is short for *form*. The *Print* part of the name tells you the intended purpose of the form. If you ever need to refer to the form inside a procedure, you can use this meaningful name.

That's all there is to creating a user form! Of course, it's not much good until you put something in it.

Add Option Buttons

Your goal in creating this form is to let a user choose one of three layouts when printing the report: all the rows, only the summary rows, or only the detail rows. *Option buttons* provide a way to select a single item from a short, predefined list. Generally, option buttons go inside a *frame*.

When VBA displayed the user form, it automatically displayed the Toolbox for forms. This Toolbox contains the same controls that are in the ActiveX Controls collection on the Developer tab of the Ribbon in Excel. You can use the Toolbox to add ActiveX controls to a form.

See Also For information about putting ActiveX controls on a worksheet, see the section titled "Creating an Error-Resistant Loan Payment Calculator" in Chapter 10, "Use Dialog Box Controls on a Worksheet."

Toolbox

Frame

1. Activate the **Form** window. If you don't see the Toolbox, click the **Toolbox** button on the Standard toolbar to display it.

2. In the **Toolbox**, click the **Frame** button, and then click near the upper-left corner of the form.

   A large frame control appears on the form. You can move or resize the frame later.

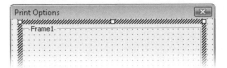

Your next task is to add the option buttons. You can avoid having to click the control button on the Toolbox each time you add a button by double-clicking the control button. Double-clicking activates the button until you click it again.

OptionButton

3. Double-click the **OptionButton** button, click in three places on the form to create three buttons, and then click the **OptionButton** button again to turn it off.

   You don't need to position the controls exactly.

4. Activate the **Properties** window, and select **Frame1** from the list at the top.

5. Type **Rows** as the value of the **Caption** property and **grpRows** as the value of the **Name** property.

   The prefix *grp* is short for *group*, which is an old name for a frame.

6. In the list at the top of the window, select **OptionButton1**.

7. Type **All** as the value of the **Caption** property and **optAll** as the value of the **Name** property.

8. With the **optAll** control still selected, type **True** as the value of the **Value** property.

   Setting the Value property to True makes this the default option.

9. Give the second option button the caption Summary and the name optSummary.

10. Give the third option button the caption Detail and the name optDetail.

11. Select all three option buttons by clicking between the bottom option button and the bottom of the frame and dragging a rectangle that touches each of the option button captions.

    The Format menu provides powerful tools for getting the controls on a form to line up properly.

12. On the **Format** menu in the Visual Basic editor, point to **Vertical Spacing**, and then click **Remove**.

13. On the **Format** menu, point to **Align**, and then click **Lefts**.

14. On the **Format** menu, click **Size To Fit**.

15. Finally drag the group of controls to the upper-left corner of the frame, and resize the frame so that it fits around the option buttons.

16. Save the workbook, press F5 to see how the option buttons will look (by clicking the option buttons), and then close the **Print Options** window.

A frame with a set of option buttons is a good user interface for selecting a single option from a predefined list.

Add a Check Box with a Related Text Box

Your form needs some way for you to specify whether to print all the months or only the remaining months. This is basically a "yes or no" choice. The best control for a "yes or no" choice is a check box. When the check box is selected, the macro will print starting with the current month.

Even though the budget analyst says that the report should start with the current month, you know that exceptions inevitably will arise. Therefore, in addition to the check box, you should add a text box that lets you specify a different start month, just to be prepared.

CheckBox

1. With the form window visible, click the **CheckBox** button in the **Toolbox**, and then click below the frame on the form where you want the check box to appear.

```
Print Options                          [X]
 ┌─Rows────────────┐
 │  ⦿ All          │
 │                 │
 │  ○ Summary      │
 │                 │
 │  ○ Detail       │
 └─────────────────┘
 □▢ CheckBox1                      ▢
```

2. In the **Properties** window, change the caption for the check box to Start with month and change the name to chkMonth.

3. Double-click the size handle on the right of the check box selection rectangle to shrink the rectangle to fit the caption.

```
Print Options                          [X]
 ┌─Rows────────────┐
 │  ⦿ All          │
 │                 │
 │  ○ Summary      │
 │                 │
 │  ○ Detail       │
 └─────────────────┘
 □▢ Start with month ▢
```

You'll now add the text box for the month immediately after the caption for the check box so that the contents appear to complete the *Start with month* caption.

TextBox

4. Click the **TextBox** button in the **Toolbox**, and then click to the right of the check box caption.

```
Print Options                              [x]
┌─ Rows ─────────────┐
│   • All            │
│   ○ Summary        │
│   ○ Detail         │
└────────────────────┘
  ☐ Start with month   [              ]
```

5. Change the text box name to txtMonth, set the **Value** property to 7/1/2007, and then change the **Enabled** property to False.

   You won't need to change the value of the month if the check box is cleared. Setting the Enabled property to False makes the contents of the box appear gray. You want the text box to become enabled whenever the user selects the check box. This is a job for an event.

6. Double-click the **chkMonth** check box control.

   A new window captioned as *frmPrint (Code)* appears. It contains a new event handler procedure, *chkMonth_Click*. The Click event is the default event for a check box.

   ```
   chkMonth              ▼   Click               ▼
         Private Sub chkMonth_Click()

         End Sub
   ```

7. Insert the following statement as the body of the new chkMonth_Click procedure:

   ```
   txtMonth.Enabled = chkMonth.Value
   ```

   This statement enables the text box whenever the check box is selected and disables the text box whenever the check box is cleared.

8. Save the workbook, press F5 to run the form, and click the check box a couple of times to confirm that the enabled state of the text box always matches the value of the check box.

   When the check box is cleared, you can't change the date. When it's selected, you can.

9. Close the form.

> **Troubleshooting** If the text box does not become enabled, make sure that you added the event handler to the check box, not to the text box.

Adding an event to the check box control makes the user interface work better, but it doesn't change anything in Excel. Even though the event is VBA code, it is still part of the user interface of the form, not part of its functionality.

Initialize the Text Box

When you created the month text box, you assigned 7/1/2007 as a default date. Since most of the time you'll want the current month in that box, you can make the form easier to use by initializing the text box with the current month. To do so, you must calculate the appropriate date for the text box at the time you display the form.

1. Double-click the background of the form.

A new procedure named *UserForm_Click* appears.

```
UserForm              ▼   Click                 ▼
    Private Sub chkMonth_Click()
        txtMonth.Enabled = chkMonth.Value
    End Sub

    Private Sub UserForm_Click()
    |
    End Sub
```

The name of the object for a form is always *UserForm*. No matter what name you give the form, the event handler procedures always use the name *UserForm*. The default event for a form is *Click,* but because you don't want to wait until the user clicks the form to initialize the month, you need a different event.

2. From the **Procedures** list, select the **Initialize** event. After the UserForm_Initialize procedure appears, delete the **UserForm_Click** procedure.

3. Enter the following statement as the body of the procedure:

```
txtMonth.Value = Date
```

Date is a built-in Visual Basic function that returns the current date, based on your computer's internal clock.

4. Press F5 to run the form.

The purpose of the date is to identify the month you want the report to start with. You'll create a macro that searches the top row of the worksheet to find a date that matches the one in the text box. The dates in the top row of the worksheet are all for the first day of the month. To find a match, therefore, the date in the text box must be for the first day of the month as well. The date that the macro puts in the text box, however, is the current date. Because it's highly unlikely that the current date is the first day of the month, you need a way to convert the current date to the first day of the current month.

5. Close the form, and then double-click the background to get back to the **UserForm_Initialize** procedure.

You're now going to create a custom function that will convert any date into the first day of the month.

6. Below the **UserForm_Initialize** procedure, add this custom function:

```
Function StartOfMonth(InputDate)
    If IsDate(InputDate) Then
        StartOfMonth = DateSerial _
            (Year(InputDate), Month(InputDate), 1)
    Else
        StartOfMonth = Empty
    End If
End Function
```

This function accepts an input date as an argument. It first checks to see whether the input date is a date or can be turned into one. If it can, the function extracts the year and the month from the input date and uses the DateSerial function to create a new date. You give the DateSerial function a year, a month, and a day, and it gives you back the appropriate date. The StartOfMonth function ignores the day portion of the input date and always uses 1 as the day instead. If for some reason the input date can't be interpreted as a date, the function returns the special value *Empty*. The Empty value is the value used when a variable has never been initialized. The Visual Basic Date function in the UserForm_Initialize procedure always returns a valid date, so if you call only the StartOfMonth function from the UserForm_Initialize procedure, it doesn't have to handle an invalid date. But whenever you write a custom function, you should write it to work in a variety of possible situations. Returning an Empty value when the argument is an invalid date is one way to make your function more flexible.

> **Tip** If you want to test a function from a form, you can do so from the Immediate window. Because the function is part of the code for a form object, you must include the form name before the function name. For example, you could test the StartOfMonth function in the Immediate window by entering the following statement in the Immediate window: *?frmPrint.StartOfMonth("May 23, 2007")*.

7. Change the statement in the **UserForm_Initialize** procedure to txtMonth.Value = StartOfMonth(Date).

8. Press F5 to run the dialog box, check the date in the month box, and then close the form.

The date should be the first day of the current month.

Many controls need to be initialized. Some controls, such as the option buttons, can be initialized when you create the form. Other controls, such as the month text box, need to be initialized when you run the form, and the Initialize event handler is the place to initialize controls when you run the form.

Add Command Buttons

Your form allows you to specify what both the rows and columns of the report should look like. You still need a way to start printing. To do that, you add a command button. In theory, you don't need a cancel button because you can always just click the Close Window button to close the form. But a cancel button is easier to understand and use, and that's the whole purpose of a good user interface.

CommandButton

1. Activate the **Form** window.

2. Click the **CommandButton** button in the **Toolbox**, and then click to the right of the **Rows** frame on the form.

3. Press and hold the Ctrl key, and drag the new button down to make a copy of it.

    Clicking the top button will print the report, but clicking the bottom one won't. Clicking either button will close the form.

    ```
    Print Options                              [x]
    ┌─Rows──────────┐   ┌─────────────────────┐
    │  ⦿ All         │   │    CommandButton1    │
    │                │   └─────────────────────┘
    │  ○ Summary     │   ┌─────────────────────┐
    │  ○ Detail      │   │    CommandButton1    │
    │                │   └─────────────────────┘
    │  □ Start with month    7/1/2007          │
    │                                          │
    └──────────────────────────────────────────┘
    ```

4. Change the caption of the top button to Print, change the name to btnPrint and change the **Default** property to True.

    Only one command button on a form can be the default. A default button is the one that is "clicked" when you press the Enter key.

5. Change the caption of the bottom button to Cancel, change the name to btnCancel and change the **Cancel** property to True.

Only one command button on a form can be a cancel button. A cancel button is the one that is "clicked" when you press the Esc key. Normally when you click a cancel button, you expect the form to close. A cancel button by itself, however, doesn't close the form. First you have to add an event handler to it.

6. Double-click the cancel button to create an event handler named btnCancel_Click and enter the statement Unload Me as the body of the procedure.

The Unload command removes a form from memory. The *Me* keyword refers to the current form. The macro statement *Unload Me* therefore removes from memory the form that contains the control whose event handler is currently running.

7. Select **btnPrint** from the **Objects** list at the top of the code window to create a new procedure called btnPrint_Click and enter these two statements as the body of the procedure:

```
Unload Me
MsgBox "Printing"
```

The first statement removes the form, and the second statement is a placeholder until you add the functionality to print the report.

8. Save the workbook, and run the form several times. Try clicking the **Cancel** and **Print** buttons. Try pressing the Esc or Enter keys.

 Pressing the Enter key or clicking the Print button should display the Printing message. Pressing the Esc key or clicking the Cancel button should make the form disappear quietly.

Set the Tab Order for Controls

Some people prefer to use the Tab key on the keyboard rather than the mouse to move the *focus* from control to control. For them, you should make sure that the tab order is logical.

1. Run the form one more time. Select the **Start with month** check box to enable the month text box. Press the Tab key repeatedly. Watch the small gray box move from control to control.

 The gray box identifies the control that has the focus.

2. Click **Cancel** to close the form.

 For this form, the tab order should be optAll, optSummary, optDetail, chkMonth, txtMonth, btnPrint, and btnCancel. If that's not the tab order for your controls, the Visual Basic editor provides a simple way to change the tab order.

3. Click the background of the form. Then on the **View** menu, click **Tab Order**.

 The Tab Order dialog box shows five controls: grpRows, chkMonth, txtMonth, btnPrint, and btnCancel. It treats the grpRows frame control (along with the controls it contains) as a single item. If a control is out of place in the sequence, you simply select the control and click the Move Up or Move Down button to put it in the right place.

4. After making any necessary adjustments, click **OK** to close the dialog box.

When you have nested controls—such as the option buttons inside the frame—you must set the tab order for the nested controls separately.

5. Select the frame box (or any of the option buttons), and on the **View** menu, click **Tab Order** again.

This time, the Tab Order dialog box shows only the controls inside the frame.

6. If the controls are not in the order optAll, optSummary, and optDetail, make any necessary adjustments, and then click **OK** to close the dialog box.

7. Save the workbook.

The tab order is easy to set, but remember that you need to set the order for the controls in each frame separately.

Preparing a Form's Functionality

The form now looks good. The next step is to build the functionality for printing the report. You need a way to change between the different row views, and you need a way to hide any unwanted columns. Excel can store different custom views of a worksheet, which you can then show later as needed. If you build some views into the worksheet, creating a macro to switch between views will be easy.

Create Custom Views on a Worksheet

A custom view allows you to hide rows or columns on a worksheet and then give that view a name so that you can retrieve it easily. You need to create three views. The first view shows all the rows and columns. That one is easy to create. The second view shows only the total rows. The third view shows only the detail rows. Hiding the rows can be a tedious process. Fortunately, you need to hide them only once, and you can use Excel's Go To Special command to speed up row selection.

1. Activate Excel. Then on the **View** tab of the Ribbon, click **Custom Views**.

2. In the **Custom Views** dialog box, click the **Add** button, type **All** as the name for the new view, clear the **Print settings** check box, leave the **Hidden rows, columns and filter settings** check box selected, and then click **OK**.

Add View		? ✕
Name:	All	
Include in view		
☐ Print settings		
☑ Hidden rows, columns and filter settings		
	OK	Cancel

You just created the first view, the one with all rows and columns displayed. You now need to create the Summary view, showing only the total rows. That means that you need to hide the detail rows, which are the only rows with labels in column B.

3. Select column **B**. On the **Home** tab of the Ribbon, click the **Find & Select** arrow, and then click **Go To Special**.

Find & Select ▾

4. Select the **Constants** option, and click **OK**.

Go To Special	? ✕
Select	
◯ Comments	◯ Row differences
⦿ Constants	◯ Column differences
◯ Formulas	◯ Precedents
☑ Numbers	◯ Dependents
☑ Text	⦿ Direct only
☑ Logicals	◯ All levels
☑ Errors	◯ Last cell
◯ Blanks	◯ Visible cells only
◯ Current region	◯ Conditional formats
◯ Current array	◯ Data validation
◯ Objects	⦿ All
	◯ Same
	OK Cancel

Only the cells in the detail rows are still selected.

Format ▾

5. On the **Home** tab of the Ribbon, click the **Format** arrow, point to **Hide & Unhide**, and click **Hide Rows** to hide the selected rows.

	A	B	C	D	E	F	G
1	Summary		Rates	Jan-2007	Feb-2007	Mar-2007	Qtr1
2	Projected Units			29000	30000	31000	90000
3	Projected Revenues			71000	73000	75000	219000
4	**Projected Pre-tax Profit**			28094.9	28332.9	31570.9	87998.7
5							
6	Variable						
13	Total Variable			7598	7860	8122	23580
14							
15	Salaries						
21	Total Salaries			16546	16546	16546	49638

The remaining rows that you want to hide all have blank cells in column D. Does that give you any ideas?

6. Select column **D**. Click the **Find & Select** arrow, and then click **Go To Special**.

7. Select the **Blanks** option, and click **OK**. Then hide the selected rows as you did in Step 5.

This is the view for the managers.

	A	B	C	D	E	F	G
1	Summary		Rates	Jan-2007	Feb-2007	Mar-2007	Qtr1
2	Projected Units			29000	30000	31000	90000
3	Projected Revenues			71000	73000	75000	219000
4	**Projected Pre-tax Profit**			28094.9	28332.9	31570.9	87998.7
13	Total Variable			7598	7860	8122	23580
21	Total Salaries			16546	16546	16546	49638
23	Total Salaries and Benefits			22337.1	22337.1	22337.1	67011.3

8. To create another view with only the total rows visible, on the **View** tab of the Ribbon, click **Custom Views**, click **Add**, type Summary, clear **Print settings**, and then click **OK**.

Now you need to create the detail view, which hides all the summary rows. The rows you want to hide have labels in the range A4:A54.

9. On the **View** tab, click **Custom Views**, and with **All** selected, click **Show** to unhide all the rows.

10. Select the range **A4:A54**, use **Go To Special** to select the cells with constants, and then hide the rows.

11. Select column **D**, and hide all the rows with blank cells.

	A	B	C	D	E	F	G
1	Summary		Rates	Jan-2007	Feb-2007	Mar-2007	Qtr1
2	Projected Units			29000	30000	31000	90000
3	Projected Revenues			71000	73000	75000	219000
7		Potting Soil	0.095	2755	2850	2945	8550
8		Pots	0.012	348	360	372	1080
9		Seeds	0.002	58	60	62	180

12. With only the detail rows visible, create a new view named Detail, again clearing the **Print settings** option.

13. Save the workbook, and try showing each of the three views. Finish with the **All** view.

Creating the views is bothersome, but you have to do it only once.

Create a Macro to Switch Views

After the views are created, making a macro to switch between views is easy.

1. Start recording a macro named ShowView.

2. Show the **Summary** view, turn off the recorder, and look at the macro.

Ignoring comments, the macro should look like this:

```
Sub ShowView()
    ActiveWorkbook.CustomViews("Summary").Show
End Sub
```

A Workbook object has a collection named *CustomViews*. You use the name of the view to retrieve a CustomView item from the collection. A CustomView object has a Show method. To switch between views, all you need to do is substitute the name of the view in parentheses. And rather than create three separate macros, you can pass the name of the view as an argument.

3. Type ViewName between the parentheses after **ShowView**, and then replace **"Summary"** (quotation marks and all) with ViewName.

The revised macro should look like this:

```
Sub ShowView(ViewName)
    ActiveWorkbook.CustomViews(ViewName).Show
End Sub
```

Next you'll test the macro and its argument by using the Immediate window.

4. Press Ctrl+G to display the **Immediate** window.

Make sure that the Excel window is visible in the background.

5. In the **Immediate** window, type ShowView "Detail" and press Enter.

The worksheet should change to show the detail view.

6. Type ShowView "All" and press Enter.

7. Type ShowView "Summary" and press Enter again.

The macro works with all three arguments.

8. Close the **Immediate** window, and save the workbook.

You now have the functionality to show different views. Creating the views might not have been fun, but it certainly made writing the macro a lot easier. Also, if you decide to adjust a view (say, to include blank lines), you don't need to change the macro— changing the view will automatically change the way the macro works.

Dynamically Hide Columns

At this point, you need to create the functionality to hide columns containing dates earlier than the desired starting month. You don't want to create custom views to change the columns because you would need to create 36 different custom views— one for each of the 12 months times the 3 different row settings. It would be better to change the columns dynamically, based on the choices in the dialog box. If the user chooses to hide columns, you'll hide from column C to the month that contains the specified month. One good way to find the month is to use Excel's Find method.

1. In Excel, select all of row **1**, and then start recording a macro named HideMonths.

2. On the **Home** tab of the Ribbon, click **Find & Select**, click **Find**, and then click the **Options** button to expand the dialog box.

3. Type **5/1/2007** in the **Find what** box, select the **Match entire cell contents** check box, and make sure the **Look in** list box says **Formulas**.

> **Troubleshooting** If your system uses a date format other than mm/dd/yyyy (the default United States date format), you'll need to experiment to find the date format that works for you.

When you search for the formula, you look for the underlying date in the cell. The underlying date uses the system date format, regardless of how the cell happens to be formatted. By searching only entire cells, you make sure that 1/1/2007, for example, finds only January (1/1/2007), and not November (11/1/2007), which differs only by the extra digit at the beginning.

4. Click **Find Next**, close the **Find** dialog box, stop the recorder, and then edit the **HideMonths** macro. Put a line continuation (a space, an underscore, and a new line) after every comma to make the statement readable.

Ignoring comments, the macro should now look like this:

```
Sub HideMonths()
    Selection.Find(What:="5/1/2007", _
        After:=ActiveCell, _
        LookIn:=xlFormulas, _
        LookAt:=xlWhole, _
        SearchOrder:=xlByRows, _
        SearchDirection:=xlNext, _
        MatchCase:=False, _
        SearchFormat:=False).Activate
End Sub
```

The macro searches the selection (in this case, row 1) starting with the active cell (in this case, cell A1), searches for the specified date, and activates the matching cell. You don't want the macro to change the selection, and you don't want the macro to activate the cell it finds. Rather, you want the macro to assign the cell it finds to a range variable so that you can refer to it.

5. Make these changes to the macro: Declare the variable **myFind** as a **Range**. Change **Selection** to **Rows(1)** and **ActiveCell** to **Cells(1)**. Add **Set myFind =** to the beginning of the **Find** statement, and delete **.Activate** from the end.

The revised macro looks like this:

```
Sub HideMonths()
    Dim myFind as Range
    Set myFind = Rows(1).Find(What:="5/1/2007", _
        After:=Cells(1), _
        LookIn:=xlFormulas, _
        LookAt:=xlWhole, _
        SearchOrder:=xlByRows, _
        SearchDirection:=xlNext, _
        MatchCase:=False, _
        SearchFormat:=False)
End Sub
```

If the Find method is successful, then myFind will contain a reference to the cell that contains the month. You want to hide all the columns from column C (the Rates column) to one column to the left of myFind.

6. Before the **End Sub** statement, insert this statement:

```
Range("C1",myFind.Offset(0,-1)).EntireColumn.Hidden = True
```

This selects a range starting with cell C1 and ending one cell to the left of the cell with the month name. It then hides the columns containing that range.

7. Save the workbook, and press F8 repeatedly to step through the macro, watching as columns **C** through **H** disappear.

You'll be changing this subroutine to hide columns up to any date. You need some way of knowing whether or not the Find method finds a match. If the Find method does find a match, it assigns a reference to the variable. If it doesn't find a match, it assigns a special object reference, *Nothing*, to the variable. You can check to see whether the object is the same as Nothing. Because you're comparing object references and not values, you don't use an equal sign to do the comparison. Instead, you use a special object comparison word, *Is*.

> **Important** A variable that's declared as a variant contains the value *Empty* when nothing else is assigned to it. A variable that's declared as an object contains the reference *Nothing* when no other object reference is assigned to it. Empty means "no value," and Nothing means "no object reference." To see whether the variable myValue contains the Empty value, use the expression *IsEmpty(myValue)*. To see whether the variable myObject contains a reference to Nothing, use the expression *myObject Is Nothing*.

8. Add the **If** and **End If** statements around the statement that hides the columns, resulting in this If structure:

```
If Not myFind Is Nothing Then
    Range("C1", myFind.Offset(0, -1)) _
        .EntireColumn.Hidden = True
End If
```

If the Find method fails, it assigns Nothing to myFind, so the conditional expression is False and no columns are hidden.

9. Test the macro's ability to handle an error by changing the value for which the **Find** method searches from **5/1/2007** to **Dog**.

10. Step through the macro, and watch what happens when you get to the If structure. Hold the mouse pointer over the **myFind** variable and see that its value is **Nothing**.

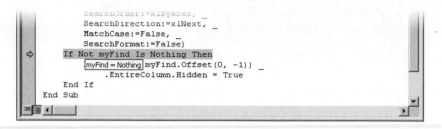

```
        SearchOrder:=xlByRows, _
        SearchDirection:=xlNext, _
        MatchCase:=False, _
        SearchFormat:=False)
    If Not myFind Is Nothing Then
        myFind = Nothing myFind.Offset(0, -1)) _
            .EntireColumn.Hidden = True
    End If
End Sub
```

If you search for a date that is in row 1, myFind will hold a reference to the cell containing that date, and the macro will hide the months that precede it. If you search for anything else, myFind will hold a reference to Nothing, and the macro won't hide any columns.

11. Press F5 to end the macro.

The final step is to convert the date to an argument so that you can search for a month other than May.

12. Type StartMonth between the parentheses after **HideMonths**, and replace **"5/1/2007"** or **"Dog"** (including the quotation marks) with StartMonth.

The revised (and finished) procedure should look like this:

```
Sub HideMonths(StartMonth)
    Dim myFind As Range
    Set myFind = Rows(1).Find(What:=StartMonth, _
        After:=Cells(1), _
        LookIn:=xlFormulas, _
        LookAt:=xlWhole, _
        SearchOrder:=xlByRows, _
        SearchDirection:=xlNext, _
        MatchCase:=False, _
        SearchFormat:=False)
    If Not myFind Is Nothing Then
        Range("C1", myFind.Offset(0, -1)) _
            .EntireColumn.Hidden _
            = True
    End If
End Sub
```

13. Now test the macro. Press Ctrl+G to display the **Immediate** window.

14. Enter ShowView "All" and then enter HideMonths "8/1/2007".

	A	B	M	N	O	P
1	Summary		Aug-2007	Sep-2007	Qtr3	Oct-2007
2	Projected Units		35000	36000	106000	37000
3	Projected Revenues		85000	87000	255000	89000
4	**Projected Pre-tax Profit**		40522.9	42260.9	121306.7	-133909.5
5						
6	**Variable**					
7	Potting					
8	Pots					

Immediate

```
ShowView "All"
HideMonths "8/1/2007"
```

15. Close the **Immediate** window, and save the workbook.

You now have macros that can handle the functionality of the form by hiding appropriate rows and columns. It's time to put the form and the functionality together.

Implementing a Form

You've created a user interface that allows you to specify which rows and columns to print. You've also created the functionality for the form. The ShowView and HideMonths macros show the appropriate rows and columns. You now need to make the user interface drive the functionality. You need to implement the form.

On this form, the Print button is what formats and prints the report. You'll put all the code that links the form to the functionality into the btnPrint_Click procedure.

Implement Option Buttons

To implement the option buttons, you need a way to determine which option button value is True. The frame control has a Controls property that returns a collection of all the controls in the frame. You can loop through those controls and determine which option button value is True.

Project Explorer

1. In the Visual Basic editor, click the **Project Explorer** toolbar button, double-click the **frmPrint** form, and then close the **Project** window.

When you have a project with several components, the Project window is often the easiest way to get to the right place.

2. Double-click the **Print** button to show the **btnPrint_Click** event handler procedure.

See Also For details about using a For Each loop, see the section titled "Loop Through a Collection by Using a For Each Loop" in Chapter 7, "Control Visual Basic."

3. Insert these statements at the beginning of the procedure, before the **Unload Me** statement:

```
Dim myControl As Control
Dim myView

For Each myControl In grpRows.Controls
    If myControl.Value = True Then
        myView = myControl.Caption
    End If
Next myControl

ShowView myView
```

This For Each loop inspects each control in the frame, looking for a value of True. You declare the loop variable as a Control (not as an OptionButton) because it's possible for a frame to contain other types of controls besides option buttons.

> **Tip** If you loop through the controls of a frame that contains controls other than option buttons, you should check to see whether the control is an option button. You can use the conditional expression *TypeName(myControl) = "OptionButton"* to determine whether the control is an option button.

The loop stores the caption of the selected option in a variable, and the macro later uses that variable as the argument when it runs the ShowView macro. What a fortuitous coincidence that you used the same names for the custom views as for the captions of the option buttons!

4. Save the workbook, and press F8 to run the form. Then press F8 repeatedly to step through the initialization procedures until the form appears.

If you press F8 to run the form, you can step through any event handler procedures triggered by controls on the form.

> **Troubleshooting** Make sure you have the form's code window active when you press F8. You can run the form by pressing F5 while either the form design window or the form code window is active, but the form code window must be active to use F8.

5. In the form, click the **Summary** option, and then click **Print**.

6. Press F8 repeatedly to step through the **btnPrint_Click** procedure.

7. Close the message box as necessary.

Option buttons can be easy to implement if you plan ahead. In this example, giving the custom views in the worksheet the same names as the captions of the option buttons made the option buttons easy to implement. If you want to add a fourth view option, all you have to do is define a new view on the worksheet and add an option button with the appropriate caption to the form. You don't need to make any changes to any of the procedures.

Implement a Check Box

If the check box is selected, the Print button event handler should run the HideMonths macro. Actually, the HideMonths macro will do nothing if you give it a date that it doesn't find. You can take advantage of that fact by assigning to a variable either the date from the month box or an invalid value.

1. In the form, double-click the **Print** button to show the **btnPrint_Click** procedure, and add the following statements after **Dim myView**.

```
Dim myMonth

If chkMonth.Value = True Then
    myMonth = txtMonth.Value
Else
    myMonth = "no date"
End If
```

These statements assign to the myMonth variable either the value from the month text box or an obviously invalid value.

2. Insert the statement **HideMonths myMonth** after the statement **ShowView myView**.

   You place this statement after the ShowView statement because you want to change the view before hiding the months; showing the custom view redisplays all the hidden columns.

3. Save the workbook, and press F5 to run the form.

4. Select the check box, type 9/1/2007 in the month box, and click **Print**.

   The worksheet now shows only the months starting from September.

	A B	N	O	P
1	Summary	Sep-2007	Qtr3	Oct-2007
2	Projected Units	36000	106000	37000
3	Projected Revenues	87000	255000	89000
4	Projected Pre-tax Profit	42260.9	121306.7	-133909.5
5				
6	Variable			
7	Potting Soil	3420	10070	3515

5. Click **OK** to close the message box.

Check for Errors in an Edit Box

What if you run the form and type *Dog* as the date? The macro shouldn't hide any columns, but it should point out the error. Also, what if you type *4/15/2007* as the date? Ideally, the macro should convert 4/15/2007 to the first day of the month: 4/1/2007. Think about all the functions you've created during this project and see whether you can find one that can convert an arbitrary date to the start date of the month.

1. Double-click the **Print** button.

2. In the **btnPrint_Click** procedure, replace **myMonth = txtMonth.Value** with myMonth = StartOfMonth(txtMonth.Value).

   The StartOfMonth function converts a date to the first of the month. If the input date isn't a valid date, the function returns the Empty value. (That was remarkably forward-looking of you to write the StartOfMonth function in such a way that it can handle invalid dates.) Once the StartOfMonth function finishes its job, if the myMonth variable contains the Empty value, you'll want to show a message and make the value easy to fix.

3. Insert these statements before the **Else** statement:

```
If myMonth = Empty Then
    MsgBox "Invalid Month"
    txtMonth.SetFocus
    txtMonth.SelStart = 0
    txtMonth.SelLength = 1000
    Exit Sub
End If
```

When you run the form, the macro appropriately displays a message box explaining the problem if you type an invalid date. After you close the message box, you should be able to just start typing a corrected value. For that to happen, however, the macro must move to the text box and preselect the current, invalid contents.

The SetFocus method moves the focus to the text box. Setting the SelStart property to 0 (zero) starts text selection from the very beginning of the text box. Setting the SelLength property to 1000 extends text selection to however much text there is in the box. Using an arbitrarily large value such as 1000 simply avoids having to calculate the actual length of the contents of the box.

4. Save the workbook, and then press F5 to run the form.

5. Enabling the month, type Dog, and click **Print**.

6. Click **OK** to close the error.

7. Type Jun 23, 07 and click **Print**.

8. Click **OK** to close the **Printing** placeholder message box.

When you put an edit box on a form, you must think about what the macro should do if the user enters an invalid value. In many cases, displaying an error message and pre-selecting the invalid entry is the best strategy. The SetFocus method and the SelStart and SelLength properties are the tools that allow you to implement that strategy.

Print the Report

The Print form now does everything it needs to do—everything, that is, except print. If you display the report in print preview mode, you can then decide whether to print it or just admire it.

1. Double-click the **Print** button.

2. In the **btnPrint_Click** procedure, replace **MsgBox "Printing"** with ActiveSheet.PrintPreview.

After the report is printed, you should restore the rows and columns in the worksheet.

3. After the statement **ActiveSheet.PrintPreview**, type the statement ShowView "All".

The finished Print button event handler routine should look like this:

```
Private Sub btnPrint_Click()
    Dim myControl As Control
    Dim myView
    Dim myMonth

    If chkMonth.Value = True Then
        myMonth = StartOfMonth(txtMonth.Value)
        If myMonth = Empty Then
            MsgBox "Invalid Month"
            txtMonth.SetFocus
            txtMonth.SelStart = 0
            txtMonth.SelLength = 1000
            Exit Sub
        End If
    Else
        myMonth = "no date"
    End If

    For Each myControl In grpRows.Controls
        If myControl.Value = True Then
            myView = myControl.Caption
        End If
    Next myControl

    ShowView myView
    HideMonths myMonth

    Unload Me
    ActiveSheet.PrintPreview
    ShowView "All"
End Sub
```

4. Save the workbook, press F5 to run the form, select the **Summary** option, limit the months to August and later, click the **Print** button, and then click **Zoom** to see the beautiful report.

Chapter11.xlsm - Microsoft Excel

Print Preview

Print | Page Setup | Zoom | Next Page | Previous Page | Show Margins | Close Print Preview

Print | Zoom | Preview

Budget

Summary	Aug-2007	Sep-2007	Qtr3	Oct-2007	Nov-2007	Dec-2007
Projected Units	35000	36000	106000	37000	38000	39000
Projected Revenues	85000	87000	255000	89000	91000	93000
Projected Pre-tax Profit	40522.9	42260.9	121306.7	-133909.5	41736.9	50474.9
Total Variable	9170	9432	27772	9694	9956	10218
Total Salaries	16546	16546	49638	16546	16546	16546
Total Salaries and Benefit	22337.1	22337.1	67011.3	22337.1	22337.1	22337.1
Total Supplies	800	800	2400	800	800	800
Total Operating	2150	2150	6450	4650	2150	2150
Total Contracts	8500	8500	25500	5500	12500	5500
Total Leases	1520	1520	4560	1520	1520	1520
Total Expenses	44477.1	44739.1	133693.3	222909.5	49263.1	42525.1

5. Close the **Print Preview** window.

The user interface of the form is now linked to its full functionality. All that's left is to provide a way for the user to run the form from Excel instead of from Visual Basic.

Launch the Form

To launch the form, you can add an unobtrusive button to the worksheet. The top-left corner of the Budget worksheet is always visible (because the panes are frozen), so you could put a button in the right side of cell B1. Rather than use an ActiveX button, you can use an ActiveX label so that you can make the background transparent and set the font color.

Label
(ActiveX Control)

1. In Excel, activate the **Developer** tab of the Ribbon, click the **Insert** arrow, and click **Label (ActiveX Control)**.

2. Drag a small rectangle in the right half of cell **B1**.

3. Click the **Properties** button on the Ribbon, and set the following property values: Change **(Name)** to **lblPrint**, change **BackStyle** to **0 – fmBackStyleTransparent**, change **Caption** to **Print**, change **ForeColor** to a blue color, change **PrintObject** to **False**, and change **TextAlign** to **2 – fmTextAlignCenter**.

	A	B	C	D
1	**Summary**	Print	Rates	**Jan-2007**
2	Projected Units			29000
3	Projected Revenues			71000
4	**Projected Pre-tax Profit**			**28094.9**
5				

4. Right-click the label, and click **View Code**.

5. In the **lblPrint_Click** event handler, insert the statement **frmPrint.Show**.

   The procedure will look like this:

   ```
   Private Sub lblPrint_Click()
       frmPrint.Show
   End Sub
   ```

   The Show method of a form displays the form. To refer to the form, simply use the name that you gave it when you created it.

   > **Tip** Ordinarily, you can't activate a worksheet while a form is displayed. When a form prevents you from selecting the worksheet, it's called a *modal form*. If you want the user to be able to use the worksheet while the form is displayed, add the argument False after the Show method. This creates what is called a *nonmodal form*.

6. Switch to Excel, turn off design mode, save the workbook, and then click the **Print** label.

7. When the Print Options dialog box appears, click **Cancel**.

   > **Tip** Instead of putting an ActiveX control on the worksheet, you could also create an ordinary macro that shows the form, and then add that macro to the Quick Access Toolbar for this workbook. Some users may not notice the Quick Access Toolbar icon, so a label may be preferable provided a pane is frozen and will always be visible.

Creating a fully usable form involves three major steps: creating the user interface, creating the functionality, and joining them together into a working tool. Now that you've created one form, you can create dozens more for your own projects.

CLOSE the *Chapter11.xlsm* workbook.

Key Points

- You can create a custom dialog box by using a UserForm in Visual Basic. The controls on a UserForm are the same ActiveX controls you can insert on a worksheet.

- When you create an application, designing the interface first helps you to identify the functionality you need.

- When you create a dialog box, always make sure the tab order of the controls makes sense for users who like to use the keyboard.

- Minimize the work your macro has to do by utilizing worksheet functionality such as custom views.

- Have fun building applications with Visual Basic in Excel!

Appendix

A Complete Enterprise Information System

In Chapter 5, "Explore Data Objects," you learned how to retrieve external data into a PivotTable report; in Chapter 6, "Explore Graphical Objects," you learned how to work with graphical objects; in Chapter 7, "Control Visual Basic," you learned how to create loops; in Chapter 8, "Extend Excel and Visual Basic," you learned how to create subroutines; and in Chapter 9, "Launch Macros with Events," you learned how to use ActiveX controls and event handlers. In this appendix, you'll see what can happen when you use Microsoft Office Excel 2007 and Microsoft Visual Basic for Applications (VBA) to put all these pieces together.

Included with the practice files for this book is a bonus application. This application is a simple enterprise information system (EIS). It uses one of Lucerne Publishing's databases in an easy-to-use, visually powerful way to display order information for each state in the Lucerne Publishing territory.

Important Before you complete this appendix, you need to install the practice files from the book's companion CD to their default locations. See "Using the Book's CD" on page xv for more information.

USE the *EIS.xlsm* file. This practice file is located in the *Documents\MSP\ExcelVBA07SBS* folder.
BE SURE TO copy the *EIS.xlsm* workbook into the trusted location you created in Chapter 1.
OPEN the *EIS.xlsm* workbook.

> **Important** Whenever you receive a macro-enabled workbook from someone else—even someone you trust—you should first open the workbook without enabling macros and use the Project Explorer window in Visual Basic to review the code—particularly any event handler procedures attached to worksheets or workbooks. Once you are comfortable that the code is safe, you can enable macros or put the workbook in a trusted location.

When the *EIS* workbook opens, the application changes the Excel window size and displays an introductory animation that leaves you with a colored, shaded map of the western United States.

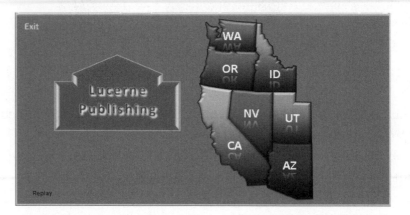

1. When the animation finishes, click the **Replay** label in the bottom-left corner. While the animation runs, click the **Cancel** button.

   The animation stops, and the procedure that controls it jumps directly to its end and displays the map. Animations are good for attracting attention, but they can be annoying to an impatient user. It's usually a good idea to provide a mechanism for bypassing a lengthy animation.

2. Click the map for **California**.

   The screen switches to display quarterly orders for a two-year period, complete with a graph.

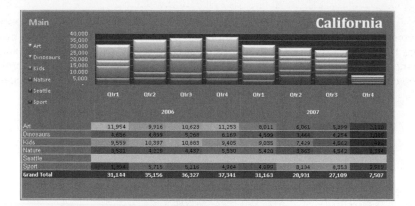

3. Look at the caption at the top of the application.

   The caption says *Lucerne Publishing EIS* rather than *Excel*. The caption contributes to the custom appearance of the application.

4. Look at the text at the top-left corner of the worksheet to see the label that says *Main*. Then move the mouse over the text.

   The font changes to signal to the user where to click. This is a simple way to navigate within the application. Rather than change the Ribbon, which you can't do directly with VBA, you can add a label.

5. Click the **Main** label to return to the map.

6. Move the mouse over the notch where Nevada interlocks with Arizona. When the mouse is over the **Nevada** part of the notch, click to display Nevada data. Then return to the main sheet, and click when the mouse is over the **Arizona** part of the notch.

   You can click anywhere within the exact border of the state to show the data for that state.

7. Try selecting a cell on the worksheet.

   This is a "look but don't touch" screen. The application makes use of a worksheet, but from the user's perspective, it could be a completely custom application.

8. Press Ctrl+N to create a new workbook.

The Excel window returns to the normal appearance it had before the application started.

With VBA macros, you can't prevent the user from opening a new workbook, but you can make your application behave properly when it happens.

9. Change the Excel application border to a noticeably different size and shape.

10. On the **View** tab of the Ribbon, click **Switch Windows**, and then click **Lucerne Publishing EIS**.

The window changes back to the look of the application.

11. Press Ctrl+Tab (the shortcut for switching windows) to see the application switch back to the size and shape you assigned. Then press Ctrl+Tab to return to the application.

12. Click **Main** to return to the main sheet. Then click the **Exit** label in the top-left corner of the workbook to close the application workbook.

This application goes beyond what you are likely to do with macros, but it may give you a sense of the limits of what a macro can do. Explore the code within it. Some of the code will be new, but after you have completed the chapters in this book, much of it will be familiar to you. This application may give you some interesting ideas to apply in the macros you create. Have Fun!

> **Tip** As mentioned in Chapter 1, "Make a Macro Do Simple Tasks," if you want to create a full-fledged application using Excel as a platform, you'll probably want to use Microsoft Visual Studio instead of VBA.

Index

A

A1 reference style, 119
Accounting format, 5
Accounting Number Format button, 5
Activate method, 82, 88
active workbook, referencing, 82
ActiveCell object, 53
ActiveCell property, 104–105
  column selection with, 105
ActiveSheet, 46
ActiveX controls. *see also* command
    buttons
  defined, 264
  vs. Forms controls, 268
Add method, 71, 75
  Name argument, empty string for, 157
  Source value, 144
  value returned by, 86
AddDataField method, 160
adjustment handles on shapes, 190, 191
animations, 336
arguments
  defined, 27
  displaying all for method. *see* Auto
    Quick Info
  for functions, adding, 240–242
  for functions, making optional, 243–244
  naming, 27
  parentheses around, 218, 219
  for PasteSpecial method, 27
  syntax in macros, 27
Array function, 88

attributes. *see* properties
Auto List Members, 45, 74
  for worksheets, activating, 89–90
Auto Quick Info, 45

B

blank cells in worksheets, selecting,
    48–49
BorderAround method, 129
borders
  on ranges, adding, 127–130
  on shapes, modifying, 192
Borders object, 129
breakpoints
  setting, 230
  temporary, 232–233
browsing object classes. *see* Object
    Browser
buttons
  From Access, 143
  Accounting Number Format, 5
  Design Mode, 268
  Macros, 8
  Object Browser, 94
  Properties, 265
  Record Macro, 6
  Save, 21
  Search, 128
  Stop Recording, 6, 7, 115
  Undo, 18
  Use Relative References, 59
  View Code, 267

C

Additional Resources for Home and Business

Breakthrough Windows Vista™: Find Your Favorite Features and Discover the Possibilities

Joli Ballew and Sally Slack
ISBN 9780735623620

Jump in for the topics or features that interest you most! This colorful guide brings Windows Vista to life—from setting up your new system; accessing the Windows Vista Sidebar; customizing it for your favorite gadgets; recording live television with Media Center; organizing photos, music, and videos; making movies; and more.

So That's How! 2007 Microsoft® Office System: Timesavers, Breakthroughs, & Everyday Genius

Evan Archilla and Tiffany Songvilay
ISBN 9780735622746

From vanquishing an overstuffed inbox to breezing through complex spreadsheets, discover smarter ways to do everyday things with Microsoft Office. Based on a popular course delivered to more than 70,000 students, this guide delivers the tips and revelations that help you work more effectively with Microsoft Office Outlook®, Excel®, Word, and other programs. Also includes 'webinars' on CD.

Look Both Ways: Help Protect Your Family on the Internet

Linda Criddle
ISBN 9780735623477

You look both ways before crossing the street. Now, learn the new rules of the road—and help protect yourself online with Internet child-safety authority Linda Criddle. Using real-life examples, Linda teaches the simple steps you and your family can take to help avoid Internet dangers—and still enjoy your time online.

The Microsoft Crabby Office Lady Tells It Like It Is: Secrets to Surviving Office Life

Annik Stahl
ISBN 9780735622722

From cubicle to corner office, learn the secrets for getting more done on the job—so you can really enjoy your time off the job! The Crabby Office Lady shares her no-nonsense advice for succeeding at work, as well as tricks for using Microsoft Office programs to help simplify your life. She'll give you the straight scoop—so pay attention!

Microsoft Office Excel 2007: Data Analysis and Business Modeling

Wayne L. Winston
ISBN 9780735623965

Beyond Bullet Points: Using Microsoft Office PowerPoint® 2007 to Create Presentations That Inform, Motivate, and Inspire

Cliff Atkinson
ISBN 9780735623873

Take Back Your Life! Using Microsoft Office Outlook 2007 to Get Organized and Stay Organized

Sally McGhee
ISBN 9780735623439

See more resources at **microsoft.com/mspress**
and **microsoft.com/learning**

What do you think of this book?

We want to hear from you!

Do you have a few minutes to participate in a brief online survey?

Microsoft is interested in hearing your feedback so we can continually improve our books and learning resources for you.

To participate in our survey, please visit:

www.microsoft.com/learning/booksurvey/

...and enter this book's ISBN-10 number (appears above barcode on back cover*). As a thank-you to survey participants in the United States and Canada, each month we'll randomly select five respondents to win one of five $100 gift certificates from a leading online merchant. At the conclusion of the survey, you can enter the drawing by providing your e-mail address, which will be used for prize notification only.

Thanks in advance for your input. Your opinion counts!

* Where to find the ISBN-10 on back cover

ISBN-13: 000-0-0000-0000-0
ISBN-10: 0-0000-0000-0

0 000000 000000

Example only. Each book has unique ISBN.

Microsoft® Press

No purchase necessary. Void where prohibited. Open only to residents of the 50 United States (includes District of Columbia) and Canada (void in Quebec). For official rules and entry dates see:

www.microsoft.com/learning/booksurvey/

Additional Resources for Business and Home Users

Published and Forthcoming Titles from Microsoft Press

Beyond Bullet Points: Using Microsoft® PowerPoint® to Create Presentations That Inform, Motivate, and Inspire
Cliff Atkinson • ISBN 0-7356-2052-0

Improve your presentations—and increase your impact—with 50 powerful, practical, and easy-to-apply techniques for Microsoft PowerPoint. With *Beyond Bullet Points*, you'll take your presentation skills to the next level—learning innovative ways to design and deliver your message. Organized into five sections, including Distill Your Ideas, Structure Your Story, Visualize Your Message, Create a Conversation, and Maintain Engagement—the book uses clear, concise language and just the right visuals to help you understand concepts and start getting better results.

Take Back Your Life! Special Edition: Using Microsoft Outlook® to Get Organized and Stay Organized
Sally McGhee • ISBN 0-7356-2215-9

Unrelenting e-mail. Conflicting commitments. Endless interruptions. In this book, productivity expert Sally McGhee shows you how to take control and reclaim something that you thought you'd lost forever—your work-life balance. Now you can benefit from Sally's popular and highly regarded corporate education programs, learning simple but powerful techniques for rebalancing your personal and professional commitments using the productivity features in Outlook. When you change your approach, you can change your results. So learn what thousands of Sally's clients worldwide have discovered about taking control of their everyday productivity—and start transforming your own life today!

On Time! On Track! On Target! Managing Your Projects Successfully with Microsoft Project
Bonnie Biafore • ISBN 0-7356-2256-6

This book focuses on the core skills you need to successfully manage any project, giving you a practical education in project management and how-to instruction for using Microsoft Office Project Professional 2003 and other Microsoft Office Professional Edition 2003 programs, such as Excel® 2003, Outlook 2003, and Word 2003. Learn the essentials of project management, including creating successful project plans, tracking and evaluating performance, and controlling project costs. Whether you're a beginner just learning how to manage projects or a project manager already working on a project, this book has something for you. Includes a companion CD with sample Project templates.

Design to Sell: Using Microsoft Publisher to Inform, Motivate, and Persuade
Roger C. Parker • ISBN 0-7356-2260-4

Design to Sell relates the basics of effective message creation and formatting to the specific capabilities built into Microsoft Publisher—the powerful page layout program found on hundreds of thousands of computers around the world. Many Microsoft Office users already have Publisher on their computers but don't use it because they don't think of themselves as writers or designers. Here is a one-stop guide to marketing that even those without big budgets or previous design or writing experience can use to create compelling, easy-to-read marketing materials. Each chapter has an interactive exercise as well as questions with answers on the author's Web site. Also on the Web site are downloadable worksheets and templates, book updates, more illustrations of the projects in the book, and additional before-and-after project makeovers.

Microsoft Windows® XP Networking and Security Inside Out: Also Covers Windows 2000
Ed Bott and Carl Siechert • ISBN 0-7356-2042-3

Configure and manage your PC network—and help combat privacy and security threats—from the inside out! Written by the authors of the immensely popular *Microsoft Windows XP Inside Out*, this book packs hundreds of timesaving solutions, troubleshooting tips, and work-arounds for networking and security topics—all in concise, fast-answer format.

Dig into the tools and techniques for configuring workgroup, domain, Internet, and remote networking, and all the network components and features in between. Get the answers you need to use Windows XP Service Pack 2 and other tools, tactics, and features to help defend your personal computer and network against spyware, pop-up ads, viruses, hackers, spam, denial-of-service attacks, and other threats. Learn how to help secure your Virtual Private Networks (VPNs), remote access, and wireless networking services, and take ultimate control with advanced solutions such as file encryption, port blocking, IPSec, group policies, and tamper-proofing tactics for the registry. Get up to date on hot topics such as peer-to-peer networks, public wireless access points, smart cards, handheld computers, wireless LANs, and more. Plus, the CD includes bonus resources that make it easy for you to share your new security and networking expertise with your colleagues, friends, and family.